ENTERPRISE SOCIAL TECHNOLOGY

Helping organizations
harness the power of

**Social Media
Social Networking
Social Relevance**

Scott K

GREENLEAF
BOOK GROUP PRESS

Published by Greenleaf Book Group Press
Austin, Texas
www.gbgpress.com

Distributed by Greenleaf Book Group LLC

For ordering information or special discounts for bulk purchases, please contact Greenleaf Book Group LLC at PO Box 91869, Austin, TX 78709, 512.891.6100.

Design and composition by Greenleaf Book Group LLC and Bumpy Design
Cover design by Christopher Bridges

Publisher's Cataloging-In-Publication Data
(Prepared by The Donohue Group, Inc.)

Klososky, Scott.
    Enterprise social technology : helping organizations harness the power of social media, social networking, social relevance / Scott Klososky. -- 1st ed.
     p. ; cm.
    ISBN: 978-1-60832-086-8
    1. Online social networks--Economic aspects. 2. Internet--Social aspects--Technological innovations. 3. Business communication. 4. Success in business. I. Title.
HM742 .K56 2011
302.30285   2010939149

Part of the Tree Neutral® program, which offsets the number of trees consumed in the production and printing of this book by taking proactive steps, such as planting trees in direct proportion to the number of trees used: www.treeneutral.com

TreeNeutral®

Printed in the United States of America on acid-free paper

11 12 13 14 15 16   10 9 8 7 6 5 4 3 2 1

First Edition

DEDICATION

Never in the course of human events have we lived in a time where tools to communicate, connect, entertain, and be productive have been handed to us in such volumes, and for free. We will one day look back and be amazed at this time and at how these tools altered our lives. The fact that we used crowdsourcing to quickly integrate the thoughts and talents of over a dozen people from around the world to produce this book is something special. I would like to thank all of the people who helped put this together, as they are very much the kindred spirits of the pioneers that once ventured into strange new lands. Today, we pioneer by using new technologies, and this is certainly the case with all of the people who invested time on crowd-SPRING.com and 99Designs.com to help us. This also includes all of the folks at Greenleaf Book Group who supported testing out a new model for producing a book. Hopefully this is the first of many in the Crowdscribed series we will be producing.

CONTENTS

I have spent the past couple of years consulting with organizations on the implementation of social technology as a tool. Among the interesting things I've discovered is the unsettling reality that social technology tools are still seen by many leaders as mere novelties rather than being used as a means to measurably improve the bottom line. This book was written because I want to move the discussion past whether the CEO should be tweeting, or the organization developing a Facebook fan page, and toward how leaders can holistically integrate the full range of social technology tools to make a truly meaningful difference in their organizations.

This book is not meant to be Social Technology 101. There are already many books available on how to write blogs, use LinkedIn, and build Facebook fan pages. Rarely do I encounter organizations today whose leaders do not have at least a rudimentary understanding of the basic social tech tools and why they need to be using them. Thus it seems fair to assume that readers of this book have tried out things like uploading videos to YouTube and sharing presentations with SlideShare.

Instead, this book is a how-to manual that will teach you a process for implementing social technology in its most powerful form. Just as personal computers, the Web, and e-commerce have caused dramatic changes in how organizations operate, social tech will also alter the way we do business. It already has.

As we have seen in the past, the operations that learn early on to leverage new technologies gain great benefits. Well-known examples include technology-driven companies like eBay and Amazon. Less well-known examples are the law firm that adopted practice management software early on and dramatically improved profitability, and the bank that installed online banking a year before any of its competitors and gained a perpetual advantage with young customers. When you implement a powerful tool before your competition, you can win market share, create wealth, and even generate social good. Considering all these benefits, it is obvious that the race is on to figure out how to leverage social tech tools to win big in business.

This book will help you put together a game plan that will deliver serious results. Not just an introduction to social tech but an in-depth explanation of its relevance, *Enterprise Social Technology* is intended for the whole spectrum of leaders–from the nontechnology person to the tech expert.

A (Very) Brief History of Social Communication

It all started with drawings on cave walls . . . OK, that may be going a little too far back! Let's start instead with the Gutenberg press, which changed forever our ability to communicate ideas, concepts, and news to groups of people. The printing press was indeed an early form of social technology; it provided an inexpensive and fast method for communication of a single message (that of the Bible) to a large group of people. It also let people broadcast news in a much more efficient way than by word of mouth.

The first *electronic* social technology was the telegraph, which at the time seemed almost magical in its ability to let someone communicate instantly over hundreds of miles. The telegraph forced people to develop a new language (Morse code) that allowed them to get messages across in just a few characters. (Looking at the twin phenomena of texting and Twitter, we see that some things never change.)

The telephone further expanded the significance of social technology and provided us with the most powerful communication device we had seen up to that point.

Next came the Internet, which provided us with e-mail, and then instant messaging, followed by blogging, microblogging, and voice and video over the Web tools (like Skype). With the explosion of mobile devices came texting and on-the-go connection to the Internet.

All this is to say that we have been socially connecting for many centuries, so the dynamic is nothing new—and we will probably never stop developing new modes of social tech. The only radical thing that the most recent social technologies have brought us is a set of tools that connect us much more effectively and much more cheaply (in fact, for free in most cases).

At times, these new communications tools also have a way of reordering entire industries. Think of the impact that cell phones are having as they bring on the death of pay phones and home landlines, or the effect of the MP3 audio file format on the music industry.

The past couple of years have seen the explosion of social technology tools at a personal level; these same tools are now rapidly being adopted in the business world. Social tech has already started to change organizational behavior and is poised to dramatically alter the way the world operates. The fact is, you ain't seen nothin' yet.

Social Tech: Playtime Is Over

Human beings like connection. We especially like connecting with people who share our interests. Give us a new form of cheap, instant, and robust communication, and we will use it to connect with people all over the world. We have done so for many years. Obviously, there were many ways of connecting with groups or communities before MySpace and Facebook existed. The significance of these sites is in the way they have improved on the traditional website by allowing us to create an online persona. Now we have clustered environments and simple tools to build our own pages, on which we can present information about our lives. Of course, some people—especially older generations—are hesitant to share information in online communities, but that attitude is swiftly changing. Today we see that very large communities are experiencing explosive growth, and new groups form every second. Ning.com, for example, is a platform that facilitates the formation of many thousands of groups while requiring very little money or effort.

Combine a multifaceted schema of communication with a sophisticated set of choices for forming communities, and—*bang!*—you have a technologically enhanced social system. And once you have a social system that gives people—both as individuals and on the behalf of larger entities—the ability to communicate seamlessly, virtually for free, and with lots of cool filtering systems, you have something that is commercially attractive. I'm talking not about e-commerce or simple online transactions, but about a whole new dimension of doing business. I'm talking about an organization's ability to communicate with and influence individuals for free, everywhere in the world.

It's become pretty clear that with the advent of the Internet, our world would never be the same. Once we created the ability for any one person to talk to billions—unfiltered and at no or little cost—we turned a corner as a civilization. The big difference between the impact of social tech and the Gutenberg Bible is one of speed. It took decades for the printing press as a tool to spread across the world. It only took months for social tech to do the same.

Look, the reality is that there will be absolute winners and losers when it comes to learning how to leverage social technology. Do it well, and you may prosper beyond whatever level you might have imagined. Blow it, and your organization may not survive—and I mean that. If you thought e-commerce, outsourcing, and e-mail marketing were powerful tools, get ready for concepts that will have an even greater impact on organizations.

When it comes to social tech, playtime is over. That's why you are about to get the whole story, chapter and verse, on implementing an organized process for integrating social technologies into your organization. The changes that will come because of social tech will be far-reaching, fast, and dramatic. The seeds of tomorrow have already been planted today, and they have begun to spring up from the ground. I am not guessing or prognosticating when I say these things—I'm simply observing the trends. What first influences individuals goes on to reform organizations, striking with a vengeance.

Let's take a look at the different types of social technology that play this role.

The Three Categories of Social Technology

Social tech is not just a collection of a few Internet applications or platforms. It is a broad movement that already includes hundreds of companies, each of which provides a unique service. From a business standpoint, it makes more sense to look at social technology not as an assortment of software applications (such as YouTube, Twitter, and LinkedIn), but as a collection of new capabilities (like user-generated content, microblogging, and e-communities) that organizations can leverage. If you really want your organization to build a powerful social tech strategy, you need to be in command of various techniques and technologies within each of the following three categories.

Social Relevance

The first category is *social relevance*. This category encompasses the online reputation of an individual or organization. Social relevance is already starting to make a difference in the world and will soon have a dramatic impact on a company's ability to sell products and services. Organizations are just starting to use online reputation management to understand the good, the bad, and the ugly of open and accessible public comments on products and services, there to be seen by anyone with Internet access.

At an individual level, a professional's social relevance will have a great impact on whether or not that person lands the job, gets the meeting appointment, or closes the sale. We are nearing the point at which we will have the ability to rate people, just as we are now rating news stories, restaurants, and businesses. Check out sites like SocialMention.com, Klout.com, or Addictomatic.com for an idea of how easy it is to verify credentials online.

Every organization needs to have a plan in place to manage its social relevance and the social relevance of its employees—and a website alone will not get you there. Here are some of the ways social relevance has been incorporated into organizational action.

Online Reputation Management

In the past, our own reputations were pretty easily controlled, whereas the reputations of others were nearly impossible to corroborate in any detail. We learned what to expect from the people and organizations we dealt with mostly by interacting with them and seeing what happened. There was simply no easy way to check the credentials of a person or company. Of course, we could contact a few (probably biased) references that someone would give us, but that was about it.

All that has changed. Welcome to the brave new world! From now on, we will all be able to check online to see what a person has done, how they think, and what others think of them. We will learn about many personal aspects of their lives that would have been completely private in generations past.

Online Rating Systems

Internet users now have online rating systems—an offshoot of online reputation management—at their disposal, providing them with the ability to rate everything from news items to teachers. There are sites for rating doctors, lawyers, hotels, restaurants, retail locations—the list goes on and on. With the power of scalability, we now can view what hundreds or thousands of past customers, patients, or clients think of an organization or provider. Frankly, I think that we will look back on the previous decades as a Stone Age—a backward era when people picked doctors, dentists, and lawyers without any input as to how good they were. We just looked them up in the Yellow Pages or got a reference from a single friend, and then we hired them. Those days are just about over. It will be a *very* different world when we all can rate service providers, and nothing but good will come out of this in the long run.

Social Media

The second category of social tech is *social media*. This includes the use of Internet and mobile media (videos, documents, photos, slide presentations, etc.) for sharing ideas, concepts, messages, or entertainment. For each type of medium, there are services that facilitate one-to-one or one-to-many communication; examples include YouTube, Scribd, Flickr, and SlideShare. Every enterprise needs to understand how to utilize these types of sites in order to be the primary provider of information in its respective field.

Here are some of the ways social media has been incorporated into organizational action.

User-Generated Content

Never before in history could any individual create a video, presentation, document, or photograph and publish it instantly for all the world to see, and for free. Whereas in the past mass media outlets (TV networks, newspapers, magazines, radio stations) were the sole filters of what would be shared with the masses, people now have the power to create any type of media they choose and share it with their friends—or the entire world—over the Web. We are already seeing the power this has to break the hegemony of governments and big media.

Citizen Journalism

Blogging, microblogging, and RSS feeds are just a few of the tools that are allowing any person to become a news source who contributes to the entire Internet—free of charge. Never before in human history could a human being witness an event or have a thought and instantly share it with the rest of humanity. And, to the surprise of many, these "ordinary citizens" often have more insightful and relevant things to say than the mainstream media does.

Real-Time News

Not only can any citizen with Web access now create and deliver news, but he or she also can do it in real time. We used to think that television was the fastest form of receiving news; reporters could interrupt the broadcast of any show to give viewers a glimpse of a news event. Now we know there is, in fact, a lag time between when an event happens and when reporters deliver the news of it. Services like Twitter, however, allow any witness to an event to deliver text and pictures within seconds of the event's occurrence.

Web-Based Rivers of Information

We now have tools that allow us to create a powerful flow of information straight to our brains. Throughout the past century or so, we have always had books, newspapers, and trade shows; in other words, we have been able to create streams of information related to our fields of interest. Today, however, we can create raging *rivers* of information that can include input from just about every thought leader on any subject, and we can get this information in real time. Social tech allows us to construct powerful collections of information that get pushed to us on any device we choose, and filtering tools help us aggregate and weed out social media so we get only the most important nuggets each day.

Social Networking

The final category of social tech is *social networking*, which is all about connecting with people through a variety of communication methods and online communities. Networking used to consist of in-person events and a Rolodex filled with business cards. Back in the day, there was a physical limit on how many people with whom we could maintain a relationship. Now, with blogs, Facebook, Twitter, MySpace, Ning, LinkedIn, Plaxo, and many other options, social networking increases the number of people you can keep in your network, eases communication on a larger scale, and allows for more frequent contact—all using tools that are free. In short, our ability to connect is blossoming right in front of our eyes.

Since business is all about connections, social networking is going to change how we sell, how we serve customers, how we resolve issues, and how we build relationships with the general public. Here are some of the ways social networking has been incorporated into organizational action.

Online Communities

For the first time, people now have the ability to instantly find others who share their own interests. Those interests can be related to entertainment, hobbies, business, or anything else. And now, not only can we easily find existing groups of like-minded individuals, but we also can use services like Ning to instantly set up a new group for any area of interest. Geography and even language are not issues any longer because our new social networking tools facilitate communication and sharing from any corner of the world.

Microblogging

Services like Twitter and Facebook have given people the ability to build frameworks of information provided by both friends and strangers and also to see inside the minds of hundreds of people each day. Microblogging, a form of connection we have not encountered in the past, consists of short bursts of user-generated content that allow people to stay current with known contacts and to follow the thoughts of strangers who have interesting or relevant things to say.

Location-Based Information

Social networking tools have given us the ability to interact with our environment and find almost any location without driving around aimlessly for hours. With a smartphone and the right applications, we can stand in the middle of a city and within seconds find exactly what we are looking for and the directions for getting there. On the flip side of the coin, businesses can identify where we are and send us information when we are in their neighborhood. We also can find out where any of our friends are in relation to where we currently stand. We can even use our smartphones to identify what we are looking at and to bring in information that relates to our location (known as "augmented reality," or AR). With AR, we can completely change how we relate to physical locations; in the future, we may even be able to walk into a store with a video visor that virtually decorates the store specifically for each of us.

Crowdsourcing

In the past ten years or so, outsourcing work to other countries has become a popular way to lower the cost of doing business. But traditional outsourcing will pale in comparison to what happens when organizations begin to truly leverage the Internet herd. Early examples of this "crowdsourcing," like the Wikipedia concept, showed us that Web users could be harnessed into doing impressive tasks for very little money or even for free. Now we have an explosion of sites like IdeaStorm.com, Mturk.com, Innocentive.com, crowdSPRING. com, and LogoTournament.com—all examples of how work can be completed when it's opened up to the Internet crowds. Businesspeople are waking up to the fact that they can farm out assignments over the Internet—often to anonymous sources—quickly, inexpensively, and competently.

* * *

Rather than an exhaustive list of concepts that fit underneath the social tech umbrella, these are merely a few interesting examples to underscore the point: Social tech is a topic that includes a far greater range of options than just Facebook. We are only a few years into this "social" era, and social technology is really just a newborn idea. We will continue to innovate with these tools and concepts for years to come. It would be naïve to think that we have fully mined all the possibilities when it comes to social technology. I suspect we are still very early in the development stages, and I predict that we will be shocked, even over the next five years, at social tech's continuing impact on business and society.

By now you should have a better idea of what social technology is all about. Let's switch gears to reveal what this book is about and how you can get the most out of it.

How to Use This Book

A tool is wasted if no one learns how to use it, and social tech is far too valuable a tool to waste. The rest of this book is a primer for how businesses can integrate social tech tools and strategies into their organizations.

I'm a hands-on kind of guy. I started my career in technology in 1981, and I have spent the past thirty years building technology companies and evangelizing tech concepts. I believe that to understand any technology, particularly social technology, you have to use it with your own hands. So when I decided to write a book about how social technologies should be integrated into organizations, I realized that I should practice what I preach: I decided to use social technology, specifically crowdsourcing, to augment *Enterprise Social Technology*. In the end, we developed a new model for crowdsourcing a published work—a model that is fast and efficient, and that provides more value than when content is created by a single source.

Here is how the system worked: I created a detailed outline for the book, chapter by chapter, and wrote the first section (this introduction) and the last two chapters myself. Then I used crowdSPRING. com to crowdsource the content for the other chapters. The whole book was then edited at least twice by both the publisher and me. In the end, we found that crowdsourcing works, even for a project as complex as writing a book. (The Afterword at the end of this book contains more information on *how* the project worked.)

In order to leverage social technology, you need to have in place a process for integrating these tools within the operations of the organization. Although no one has more than a couple of years' experience in this area, I am lucky enough to have worked with a number of clients and to have had the opportunity to refine a twelve-step process for successfully helping an organization quickly gain value from social tech. Each of the chapters from this point forward represents one of these twelve steps. We will describe each step in detail so you get a clear picture of the concept and why it is important.

Note that these steps are presented in a logical order, but you do not need to tackle them consecutively. In many cases, different people within an organization can work on completing the steps concurrently. Still, we typically try to get organizations to implement these steps within ninety days, because we have found that committing to a short deadline keeps the task of implementing social tech from getting lost among the other tasks in a wasteland of good intentions. This ninety-day time frame can be adjusted based on the size of an organization. A smaller company can probably accomplish this goal faster; a larger one may want to allow time for more people to be involved in the process. What does not change is that organizations of all sizes should complete some form of all twelve steps. As mentioned before, there are large rewards for the organizations that learn to use these tools more quickly than their competitors.

As you go through the steps, we will provide resources and tools that will help you with the completion of each one. Look for the icon seen here in the right margin, which indicates that an additional online resource is available on our website.

Now let's get started.

–Scott Klososky

CHAPTER 1

Setting Social Tech Goals

Social technology is not a magic wand. You will not mysteriously begin to prosper once you start using it. If you are in business, you want to make profits, and there are two simple ways to do so: You must either increase sales, which can be done by leveraging social campaigns, or lower back-office costs, which can be accomplished by improving collaboration and communication and by leveraging concepts such as crowdsourcing to find new ways to achieve tasks for less money.

Even if you are part of a nonprofit or public entity (and thus driving profits may not be your objective), there will be specific goals you want to realize, and in most cases social tech tools can help you get there. That's what this first step is about—identifying where "there" is. The key to creating order out of chaos is to clarify what your organization wants to accomplish through social technology. That means setting clear and measurable goals. This sounds like a basic concept, yet it seems that most organizations do not have a concise list of what they hope to achieve through the use of social tech; all they have is a fuzzy sense that they want to learn how to use it.

The quality of your goal setting determines the quality of your results. Social tech goals help people think about how to accomplish big things, and they help set the strategic endpoints that people will work toward. Without them, any social technology strategy will veer off course and be ineffective in the end. And it's not about setting just any goal—it's about setting the right kinds of goals in the areas that will drive results.

Here are a handful of examples of goals that your organization might find useful to strive toward:

- Create more prospects and customer leads.
- Increase sales and peer-to-peer sales reviews.
- Improve internal communications and morale (especially if you have offices in various parts of the world).
- Build brand awareness and track the effectiveness of the current brand.
- Improve customer service and product support.
- Improve your ability to recruit top-notch talent to your team.
- Increase market intelligence by collecting customer feedback, encouraging customer community and identity, and collecting information about competitors.
- Lower operating costs by using crowdsourcing as a means for completing tasks faster and less expensively than at present.

It is best to focus on a few core goals as opposed to trying to arrive at all of them in a short span of time. And often, reaching one or two key goals can then lead to further success with secondary aspirations.

As you set your goals, keep in mind all three areas of social tech. Too many companies focus solely on social networking and how they can connect with customers and prospects. Setting goals for how many connections you can create and how many leads you can generate through social networking is a great idea, but you must also consider your organization's objectives in the areas of social relevance and social media. These goals may relate to the following:

- Online reputation (How many mentions will you aim for? What is a desirable sentiment ratio—or approval rating—among customers?)

- Online influence (What is your ability to influence online discussions about your products, or brand?)
- Social media engagement (How many views will you try to get? What click-through rate will you aim for?)

Also, remember to write down every goal so that you can keep track of your organization's progress. Finally, consider the following section before your organization sets its sights on any targets.

Characteristics of Effective Social Tech Goals

Goals that generate effective gains in terms of social technology generally share seven characteristics, each of which is explained below.

1. Effective Goals Are Well Thought Out

Social technology goals should be co-created by several key team members within the organization and aligned with wider organizational goals. They should reflect the company's values, mission, and vision. Thus, when setting these goals, the organization should ask itself not "What do we do?" but "Why do we do what we do?" Only when this purpose is clear are social tech goals assigned and aligned with the company's broader mission.

For example, Absolut Vodka put on an event that was a success largely because the company wisely linked its social tech goals to its history of supporting artists. Absolut used social networking to drive attendance of a special one-day event in Toronto featuring Canadian multidisciplinary artist Justin Broadbent. Broadbent transformed the unused third level of a subway station into a multimedia installation—a fantastic juxtaposition against the standard drab, gray subway-station environment. During the daytime, the venue was a vibrant art exhibition, and as evening descended, it transformed into one of the hottest VIP parties in Toronto.

Absolut created a Bluetooth network for the party and a Facebook page where people could sign up for the guest list. Twitter was used to update attendees on further details as they became available. The VIP guest list reached capacity within forty-eight hours of the campaign launch, so Absolut focused its efforts on the daytime event, pushing messages to enabled devices through the Toronto Bluetooth network. Between that Bluetooth network and the company's own, Absolut achieved an overall 7 percent opt-in rate—which, compared to traditional or online media rates, was very satisfying. The company achieved its goals of a full guest list and a high Bluetooth opt-in rate.[1]

Absolut set goals for this event based on the company's previous support of artists; in the past it had commissioned sculptors, glass designers, musicians, fashion designers, and more than three hundred painters as part of its media campaigns and promotional events. Thus the campaign in support of the Justin Broadbent event fit into the broader organizational strategy. The immediate goals for the exhibition and party were well thought out by the entire team; they formed a carefully planned step toward the final goal of increased consumer engagement.

2. Effective Goals Drive Desired Results

It is crucial that social tech goals be tightly linked to the results the organization hopes to see once those goals are met. The clearer the desired results, the more likely the organization is to reach its goals—particularly if everyone within the organization understands the purpose behind them.

Tying goals to results helps an organization focus on whether its goals are about the statistics or about the effects. For example, a lot of organizations are concerned about their number of Facebook friends or Twitter followers—but these indicators shouldn't matter nearly as

---

1   Phil Barrett, "Social Media Drives Absolut Vodka Pop-Up Event," *Burning the Bacon with Barrett* (blog), August 19, 2009.

much as the more tangible results of sales, transactions, and valuable conversations do.

3. Effective Goals Are Measurable

There should be specific criteria against which results will be evaluated and a set methodology for measuring these results. Measurements should be carried out on a regular basis and reported back to the wider team in order to reinforce the value of the organization's goals.

Social technology tools make it very easy to calculate these measurements and determine how effectively goals are reached. Consider Sony Pictures' rebranding of RockYou's "Vampires" application for the movie *30 Days of Night*. The Vampires app already had over three million installs on Facebook when Sony Pictures put banner ads on the rebranded application, promoting the movie and a related sweepstakes. The campaign, which was to go live for only three weeks, set the goal of obtaining ten thousand sweepstakes entries. By the end, there were 59,100 entries, plus 11,642,051 visits to the bite page and 17,652,567 to the stats page. These results exceeded Sony's expectations, and the clear metrics provided by Facebook allowed the company to objectively evaluate the effectiveness of the campaign.[2]

4. Effective Goals Force the Organization to Stretch

Effective goals compel the organization to reach beyond standard expectations and to challenge its limits. Setting goals that are reachable but that also require increased energy and focus helps the team get excited and connect to a broader vision of what is possible.

For example, charity: water is a New York–based nonprofit that builds wells in thirteen countries, including Liberia, India, and Honduras, to provide people with clean water. In approximately

---

2   Jeremiah Owyang, "Case Study: How Sony Leveraged a Popular 'Vampire' Facebook Widget to Reach Its Community," *Web Strategy* (blog), January 29, 2008, http://www.web-strategist.com/blog/2008/01/29/case-study-how-sony-leveraged-a-popular-vampire-facebook-widget-to-reach-its-community/.

two and a half years, charity: water has raised $9.7 million and has funded 1,341 clean water projects that serve 727,110 people. The charity had to be ambitious to even try for these results, but by setting clear organizational goals and encouraging a broad vision that forced the organization to stretch in order to achieve those ambitions, charity: water engaged its stakeholders, built brand awareness, and met its goals through the use of social tech.

Donors can watch four short videos–posted online daily–of charity: water's drilling activities and can ask questions of the local drilling team via e-mail or Twitter. They also can view in real time information about every well that is built, through photos, videos, and GPS coordinates on Google Earth. The organization also pushed itself beyond its normal limits by partnering with Twestival to host a virtual, multicity fund-raising campaign through Twitter, which raised a quarter of a million dollars and increased global awareness of the world's water crisis.[3]

5. Effective Goals Are Taken Seriously

Organizational goals should be legitimate promises the company makes to itself, as opposed to hollow statements that are unlikely to result in change. Team members must feel as though they are significantly contributing to a collective vision of success, rather than laboring to meet a goal that no cares much about.

6. Effective Goals Are Owned by a Specific Person or Group of People Who Are Held Accountable for Their Attainment

Although the entire team should feel ownership of the purpose behind the organization's social tech goals, certain people need to take ownership of the execution of these goals. That way, a specific representative can be held accountable for overseeing the process,

---

3   "Case Study: charity: water," ThinkSocial blog, May 26, 2009, http://think-social.org/case-study-charity-water.htm.

and there is no confusion about whom to address if objectives are not reached. Sometimes having a team delegate responsible for achieving each goal can make all the difference.

7. Effective Goals Provide Strong ROI

The attainment of preordained goals should yield a sufficient return on investment (ROI), and the metrics for measuring this ROI should be laid out from the start.

Social Tech Goal-Setting Success Stories

Let's look now at an example of a company that reaped the benefits of good goal setting. When Mr. Vintage, Australia and New Zealand's largest pop culture T-shirt importer, ran a social tech campaign in July and August 2009, it set the following primary goals:

- Create brand awareness.
- Build stronger customer relationships and a customer community.
- Turn happy customers into raving fans.
- Leverage mainstream media coverage.

A secondary objective was to practice innovation and give the Mr. Vintage team an exercise in thinking outside the box.

Instead of running a campaign focused on a sales pitch, Mr. Vintage wanted to thank its existing fans while building up its online following. The company also took into consideration the fact that July and August are winter months in the southern hemisphere, coming up with a campaign that would appeal to most Kiwis and Aussies on a cold, gray winter's day: a two-day social media competition, during which the company gave away one $100 T-shirt voucher every hour and offered a grand-prize trip for two to Fiji.

To enter, people had to join the mailing list, become a fan on Facebook, follow Mr. Vintage on Twitter, and e-mail friends about the competition. By the end of the campaign, the results were clear and positive: more than five thousand additional Facebook fans, more than seven thousand new mailing-list subscribers, and more than fifteen hundred added followers on Twitter.

While the competition was running, Mr. Vintage ranked as the fifth-highest trending topic on Twitter—right up there with Google, Michael Jackson, and CNN. Numerous blogs featured write-ups on this originally small, local competition.

The woman who won the trip was in her mid-thirties, had never been overseas, had three kids, and had just lost 132 pounds. She ended up taking the whole family overseas (paying extra for the kids)—and all of this made a great human-interest story. Mr. Vintage was able to get the winner on national TV, where she appeared on the major morning and evening talk shows in New Zealand. The company also managed to get the winner's flight from Air New Zealand free of charge, by explaining that the partnership would give Air New Zealand exposure within Mr. Vintage's growing community. For Mr. Vintage, the total cost of the entire campaign was less than $2,000.

Because the goals of this campaign were so well thought out and consistent with the overall organizational strategy, the company's efforts were successful—proving that good goal setting leads to positive results.

British Airways is another example of a company that has successfully tied its social tech goals to larger organizational goals. One of the airline's overarching objectives is "to be the world's leading global premium airline."[4] With this in mind, British Airways launched an online platform called Metrotwin, which links New Yorkers and Londoners through a Web community that provides recommendations about shops, bars, restaurants, parks, and neighborhoods.

---

4 "Our Strategy and Objectives," British Airways, accessed September 14, 2010, http://www.britishairways.com/cms/global/microsites/ba_reports0809/our_business/strategy4.html.

Metrotwin helps users navigate the vast amount of Internet information about the two cities, enabling them to find the best content quickly, often through Amazon-style recommendations.[5]

Building an online community around the sights and accommodations of two world-class cities clearly aligns with British Airways' organizational goal of becoming the world's leading premium airline. The company also uses the site to publicize the technological prowess of the Airbus A318 for its London–New York route. The aircraft was retrofitted to include in-air Web connection, e-mail, and SMS facilities, standards that are in line with another of British Airways' goals: to demonstrate the airline's relevance in the twenty-first century. In alignment with this goal, the company also provided its first-ever press trip targeting travel bloggers.[6]

Until the creation of Metrotwin, British Airways had been a significant player with a traditional approach to PR. But these social tech goals that dovetailed with bigger organizational goals helped update the company's image and paid off for British Airways in a big way.

The founder of BBGeeks.com, a comprehensive online source for information on BlackBerry devices, talks about the importance of one of the other characteristics of good goal setting: assigning responsibility for meeting the goal to one person or group. When BBGeeks first came to Twitter, the organization was unsure of how to proceed with building a commercial social networking account. It registered, put up a basic logo, and remained static. It followed a few personal friends and posted a few conversational tweets. By the end of the first month, BBGeeks had about one hundred followers, but still lacked purpose and direction. The account remained quiet for another four months, until the organization did a bit more research and ventured into social technology once again.

---

5 Darren Davidson, "British Airways launches social media network," *Brand Republic* News blog, September 23, 2008, http://www.brandrepublic.com/News/848300/British-Airways-launches-social-media-network/.

6 Kevin May, "British Airways targeting social media with first trip for bloggers," *Tnooz* (blog), May 3, 2010, http://www.tnooz.com/2010/05/03/news/british-airways-targeting-social-media-with-first-trip-for-bloggers/.

BBGeeks' second attempt at developing social tech goals was a bit more structured, but there was one difference that would prove to be crucial: A single staff member was assigned to become the company's "voice" on Twitter. This staff member was not dedicated solely to Twitter—he spent only about thirty minutes a day on this task. But simply establishing him as the go-to guy ensured that the posts were now written thoughtfully by an actual person rather than being auto-tweeted. The BBGeeks employee in charge of the account also found BlackBerry users on Twitter and followed them, hoping that in return they would follow the company. The company encouraged this employee to post off-topic comments and to join in the conversation with other Twitter users, even if it wasn't always Black-Berry related. He also started doing small Twitter giveaways here and there, offering branded T-shirts and stickers, and occasionally he tweeted about special "Twitter only" discounts at BBGeeks.com's software and accessories store.

This time around, the company's efforts proved far more successful. Over the next three months, the number of BBGeeks' Twitter followers rose by four hundred and the organization won exclusive press conference tickets through its followers. It also used Twitter to receive instant customer feedback and content ideas for its website. Twitter became a valuable tool in the company's branding efforts, content development, online traffic improvement, revenue growth, and back-link generation.[7]

Rule Number One for Goal Setting: Review Progress Regularly

While attempting to set goals for integrating social technology into its PR strategy, the most important thing for an organization to remember is that it should review progress regularly until the end of

---

7   Rae Hoffman, "Twitter Case Study of a Commercial Brand," *Sugarrae* (blog), August 6, 2008, http://www.sugarrae.com/an-actual-non-big-brand-twitter-case-study/.

the time frame established for those goals. At that point, the company must consider lessons learned and then set new objectives, so that its social tech goals are constantly evolving in context with the overall organization. Or, said more simply, you must *inspect* what it is that you expect . . .

Disney's MySpace campaign for its 2006 dance movie *Step Up* demonstrates the importance of this rule. The film's MySpace profile gained more than 156,000 friends, boosted DVD sales, and turned the sequel, *Step Up 2: The Streets,* into a surprise box-office hit. The results were clearly measurable: An in-theater Nielsen survey given during the sequel's opening weekend showed that *Step Up 2* was more noticeable than its predecessor because of its MySpace profile. Fifty-eight percent of those people with a MySpace profile of their own recalled seeing an ad for or information about the sequel, whereas only 26 percent of those without a profile remembered seeing anything about the movie.[8]

Most important, as the process of releasing the movie evolved, so too did the social tech platform. The MySpace page was not simply a static online billboard for the movie; Disney invested time and energy into making the MySpace site enjoyable and interactive. It provided an avenue for users to interact with the movie's director and stars and ran a range of competitions, including chances to appear in the next movie and to see an advance "Black Curtain" screening of the current film, where the winner could interact with actors from the movie. These measures built considerable brand awareness and established an informal street team for the brand.

The only way to sort through the chaos of social technology and get rolling quickly with promoting your brand is to have clearly defined goals that create a direction for your organization's dedicated team, some of whom may be using social tech tools for the first time.

---

8 Michael Bush, "What Is Marketers' Biggest Challenge When It Comes to Social Networks?" *Advertising Age,* March 17, 2008, http://adage.com/digital/article?article_id=125712.

Once everyone accepts these goals, you'll need the peoplepower to get there—the team that will make it all happen.

Since the costs of using social technology are minimal, the biggest investment you'll have to make is an investment in your team. Assembling that team wisely is the topic of our next chapter.

KEY POINTS

- The quality of your goal setting determines the quality of your results. Do not be sloppy or careless when setting goals. Although this step may seem basic and overly simplistic, our experience shows that teams that carefully set goals and commit to them succeed at a much higher rate than teams that gloss over this area.

- Social tech goals must dovetail with the overall organizational strategy. Social tech is merely a tool that can be used to achieve your overall goals. It is not a magic bullet that will explode into success on its own.

- The results you expect to receive from hitting your goals need to be documented and communicated. Writing goals down and reviewing them regularly has a way of making them more of a priority—especially when they are presented to executives as commitments.

- Effective goals share certain characteristics: They are well thought out, they drive desired results, they are measurable, they force the organization to stretch, they are taken seriously, they are owned by specific people who can be held accountable, and they provide strong ROI.

 To access a copy of our social tech goals shell document, go to EnterpriseSocialTechnology.com and click on the Resources section.

CHAPTER 2

Assembling the Social Tech Team

The ease with which one can set up a social networking account belies the amount of time it takes to do it the right way. Your company's customer base and reputation were not established overnight, but you can destroy this foundation overnight with a hastily implemented online presence.

Social technology is just that: social. It is not a one-man or one-woman operation. When you bring your company into the world of leveraging social tech tools, you want your entire team's buy-in and input. This will include the employees to whom you entrust your social relevance, your social media, and your social networking. Clearly this responsibility is more than one or two people can or should be held accountable for.

The current chapter will help you to set up a social technology team by addressing the following issues:

- Why does your organization need a team?
- Who should be on the team?
- What should each party bring to the team?
- What kind of implementation timeline is reasonable to expect from the team?
- How should the team's progress and success be measured?

Why Does Your Organization Need a Team?

Remember when social tech really began to take off—when all the potential customers and clients started to hang out on Facebook, Twitter, MySpace, and various blogs, and companies needed to figure out how to reach those prospects? Suddenly social tech jobs like this one started popping up:

> New Media/General Marketer: This is a preliminary posting for a position we are beginning to search for here at Aflac corporate headquarters. We don't have the specifics yet, but we are looking for high-level professionals with ad agency backgrounds and advanced knowledge [in] new media, Web 2.0, and social networking. If you are qualified and interested, please forward your resume and salary requirements to me at [exampleaddress]@aflac.com. There are several opportunities in our marketing department, and [the] salary for these positions has not yet been determined.[9]

New media positions were rapidly being created. It seemed that although few people had a real handle on what new media was or what exactly the person in charge of it should be doing, it was the latest trend, and companies started thinking they had better get on board.

One statewide daily newspaper incorporated a new media department that mainly consisted of one person who was deemed a "creative." Management was enthusiastic about the idea, and the person in charge of new media was effectively given carte blanche to explore the possibilities of social marketing. He partnered with another employee, and they created an online extension of the newspaper that encouraged crowdsourced journalism: Ordinary citizens

---

9 Aflac job listing, quoted in Kipp Bodnar's "Uncase Study: How AFLAC Should Assemble a Social Media Team to Build for Long-term Success," *Digital Capitalism* (blog), February 25, 2009, http://digitalcapitalism.com/2009/02/building-an-corporate-social-media-team/.

could post news stories, events, pictures, and editorial blogs. This two-employee department even created a weekly live video broadcast that streamed across the Internet. People from all over the country could view and comment on the broadcast, and they could interact with professional journalists and fellow viewers.

The site started out doing rather well, but it quickly became apparent that the project was still highly experimental, with little actual buy-in from other departments and no real sense of where it was headed. Content became confusing and meandering, and interactions with followers grew inconsistent. The so-called new media department eventually floundered and faded away, although the online extensions it built remain fairly active. It simply was too much of an undertaking for one or two people.

When DigitalCapitalism.com posted an article that shared Aflac's new media listing (page 28), the website advised the company on the best way to go about hiring for this type of position. The article shows the importance of having a social media team, but it also makes the point that it isn't necessary to scramble for the funds to hire an outside social media team or agency. In fact, the best team you can assemble will include the people who already know your company and what it does best: your own employees.

Who Should Be on the Team?

Writer Amber Naslund, considered one of the leading experts in assembling social technology teams, says, "When I refer to a team, I mean exactly that: a group of people inside your organization [who] are tasked with strategizing, executing, and stewarding social media initiatives inside your company."[10] Ideally, your team will integrate people who are able to multitask—who don't mind jumping between

---

10 Amber Naslund, "Building a Social Media Team," SlideShare presentation, February 2010, http://www.slideshare.net/AmberNaslund/building-a-social-media-team.

social tech tasks and the other components of their jobs—and people who are willing to let their job descriptions evolve with the market.

An overly conservative approach to social technology might seem safer initially when your company is considering legal and IT concerns. But Facebook walls that don't allow any posts and Twitter accounts that are followed by nine hundred and fifty users but that follow none in return are quickly labeled as glorified commercials. This style of social networking implies a dismissive attitude to customer concerns and feedback, and it makes the company appear arrogant and incurious about what else is happening in the industry.

Andrew Webb covers these concerns in a blog post titled "5 Barriers to Entry for Corporate Social Media."[11] He says:

> For many organizations the biggest concern is over losing control if they enter the social media jungle. Drilling deeper, [one finds that] these concerns include the following:
>
> - Fear of opening the floodgates to customer views in public
> - Ability (and therefore associated cost) to respond and engage with the volume of discussions being generated
> - Damage to [the organization's] image/values caused by inappropriate or offensive content posted to any of [its] online assets
> - Concern about what employees might say about the business to customers or prospects
> - Cost in terms of resources, infrastructure, and time to successfully implement a social media strategy and solution

These are concerns that can and should be addressed by a variety of talent, including representatives from the marketing, information technology, human resources, public relations, sales, and

---

11 Andrew Webb, "5 barriers to entry for corporate social media," company blog of Optaros, September 14, 2009, http://www.optaros.com/blogs/5-barriers-entry-corporate-social-media/.

management teams. If you keep in mind Naslund's recommendation that this diverse social tech team "strategize, execute, and steward" social technology communication, most of these barriers can in fact become doorways to new opportunities for your business.

Depending on the size and nature of your operation, the number of social tech team members and the departments from which they originate will vary. You certainly will want the team to include people from customer-facing departments—sales, advertising, marketing, corporate communications, customer service, or otherwise. The team should also include people from the HR department—whose role will be to ensure that personnel policies are not being violated—and representatives of the organization's legal interests, to ensure that copyright and confidentiality are not violated. By including members of the IT department on the social tech team, you will ensure that your use of social technology tools doesn't increase the risk of introducing the latest Trojan horses and other viruses to your customers.

It is also important to consider the temperament of team members. You do not want to fill the team with raving fans of social tech because they might lose perspective on the overall organizational goals. Nor do you want an executive-level team that includes no members who use social tech themselves. A combination of skills and mind-sets works best.

As you consider who should join your social tech team, you also need to think about what each individual should bring to the group.

What Should Each Party Bring to the Team?

Your company's departments and staff members will differ from those of any other company, but there are basic expectations and responsibilities for members of the social tech team that apply to all organizations. First, each representative should come to the table with an open mind. Deciding ahead of time that the Internet is nothing more than a hive of predators, credit card thieves, and sexting teens, all of whom are waiting to destroy your company's reputation and finances, will get you exactly nowhere. Think in terms of possibilities.

Second, members need to be able to work as a team; they must be able to invest some time in learning about the technology they are using, and they must be willing to learn from one another. This means the young and technologically savvy must be willing to accept guidance from senior staff, and management must be willing to allow some creative and experimental latitude among younger staff who have already developed their own social tech presences.

Younger, more creative staff might have the ability to incorporate a wide variety of graphics, music, or videos into social technology sites that make the sites fun and interesting to visit. But they might not realize—as senior staff members do—the legal and copyright ramifications involved. They also might not fully understand that the artfully constructed skull-and-crossbones graphic they found just isn't appropriate for the line of children's clothing your company distributes. In this situation, a gentle, guiding hand from a senior staff member can save a great deal of misunderstanding.

Conversely, it is a wise company that follows what its younger technology entrepreneurs are doing online and looks for ways to incorporate those skills into its own social tech efforts. One traditional local television station hired a young camera technician with both a talent for social technology and the drive to implement it. Because the station was reluctant at first to hear his ideas or to embrace the social technology he negotiated so effortlessly, he started doing his own news and local event broadcasts on the site, using YouTube, Facebook, Justin.tv, podcasts, and live chat. The audience response was excellent, and it wasn't long before the technician's employer inquired as to whether the station might use some of his productions for its larger audience. It was a win-win: The television station found a new audience willing to comment on and share stories the station ran to people outside the normal television broadcast range, and the technician became an asset to the station by learning sound journalism practices from his traditional and more experienced employer.

So, keeping in mind that–in addition to shared enthusiasm for company goals and new experiences–a variety of skills, experience levels, and knowledge bases make for the most productive social technology team, consider the following outline listing the skills that social tech team members from various parts of the organization should bring to the group.

The IT Department

Don't be surprised if your tech people are among the most reticent to adopt social technology. The Internet highway can be mean streets for the uninitiated, and IT has to fix the computers and networks that become compromised. Your IT people should be able to keep your team up to date on the latest virus threats and what to watch out for (e.g., Facebook's infamous Koobface), what capacity your server has, how much bandwidth is available, how many megabytes of uploading and downloading are allowed per month, and what potential coding or privacy problems are caused by various applications.

The Legal Department

Twitter allows for 140 characters per tweet; you don't want 125 of them taken up with disclaimers. However, your legal department can keep you out of hot water by offering advice on copyright and confidentiality issues. You will find that your legal advisers are crucial in early social tech meetings when you are determining what logos, taglines, and other materials can be used and as you develop your social technology policy, covered in chapter 3.

The Executive Team

Your CEO need not be present at every planning meeting, but he or she should be aware of what the company's plans are and should have representation on hand. Management's representation on the team will ensure that the company's goals remain the main point of focus and will update other managers or company leaders on strategy and progress.

The Marketing Department

The marketing people on the social tech team are those whose job it is to sell your service or product. They might be doing a great deal of your actual social tech news and status updates. A mix of marketing traditionalists and early adopters is ideal.

The Communications Department

For the best result, you should allow customers, clients, and perhaps even competitors to comment upon, ask questions about, and otherwise interact with your social technology sites. How will complaints be handled? How will questions be answered? How will false claims about your product or service be addressed publicly? Public relations and communications employees can bring ideas for meeting these challenges and using social tech interaction to the company's advantage. The way a company publicly handles an unhappy customer can say far more than a traditional advertisement.

The Web Technician

This will be the team member who handles the building and maintenance of your website. When the creative members of the team generate ideas, the Web technician informs the team what kind of coding and applications will be required to integrate these ideas into the site. IT team members then make sure the site doesn't exceed server capacity, and legal team members ensure that it's all kosher from their perspective.

* * *

Notice that members of the social tech team are interdependent on one another's feedback in order to succeed. Amber Naslund and other social tech team experts caution against placing all this responsibility on the head of one "social technology guru." Not only is it too much for one person to handle, but it's also paradoxical to have one lonely guy or gal in a cubicle somewhere who is in charge of your biggest networking tool. Blogger and social media adviser Chris Brogan posted this insight after watching a football game:

> We think about companies using social media and we name their one person assigned to the task. Sometimes a company will have a few more employees doing it, but then they're just shadows of the functions of the "main" person doing it. [And yet] a team isn't made up of only quarterbacks . . . We're building a cluster of solo players out there on the field when what is necessary is a team methodology with all kinds of touchpoints, system connectors, and deeper communications/strategy channels.[12]

Most important, your team needs to be willing and able to invest the time to meet with one another regularly for a period of at least twelve to eighteen months. Monthly meetings are crucial in order to form a strategic plan for launching social technology; they can be conducted in person or over Skype, GoToMeeting, or other digital conference tools. It is very important that all members are allowed to provide input and offer feedback.

What Kind of Implementation Timeline Is Reasonable to Expect from the Team?

Expect your team to stay together for at least two years, and give it at least twelve to eighteen months to implement its initiatives. It may not be necessary to have a permanent social tech team, but for

---

12 Chris Brogan, "Social Media Needs to Become a Team Sport," ChrisBrogan.com, November 23, 2009, http://www.chrisbrogan.com/social-media-needs-to-become-a-team-sport/.

practical reasons the team will need to be in effect for at least that amount of time. Twelve to eighteen months sounds like a long time to completely implement a Twitter strategy, but your social strategy will not be just about deploying the profile and linking it to your website. It takes time to build relationships online, get the word out about your presence, and see what kind of an impact it's having.

Be realistic about the timeline you set for implementation. Your Facebook page or LinkedIn group might not have five hundred fans or members by the end of the first week. It will take some time. Jennifer Van Grove, associate editor of social media powerhouse Mashable, offered the following advice on social tech timelines:

> Oftentimes, small businesses approach social media as a platform for quick wins, and a way to create immediate buzz. If only it were so simple. The reality is, as with everything, you need to be realistic about what social media can do for you in the short term, and you need to approach your social media marketing efforts with community in mind. Do communicate [to] all team members involved that though social media is a great way to get the word out, [that] success will not happen overnight.
>
> Be realistic and set achievable goals. If you approach your social media strategy with an honest desire to truly connect with customers, clients, and like-minded individuals online, and [you] possess an active interest in learning, then you can realistically start to see tangible results in three to six months.[13]

In that first phase you will start to see interaction with customers, but then you will also see the communications challenges that present themselves and the effect they have on your company's IT resources

---

13 Jennifer Van Grove, "5 Tips for Managing Social Media Marketing Expectations," American Express's Open Forum website, July 27, 2009, http://www.openforum.com/idea-hub/topics/technology/article/5-tips-for-managing-social-media-marketing-expectations-jennifer-van-grove/.

and staff time. Team members must ask themselves, are the sites on which you have chosen to develop a presence working for the company? Has senior management had time to take notice of the activity, and what are their initial thoughts? On other points it might make sense for IT, legal, and human resources team members to weigh in more heavily. For example, are some sites more of a time drain to manage and maintain than others, without any real value return? How is the staff representing the company online—ethically, legally, and with a professional yet approachable demeanor? Be sure to include enough space in the implementation timeline to give the team time to answer these questions and let them see where social technology in general is trending.

Changes can take place drastically and quickly in the world of social technology. MySpace started in 2003 as a social networking site for musicians, evolved to reach a much wider audience, and then returned to its musical roots when general MySpace users more recently migrated to Facebook. In 2009, social database Socrata (formerly Blist) began hosting lists of government information and other information of interest to the public. One list names several social networking sites of interest to a particular demographic, most of whom are on Ning. However, fourteen months after the last update to this Socrata list, Ning publicly announced plans to go from a free to a pay service. Will that database listing still be relevant, or will all those sites have moved or dismembered?

After twelve to eighteen months, the team should evaluate whether the sites it's been using are still relevant to the business. Have they changed from no-fee service to a tier-based fee service? Did they promise to be the next big thing and then fizzle right out of the gate? Is your website experiencing an inordinate amount of downtime or outages as a result of increased traffic or coding incompatibility? And are there new aggregators or other streamlining tools you can use to gather and broadcast information? (Tips on this last point will be covered more fully in chapter 5.) The team should observe, question, examine, assess, reassess, and meet, meet, meet. The information it gathers and the experiences it collects will aid you greatly in crafting your social technology policy. Giving the team adequate time will also give members time to track and analyze social tech stats for potential return on investment.

How Should the Team's Progress and Success Be Measured?

After the team has met and continued to evaluate data for some time, you can gather some basic numbers: How many people are following you on Twitter, and how many are you following in return? How many Facebook users "like" your page? What new information about your industry have you been able to gather? There are a number of excellent tools, such as Google Analytics and Radian6, for analyzing Web traffic and online brand reputation—and these are not the only measures of success you will be tracking. Tools for measuring traffic and return on investment will be covered more fully in chapter 9.

Social tech–savvy libraries track statistics for almost everything they do; this information is critical to grant writing and the creation of annual reports. In addition to traffic coming through the door and materials circulated, the statistics these librarians look at include reference questions collected from e-mail, Facebook, Second Life, Text a Librarian, Twitter, LinkedIn, and so forth. One rural library mentioned on its LinkedIn profile that it offered passport services; a Chicago HR firm that needed help processing six hundred passport applications picked up this information. Networking this request through social technology sites landed the library the job—and $15,000 worth of execution-fee profits. Those are numbers management can appreciate.

New accounts landed, new product launches from suppliers or competitors, and emerging technology in your industry are just a few of the other things you'll expect to be tracking. As staff members get more comfortable with social technology, more interactive with customers, and more efficient in gathering and disseminating information within your company's legal, professional, and technological bounds, you will begin to see your business take off exponentially.

Wrapping It Up

As discussed at the beginning of this chapter, social technology is not a solo sport; it requires a team effort. Hiring an "expert" who will have the sole responsibility for implementing and managing social tech is not a wise approach. If you are part of a large organization, hiring an expert makes perfect sense, but that expert will need to lead a team that incorporates representatives from all departments: IT, legal, PR, sales, marketing, management, human resources, website maintenance, and possibly others, depending on the nature of your organization. Each team member should have an open mind and a willingness to commit to monthly meetings over a twelve-to-twenty-four-month period to discuss the company's technological capabilities. During this period, the team should monitor how communications are disseminated and how questions or complaints from clients, customers, or other members of the social network are addressed. This should provide the team with enough information to start tracking and providing statistics for reporting on ROI and to begin developing and writing a social technology governance policy—the topic of the next chapter.

═ KEY POINTS ═

- In order to implement a suite of technologies as pervasive and sophisticated as social tech, a team approach will yield results faster. When a social tech team is established, responsibilities can be spread out among members, and knowledge will be better communicated throughout the entire organization if leaders relay the team's actions to their respective departments.

- The people who are picked for the team must have different personal styles of using social tech and different proficiency levels with social technology tools.

- Each member of the team should have specific responsibilities and be held accountable for the completion of his or her tasks.

- The team must meet on a regular basis (monthly at the least) for a minimum of twelve months. If social tech tools are successfully embedded in the fabric of the organization at that point, the team can be disbanded.

- Using a cross-discipline team approach facilitates the spreading of information and social tech knowledge throughout the organization.

 To access a copy of our social tech teams shell document, go to EnterpriseSocialTechnology.com and click on the Resources section.

CHAPTER 3

Internal Governance Policies

In baseball, a well-executed play is always a thing of beauty; a poorly executed one is a train wreck to watch. The purpose of this chapter is to help you develop a playbook—an internal governance policy—so that all employees know their positions when the proverbial social technology ball comes their way.

For some strange reason, many organizations seem to believe that employees and management will just adopt the appropriate social technology practices on their own. This is a dangerous attitude; when any person can speak for the organization in a medium that allows millions of people to see that communication forever, you have a recipe for disaster. And do not make the mistake of thinking that blocking social tech usage on company computers is going to mitigate that danger. Your employees have access to social tech tools on their mobile devices and personal computers, and what they say to the world from those devices looks *exactly* like what they might say from your computers.

Does Your Organization Really Need a Policy?

When does your company need a social technology policy? Is it when it's big enough to have marketing and IT departments? Is it right after a very embarrassing and very public social tech mistake?

No—your company needs a social technology policy as soon as it makes the decision to engage in social technology, regardless of whether you employ two people or two thousand. Having this policy in place protects both the company and its employees, and thus it is to everyone's advantage.

What happens when employees aren't educated about what constitutes proper use of social technology? Consider the infamous case of Heather Armstrong, the writer and publisher of an enormously popular blog called Dooce (dooce.com). Her blog started as an off-hours activity for entertainment purposes, but things quickly went south. Her blog distinguished itself from many others in its sarcastic and crass tone, and Armstrong felt many readers came and stayed because her writing was funny. She didn't use anyone's real names in her discussions of her work and her family, but eventually her frank and often unkind writing was discovered by her brother, who sent it to the rest of Armstrong's family. According to Forbes.com,

> [in 2002], someone anonymously e-mailed Armstrong's blog to her boss, which resulted in her being fired (and entered into the Internet lexicon: to be "dooced" is to get canned from your job because of your blog). "My boss was in tears," she says. "I felt like the worst human being on the face of the earth."[14]

As the news of Armstrong's real-life drama spread, many of her readers became hostile, and her parents didn't talk to her for months. Heather was eventually able to rebound, albeit with a new policy: Now she never says anything on her blog about someone that she wouldn't say to that person's face.

What's the lesson here? TMI (too much information) can get an employee dooced. On the other hand, too little information—and too

---

14 Kiri Blakeley, "Dooce's Dilemma," *Forbes*, July 17, 2009, http://www.forbes.com/2009/07/15/dooce-heather-armstrong-forbes-woman-power-women-blog.html.

much control in the hands of too few people or only one person—can be equally disastrous for a company.

One state association recently ran into some issues with carrying out the directives of one of its subcommittees. This particular committee annually awards recognition to children's book authors from a pool of nominees whose names and information are entered through a form on the association's website. The forms and contact information were overseen by one person and one person only. Unfortunately, when that person left the committee to attend to other personal and professional matters, the contact system, documents, and everything associated with networking on behalf of that committee went with that individual. All social technology accounts had been attached to that one person's e-mail account, and logins and passwords were unknown to fellow committee members. Nominations and questions went unanswered, and the angry telephone calls from potential customers to the heads of the association began to accumulate.

A little strategic planning in the form of an internal governance policy can save everyone from headaches such as these down the road.

What Is the Purpose of the Policy?

People use social technology for any number of reasons. Most are very forthcoming about these reasons, listing them in their social profiles: to network with other professionals; to self-promote; to reconnect with old friends; to keep up with loved ones; to discuss their views on religious, political, or cultural news; to just have fun and play games. Most employees would understandably feel encroached upon if their supervisor were to suddenly take issue with their after-hours Mafia Wars activities on Facebook. Conversely, the employer has every reasonable right to expect that the Mafia Wars are not happening on company computers and networks during company time, and certainly not using the company's social networking accounts. This sort of activity is as blatantly unprofessional as using the company vehicle for a personal road trip.

Therefore it is important to set firm limits specifying that what the company sets up belongs solely to the company and is to be used entirely for the professional benefit of the company. Your social technology policy will help to define the purpose(s) of the company's social presences and will establish firm boundaries to keep business on track and employees out of legal difficulties. And that policy must be conveyed with crystal clarity throughout the organization. Radio personality and "Digital Goddess" Kim Komando writes:

> In order to give staff members the feelings of autonomy and ownership, they need to know the rules . . . Every company that uses computers—from the smallest to the largest—should have a written policy on computer and Internet use. I make all employees sign our computing policy on their first day of work. And you should, too. This way, they know that you mean business and that the computers and Internet access lines are intended to further the company's goals.[15]

Engaging your employees as individuals on behalf of your business is not only the future of business marketing; it's the here and now. Steve Rubel, director of insights at Edelman Digital, had this to say at the 2009 Mediabistro Circus: "Companies will need to put faces on the brand in order to win acceptance . . . [because] people trust other people to introduce them to brands . . . Companies have to put their individual employees out there and let them become

---

15 Kim Komando, "Why You Need a Company Policy on Internet Use," Microsoft. com, accessed June 1, 2010 http://www.microsoft.com/smallbusiness/resources/ management/employee-relations/why-you-need-a-company-policy-on-internet-use. aspx (page discontinued).

brands."[16] But the company "brand" created and reinforced by an employee's social media activity cannot go unchecked as an employee's individual presence might. Writer Alex Goldman, in an article for InternetNews.com, adds, "[Companies] need to make policies fast, because the youngest people at any company are already on social networks."[17]

How Does Your Organization Write a Policy?

By now, surely you see the wisdom in having a social technology policy. But how do you begin? There are many excellent social technology policy templates available that will show you what other companies are doing, but you really will want something tailored to your company's needs.

First, it's important to understand the difference between a *policy* and a *procedure*. This distinction will keep you from writing a policy so bloated with micromanagement detail that most people will end up signing it without even having read it properly. California Polytechnic State University has a nice, concise breakdown of the essential differences between the two:

> **Policy:** The formal guidance needed to coordinate and execute activity throughout the institution. When effectively deployed, policy statements help focus attention and resources on high-priority issues—aligning and merging efforts to achieve the institutional vision. Policy provides the operational framework within which the institution functions.

---

16 Alex Goldman, "Companies Need Social Media All-Stars," InternetNews.com, June 4, 2009, http://www.internetnews.com/webcontent/article.php/3823566/Companies-Need-Social-Media-All-Stars.htm.

17 Ibid.

> **Procedures:** The operational processes required to implement institutional policy. Operating practices can be formal or informal, specific to a department or applicable across the entire institution. If policy is "what" the institution does operationally, then its procedures are "how" it intends to carry out those operating policy expressions.[18]

In addition to keeping your policy to a practical and readable length, you will also want to aim for a policy that doesn't need constant updating, which could add to confusion and possible inadvertent violation. Procedures may vary from department to department, or even from person to person. They usually are informal and allow for the occasionally necessary degree of flexibility. So, rather than descend upon your staff like Moses with the Ten Commandments, consider keeping to the basics; this should keep everyone productive and out of trouble.

The list of sample policies at the end of this chapter are a place to start, but here are a handful of basic guidelines that you may want to consider putting into your policy document.

1. Keep in Mind the Professional Purpose of Social Tech

Most employees will already have at least one personal social networking profile for their own individual reasons. When it comes to the use of social tech tools on the organization's behalf, however, establish the boundaries of acceptable use for your company. Let everyone know that the social media site is a place for professional networking, not to be hijacked to further a personal agenda, but rather to put friendly, "human" faces on the company. It needs to be clear that the social tech tools must be used to further the organization's overall goals and are not merely playthings.

---

18 "Policy vs. Procedures: A Guideline," California Polytechnic State University, accessed June 1, 2010, http://policy.calpoly.edu/cappolicy.htm.

2. Take Responsibility for Your Content

The policy should instruct employees to regard anything they post on any social technology site on behalf of the company as something they are saying on national TV. They should assume their boss (be it an actual supervisor or simply the customers they serve) is watching everything they write, because chances are very good that this is exactly what's happening. All employees should pay attention to grammar and spelling. Social tech communication is still professional communication, as much as if it were written on company letterhead. No one should make crude references, and all individuals should be ready to prove or defend any claim they make. There may be only fifty people following your company's Twitter account, but if just ten of those people forward to their entire network something an employee said, those words could be seen by thousands in an instant.

3. Encourage Authenticity

If your company's tweets and blogs are starting to look like junk mail 2.0, with constant sales pitches and no interaction with followers, you will lose business and tarnish your reputation. People do not like to be spammed, and over-advertising is perceived as spamming. Allow your employees to add associates or friends to the company's network, to monitor what other people in your industry are doing or saying, and to engage in discussion. The policy might state the employees shouldn't be afraid to leave the chat box open on Facebook or to check incoming messages on LinkedIn. Corporate speak should be avoided in addressing customers and constituents; employees should write social media communications in the same manner as a normal human being would speak.

4. Know Your Audience

Be mindful that what your employees write today will be read by people who haven't even started following your company's online presence yet. Instruct employees not to make too many pithy comments about recent events or references that no one will understand in a few months. Social tech participants should understand what your audience finds valuable and the tone of voice they find most attractive. Employees should be sure that their sense of humor will be understood (sarcasm doesn't always translate!) and that their writing style reflects a communication style your audience will appreciate. An employee's personal style may not be the best fit for the people who will receive the content he or she writes; nonetheless, in a professional setting the employee should be willing to meet the audience's preferences instead of holding on to his or her own.

5. Exercise Good Judgment

The type of good judgment necessary in the use of social technology is probably already covered in your workplace policies or in labor law, so look for any policies there that might also apply to online communication. Simply put: If it's taboo in the workplace, it's taboo in the organization's social tech communication.

6. Keep the Concept of Community Holy

Your policy should be written to ensure that once you have a number of people connected to you through social technology, no one in the organization abuses the privilege of having a large group to interact with. Do not let other entities use your account to address this group, and do not bombard your audience with irrelevant personal thoughts. Do not invite them to join a new group every other day. Do not use the group as your own personal self-help organization. There is a responsibility that comes with the blessing of having a large community of connections—do not decimate this resource by mishandling it.

7. Create Value

The company's social technology policy should emphasize the importance of providing value to your social tech connections; advise employees against talking just to amuse themselves. If you waste people's time by passing on drivel to them, you will be unfriended and unfollowed pretty quickly. If your employees consistently post interesting, creative content, on the other hand, soon you will not need to seek out your clients; they will come looking for you. According to Web information site Alexa.com, as of this writing, Facebook, Twitter, YouTube, and Blogger are all consistently in the top twelve sites people visit on the Web. Social tech sites aren't just hosts for profiles anymore; people use them as search engines. Your social tech policy must ensure that employees use the tools at their disposal to bring meaningful value to the Internet community.

8. Do Not Engage in Flame Wars

Regardless of what someone says about the organization or its products or services, getting dragged into an online war of words never benefits anyone. Because of the anonymous nature of the Web, you never know whom you might be engaging in a vociferous argument. Every employee must realize that every word he or she says could end up being publicized in places no one ever expected. Company policy should state that when an employee finds someone who has attacked the organization online, he or she must leave the comment alone or must address it in a professional manner, with countering facts and/or an apology.

* * *

Sharyln Lauby points out the importance of many of these areas in her article "10 Must-Haves for Your Social Media Policy,"[19] which,

---

19 Sharyln Lauby, "10 Must-Haves for Your Social Media Policy," *Mashable* (blog), June 2, 2009, http://mashable.com/2009/06/02/social-media-policy-musts/.

along with Debra Littlejohn Shinder's "10 Things You Should Cover in Your Social Networking Policy,"[20] is a great read for further ideas and perspectives.

In addition to these important guidelines, your social tech policy should cover two other areas: legal policies and archival considerations.

Legal Policies-Copyrights, Fair Use, and Employee Monitoring

Your policy must institutionalize respect for copyrights and fair use. The ease of the copy-and-paste function in no way diminishes the stringency of copyright laws and the importance of crediting sources. If you see something interesting and informative, by all means pass it on, but do unto others . . . Plagiarism isn't just a concern for college term papers—it can land your company in major legal hot water.

You'll also want to be careful of how you use computers to monitor employees' behavior. In early 2010, a Pennsylvania school district came under heavy public scrutiny and legal fire when parents learned that laptops the schools had sent home with students were potentially being used to monitor children's activities in their households—without the children's or parents' knowledge or permission. Although the central issue in this case was use of webcams to monitor student activity, the legal risk of covert monitoring also applies to the observation of employees on corporate computers.

Granted, you are probably not looking at installing keyloggers or spy cams on employee computers—you just want the ability to safely monitor and manage how your employees use the company's social technology. But the message from above holds true here as well: A little policy now can save you a lot of grief down the road. It can

---

20 Debra Littlejohn Shinder, "10 Things You Should Cover in Your Social Networking Policy," *TechRepublic* (blog), July 14, 2009, http://blogs.techrepublic.com. com/10things/?p=875.

also save your company from the sort of class-action lawsuit that the Pennsylvania school system in question is facing.

Archival Considerations—Social Technology as Public Record

Remember that your social technology presences are not only part of your company's overall public relations; they are also part of your public records, and they need to be treated as such. Careless handling of e-mail or social networking accounts can land employees and businesses in hot water.

ARMA International (formerly the Association of Records Managers and Administrators) has excellent resources for safeguarding your business records under GARP, or Generally Accepted Record-keeping Principles. ARMA lists eight basic recordkeeping principles, including the Principle of Protection, which states:

> A recordkeeping program shall be constructed to ensure a reasonable level of protection to records and information that are private, confidential, privileged, secret, or essential to business continuity . . . This requires protecting information from "leaking" outside the organization. Again, this may take various forms—from preventing the physical files from leaving the premises by various mechanical and electronic means to ensuring that electronic information cannot be e-mailed, downloaded, or otherwise proliferated by people with legitimate access to the system. Sometimes, this information should not even be sent by e-mail—even among parties who have access to it—because such an exchange can jeopardize its security. *An organization must also safeguard its sensitive records from [being made] available on social networking sites and chat rooms by employees who may either inadvertently or maliciously post it there. It is prudent to have such safeguards clearly*

defined in organizational policy and, if necessary, to monitor sites for any postings that may violate this rule [emphasis added].[21]

To avoid harmful leaks and improper handling of sensitive company material, employees must be fully aware of the repercussions their online activities might yield. In an early 2010 article titled "Social Networking Policies: Best Practices for Companies,"[22] attorney Steven C. Bennett recommended several key components, including the following, that should be addressed by your company's policy in order to maintain a positive presence in the public record:

- **Competence.** Employees should be able to demonstrate proficiency in social networking—or at least the ability to learn it—before using this technology on the company's behalf.

- **Purpose.** Networking done on company time ought to be for company use.

- **Respect.** Online discussion about other staff members without their prior consent or knowledge is strongly discouraged. Interactions with other people on social sites must at all times remain professional.

- **Confidential information.** Bennett refers back to ARMA in his article and iterates that proprietary or confidential business information—whether in text, audio, video, or photographic format—should not be placed on social networking sites.

- **Disclaimers.** Employees might be speaking on behalf of the company, but their own opinions must be stated as such and made clearly distinct from the company's opinions.

21 "Principle of Protection," ARMA International's Generally Accepted Recordkeeping Principles, accessed September 10, 2010, https://www.arma.org/garp/protection.cfm.

22 Steven C. Bennett, "Social Networking Policies: Best Practices for Companies," The Metropolitan Corporate Counsel, January 5, 2010, http://www.metrocorpcounsel.com/current.php?artType=view&artMonth=January&artYear=2010&EntryNo=10521.

Who Should Craft the Policy?

An effective policy will cover most of the behavior expectations and legal concerns listed by Steven Bennett, regardless of who is involved in generating it. In fact, Bennett's article (which is well worth reading in its entirety) suggests pulling your whole team into the process of crafting a social networking policy:

> The rapidity of change in this area of law could create confusion, indecision, and mistakes for many companies. But there is no "head in the sand" solution to the problem . . . Start with some form of survey or assessment of current social networking practices within the organization and the needs of the organization going forward. A policy that does not fit the actual circumstances of the company may be ignored, and thus do more harm than good.[23]

Since so many of the standards of conduct in your policy will address employee behavior and legal concerns, it is entirely appropriate and advisable to bring in your human resources, legal, and operations departments to review the wording and to add comments. They will probably decide to format the policy as a numerical or bulleted list that requires each employee's interaction as he or she initials or otherwise acknowledges each point. The policy should then be posted somewhere public, allowing all staff members to refer to it easily and often. And, given how rapidly social technologies evolve and the laws change, it should be reviewed periodically and updated as needed by the human resources department or the person charged with employment policies.

Remember that your *procedures* may vary from person to person and do not necessarily need to be written into the *policy* itself.

---

23 Ibid.

How Should Your Organization Distribute the Policy?

You can make your policy available to your employees in print or digitally, but to be effective, there should be a record of the policy having been read and acknowledged. Recall that on this topic, Kim Komando says, "I make all employees sign our computing policy on their first day of work." Steven Bennett suggests these measures: "Make sure that any policies the company adopts are easily accessible to employees. Include them in orientation materials and employee manuals. Consider including reference to them on start-up screens for company-issued computers. Consider whether acknowledgments (through 'click wrap' or 'browse wrap' agreements) may strengthen compliance with company policies."[24]

In addressing the ethics of the policy distribution issue and policy implementation overall, writer Tony Bradley suggests that IT administrators set up monitoring systems that simultaneously fulfill the needs of the company and protect the privacy rights of employees. The first step to doing this, says Bradley, is coming up with a written Acceptable Use Policy (AUP) that employees must agree to and sign. He says the AUP should lay out what empoyees can and can't do, and that:

> the AUP should also specify what the consequences of noncompliance are, or how violations will be handled, and it should stipulate that the company retains the right to monitor any and all communications and network activity.[25]

Bradley emphasizes that monitoring employees' activity online without notification can be considered an infringement upon their privacy.

The most important point to remember with getting the policy out is that it must be read by the people whom it is intended to

---

24 Ibid.

25 Tony Bradley, "Ethics of Monitoring PC Activity," *PC World*, February 19, 2010, http://www.pcworld.com/businesscenter/article/189806/ethics_of_monitoring_pc_activity.html.

impact. Depending on the size of your organization, a variety of distribution methods might be effective. Policies are worthless of they are not distributed in a way that is readable, and in a format that is easily digested. Nor would it be wise to bury this policy in a mountain of employment documents so that it gets overlooked when a new employee starts. However you choose to broadcast and deliver this policy, you must also find ways to hold people accountable for reviewing it.

Sample Policies to Get You Started

IBM is one of many entities to have established and publicized its social networking policies. If you would like to see how some of the most prevalent and experienced names in social technology address their policies, here are some links to get you started:

- IBM Social Computing Guidelines (http://www.ibm.com/blogs/zz/en/guidelines.html)
- Sample social networking policy from IT Business Edge (http://www.itbusinessedge.com/cm/docs/DOC-1257)
- Social Media Governance's Policy Database (contains policies from more than 150 companies and networks; http://socialmediagovernance.com/policies.php)

Final Thoughts on Social Tech Policy

If you are using social technology in the workplace, having a policy to manage how it is used is not an option. Such a policy protects your company from misuse of the technology by employees lacking in experience or guidance, and it can protect your company from legal problems related to this misuse. It also protects your employees from many of their own problems, including loss of their jobs for inappropriate online activity, and implementing it is a great opportunity to educate your employees on the best use of social tech tools. Your social tech policy should define boundaries and access–who is permitted to do what–and should not put too much control in one person's hands. There is no one-size-fits-all policy, but most will address the following components:

- **Confidentiality.** Corporate information must not be revealed without authorization.

- **Consent.** You must obtain consent from clients, coworkers, and any other parties before mentioning them on any social media site.

- **Consequences.** Outline specifically what actions will be taken if the policy is violated.

- **Copyright.** Trademarks, logos, and content belonging to others should never be used without authorization.

- **Disclaimers.** Blog posts and other online comments should clearly state whether they are an individual's opinion or the opinion of the organization.

- **Prioritization.** Social technology should be part of the job but not all of it; other tasks must still be accomplished.

- **Professionalism.** Posts, tweets, and updates should reflect a professional demeanor, voice, and writing style.

- **Respect.** At all times, employees should respect the company, its allies, its competitors, its clients and customers, and the general public.

In the next chapter, you will be taking the social technology you have decided to implement and looking at ways to integrate it with your existing Web properties, such as the company website. The policies you put in place will go a long way toward reassuring your Web master of what he or she may expect to come across on the home page of your website, and they will help the Web master understand what social technology elements will need to be integrated into the site's coding.

═ **KEY POINTS** ═══════○═══════════○═

- Without a solid policy document in place that is understood by all employees, there will be chaos in the organization's use of social technology tools. The consequences of this chaos could be dramatic: people spilling internal information onto the Web, employees commenting about customers in a public forum, or the embarrassment of the whole team when one member uploads inappropriate content.

- The policy document should provide a combination of rules, guidelines, and best practices. It should not consist simply of rules and regulations; it must also help people understand the ways to use social tech successfully.

- The policy document needs to be a living document that is updated every six months or so.

- Representatives from a combination of the HR, legal, and IT departments, along with the operations department, are normally needed in order to create an effective document.

- It is a good idea to have employees sign this document to signify that they have read it and understand what it says.

 For additional resources to help you build your own social tech policy document, go to EnterpriseSocialTechnology.com and click on the Resources section.

CHAPTER 4

Integrating Social Tech with Your Web Properties

Anyone who has experienced childhood in rural India may recall the town criers who would regularly visit their village. These energetic, vocal people would rush to different villages in their bullock carts or bicycles, beating on their drums and blowing on their trumpets to gather a crowd of curious villagers who wanted to hear the news they had brought. The undivided attention the criers got was amazing—everyone got out of their way, gave them their complete attention, and offered them buttermilk and food when they were hungry. This was a first introduction to word-of-mouth advertising.

Today, the business equivalent of the town crier is the formidable combination of a company's website and social technology. But in order for a company's Web presence to be an affective "crier," these two components—website and social tech—must work in conjunction with each other.

At this point in time, it seems as though almost all organizations have websites, and most of them are very finely designed; the content is search engine optimized and the design eye-catching and ergonomic. But there is a troubling trend among many businesses: They do not understand that websites and social tech are two pieces of the same digital marketing strategy, and that these two pieces need to be bolted together. In fact, some companies have completely separate strategies for these two areas. This is a horrible waste of opportunity.

Destination Versus Conversation

Today's online constituents must be given the opportunity to access corporate content via whatever avenue is more comfortable for them—either through a company website that links to social tech pages or through social tech pages that link back to the company website. The social tech pages should act as windows to the corporate website and should provide discount offers, news, and so on; the website is the "destination," and social tech tools provide the "conversation." The *destination* is a place you go to only when you have a specific reason to do so, and that might happen every now and then. But the *conversation* can happen every day; it builds relationships with users and gives you a chance to link back to the destination (the company website)—but only as necessary, every once in a while.

Unfortunately, many corporate websites have become formal, black-tie dinner affairs that just a few people attend. Website visitors watch the events from behind plate glass, applaud, and then go home. As user-friendly as your company's site may be, there are few meaningful ways for people to interact with a corporate website. However, social technology now gives companies access to the massive jeans-and-T-shirt crowd hanging out outside the formal event. Social tech is more like a rock show, where the crowd is immersed in the music, screaming along with the scorching lead guitar and shouting out requests to the band. Today's organizations must understand that they are facing not a captive audience of suited-and-booted executives but a jovial and robust crowd. This unruly crowd may not know exactly what it wants, but it *does* know what it doesn't want.

Can an organization survive with only a social tech presence and no corporate website? Certainly not. The website provides authority, whereas the social pages provide the company with an informal method of reaching out and give the company a human face. There-fore, any strategy that the firm adopts must regard the website as a destination and social tech as a conversation. Both the Web proper-ties and the social tech strategies should be focused on serving spe-cific groups of constituents, and those groups will frequently overlap. Consider them as two faces of the same coin; though each side of a quarter is different, the two combine to form valid currency. One entity without the other dramatically cripples the potential of both.

Seven Steps to a Unified Web Presence

With this in mind, let's discuss the nuts and bolts of connecting Web properties with the world of social technology.

Social networking tools have a remarkable ability to attract cus-tomers with very brief statements, and they can lead Internet users to valuable content located on the corporate website. The corporate website, on the other hand, can encourage visitors to engage the com-pany by prominently linking to its social tech presence. The figure on page 62 illustrates the seven steps involved in making the connection between these two parts of a company's Web presence.

Step 1: Identify Your Constituents

Every organization has a set of constituents that it can expect to visit either its Web properties or its social technology pages (or both). These constituents might be customers, vendors, partners, devel-opers, or other entities with which the company has a relationship. When there is deep segmentation between the two sets of constituents, multiple social tech and website destinations are generally necessary.

Consider Intel, which has constituents that include develop-ers, hardware assemblers, commercial customers, and fans who enjoy using Intel products. There are sharp divisions between these groups; developers are "geeks" who need core information about the

1 Identify Constituents
that are common (e.g. customers,
prospects, vendors, members, partners).

2 Identify Actions
that you want constituents to take while visiting
the Web properties (e.g. purchasing, downloading
files, filling out forms).

3 Create Conversation
with consituents after identifying best methods (e.g.
Facebook, Twitter, text message, blog).

4 Define Information
that is valuable to constituents, and communicate this
recipe to them from time to time. This will earn the right to
advertise every once in a while.

5 Define Communication
and the organizational voice style you want to use (e.g. funny,
sarcastic, intelligent).

6 Send Advertisements
to earn the right to send ads, coupons/specials once in a while to drive
traffic to the Web properties.

7 Use Web Properties
to drive people to take the actions you are targeting.

company's products, whereas commercial customers need to know about rates, payment terms, and so forth. Each segment requires a different strategy.

Your Web properties should be designed with your three to five most important visitor categories in mind, and specific paths through the Web properties should be developed for each. These paths should eventually drive your constituents to take specific actions, which might include filling out a form, buying a product, or downloading a white paper.

We also want to connect with these same constituent groups through social tech tools. For this reason, we must develop constituent-relevant conversations and build strong relationships so that we *earn the right* to send them links that drive them to the destination (website), from which point they will drop into the action funnels we've created.

You eventually want to have a large number of target constituents who view your content through social channels and then forward the destination links to their friends. This creates a wonderful eWord-of-mouth dynamic that will multiply your marketing efforts and give your content a better chance of going viral. For example, if you have strong eWord of Mouth and are connected to one thousand constituents through your social tech pages, when you send a link with a discount offer, it may end up being seen by ten thousand people. In this case, you might have a 300 percent redeem rate over what that rate would have been had the offer reached only the people directly following you.

Step 2: Identify the Actions You Want Your Constituents to Take

The constituents you identified in the first step will visit the corporate website for a specific reason and will then react by taking certain actions. Which actions you drive constituents to take depends heavily on what you are trying to accomplish with a website or social tech account. If you are a B2C (business-to-consumer) organization, you might want people simply to buy a product. If you are a B2B (business-to-business) operation, you might want a prospect to identify him- or herself by filling out a contact form.

The best websites provide visitors with several options for the types of action they could take. For example, you might hope that in the best-case scenario a visitor will fill out a client request form so you can capture his or her contact information and interests. But since only a small percentage may take that action, you can also provide a less invasive action, such as downloading a white paper in exchange for the visitor's e-mail address.

The goal is to design specific actions for specific types of visitors, to drive each set of visitors to the site by using targeted social tech strategies, and to employ a measurable system for meeting both their needs and yours.

Step 3: Create Conversations

Social technology networks now number more than three hundred and counting, and the social technology channel used for a particular conversation defines the conversation. Sites like Orkut, Facebook, Twitter, and Foursquare each appeal to a niche set of members with focused interests. It's up to you to decide on which your organization site(s) should have a presence and which will best facilitate the conversations that will engage your target constituents. Remember, you can easily get lost in the crowd if you fail to focus on a specific category of social tech user.

Each social tech tool has its own strengths: Twitter allows users to "talk" to people several times a day; Foursquare is location-based; Facebook groups give users a strong sense of community. Once you have chosen the channel that will best serve your constituents, be ready to spend several months developing your voice and content. It often takes a while before word gets around about the value of your conversation, so don't kid yourself into thinking that you will be able to turn on a new channel and get thousands of followers the first week. Building conversations is a long-term activity that takes an investment of time, energy, and patience.

Step 4: Define the Content Visitors Want

This step involves initiating your interaction with prospective followers by identifying the types of information that will draw them in. Remember that a prospective follower will look over your company's social tech account and immediately form an opinion about whether he or she wants to join your group or follow you. Information you disseminate through social tech should be helpful, relevant, and interesting. If the content is for writers, give info about writing techniques, freelance opportunities, and so on. If the content is about an upcoming book, give info about how the book fits into the genre that the author's potential readers are already interested in.

In order to successfully supply your members, followers, and visitors with a valuable stream of information, you will need to consciously define the types of content you are going to deliver. Most successful conversation streams contain a mixture of content types, all of which offer value to the recipient. Offering value is the most important aspect of your content; if your first thought is of the content that most interests you (the provider) rather than the recipient, you will die on the vine of irrelevance.

Once you have mustered enough support through a steady supply of strong content, you can send out or post an occasional advertisement or coupon—but only occasionally. You must *earn* the right to market to people; otherwise you will be spamming them. You can only earn this right by providing value in much greater proportion to your selling activities. When you've done this, you can then link users back to the corporate website, where they might be convinced to take one of the predetermined courses of action you've set up.

Step 5: Define Your Communication Style

Companies who successfully use social tech develop distinctive online communication styles. For instance, Intel, Oracle, and Microsoft each use an authoritative voice. Your organization may find more value in being funny, sarcastic, or imploring—there is no fixed rule except that you must consider your constituents and what is likely to appeal to them. A tweet asking for donations to a charity should use a grateful tone, whereas a tweet directed at salespeople should speak clearly and get straight to the point. Brainless wit or gallows humor should be avoided (unless your market is fraternity members), and depreciating any race or religion is never acceptable. Never talk down to Internet users; no one likes to be patronized over the Internet by an unknown company.

The voice you create for your social tech communications should reflect the values and culture of your organization. It might also come in several different flavors based on the channel or audience. If you are a franchisor, for example, you might use a slightly different voice to talk to the general public than you do with your franchisees. This does not mean that you speak to the public in an inauthentic way; it just means that you might use more humor and lightness with the public and be a bit more businesslike with franchisees.

People are generally jaded when it comes to corporate speak; they want even the largest organizations to address them as human beings. So whether you are using Twitter, a blog, or Facebook to interface with constituents, you must develop a personable, consistent, and believable voice that is attractive to your target audience. Once again, the reward for doing this well is that you will build goodwill, which in turn earns you the right to sell to your followers every now and then.

Step 6: Send Advertisements

Now that you have picked the right channels for your audience, have created a valuable stream of information, and are delivering it in the company's unique voice, it's time to form a strategy for embedding advertising and promotions into the conversation. If the product or service you're promoting is useful and relevant to your constituents, they will visit the Web property and carry out the specified actions. However, you'll probably need to provide incentives—perhaps in the form of online-only bonuses or discounts—to get them there.

Recent studies show that the number-one reason a person provides his or her contact information to a company is in return for a discount or a free product or service. It is much the same with click-through from social tech to corporate websites; if you want to drive people from a conversation to your Web destination, be ready to offer something of real value. The great thing about this type of marketing is that it is completely measurable. You can see exactly how many people are following your social tech accounts, and you can measure the actual click-through rate by sending people to a discrete Web page. This allows you to test various forms of incentives. Eventually, you will find the right incentive and attain the traffic levels you desire. The question, then, will always be whether the cost of the incentive is worth a good click-through rate.

Step 7: Use Web Properties

The last step is to leverage Web properties so that visitors take the actions you want them to take once they arrive at your destination. Social tech content consists largely of short bursts of information that titillates more than it informs. It is designed to hook the follower so that real action can be taken at the website, where you can provide detailed information about your organization and products and where you have assembled the funnels that will lead the visitor to the desired action. The website can contain e-commerce capabilities, contact forms, and software downloads. It is where we turn our hard work of creating a valuable conversation into the action that will move us closer to our overall organizational goals.

A corporate Web property functions great as a destination, but it fails miserably at providing the ongoing connection that keeps a relationship fresh. Combining your Web properties and your social tech channels is like combining peanut butter and jelly: Each is pretty good on its own, but together they create something much more valuable.

Dell has done a great job of collecting Twitter followers, to whom the company can send special offers that require a subsequent visit to its website. After getting its start by using Twitter coupons to move outdated and repaired inventory, Dell is now increasing sales of its regular products. Both JetBlue and Southwest Airlines are also finding success with using Twitter to deliver promotions and fill planes that have empty seats.

Whole Foods has nearly two million followers on Twitter, and the company provides a valuable stream of information—healthy food choices, recipes, new product information—for its target audience. Through its social tech presence, Whole Foods routinely provides links that drive people back to its website.

* * *

You will need to take plenty of time to implement this seven-step process, and it will usually take a few iterations before you obtain satisfactory results. Don't be afraid to experiment with the content, voice, and style of advertisements until you find the best combination for growing your organization's follower base and getting strong click-through rates from your social tech pages to your Web properties.

Measurement Systems

It is very important to measure the performance of this seven-step integration process once you have implemented it. If you don't measure the results, there is no way of knowing what's working and what's not. There are plenty of measurements you can take to evaluate the strength of the link between your social tech accounts and your Web properties.

For example, once you post a link to your followers, fans, or group members, you can immediately measure the percentage of people who clicked through that link. Then you can measure how many of those users took the course of action you set up at the website; for the people who didn't take action, you can track what they did at the website and determine what might have impeded their progress. In some cases, just getting a follower to go to your site—even if that person didn't take action—can be a positive step; at least he or she has become aware of the site and what it provides.

Measuring ROI

Measuring your return on investment is a good way to understand the value of putting social tech to work as a method of driving actions within your Web properties. A substantial amount of time is spent in the planning stages of social tech strategy, and there are both fixed and variable costs involved in the assembly and nurturing of your base of constituents. Creation of assets like fan pages and content streams takes company resources, and if external consultants are hired to help, you must include the amount paid to them as part of the investment. The ultimate return on this investment is the increase in sales obtained through the combination of social tech lead generation and Web property actions.

Make sure to measure the results of your efforts over a long enough interval. Social tech sometimes requires months to bring measurable returns; you must develop a strategy and gather a critical mass of fans. If in the first week you don't get the amount of hits you anticipated, do not be disheartened. Keep at it. Your return on investment must be measured continuously over a long period of time, and the ratio of what you spent on social tech versus what you've received will be very much out of balance for the first few weeks and months.

A few methods that facilitate ROI measurement are explained in the section below. This list is not exhaustive; it's simply meant to get the ideas flowing.

Social Tech Connections Versus Web Property Visitors

Social tech pages offer very clear indicators of the number of fans, members, followers, or friends you have. It is also quite simple to measure the number of visitors to your Web properties. These numbers can be compared, so you'll know definitively which is more popular. Remember, this is not a competition between the two components; social tech is meant to drive visitors to the website. If the

Web properties predate the social tech accounts, it can be assumed that any sharp rise in website visits is probably due to social tech.

Social Tech Ad Conversion Rates

If you provide useful, relevant content through your social tech accounts, you have earned the right to advertise—albeit sparingly—to your social tech connections. Knowing the number of visitors to your social tech pages, the number of people who click on ads, and the number of visitors to the corporate website will tell you how effective the ads have been in motivating customers. If the conversion rate is low, the ad has to be reworked.

Number of Visitors Who Take Action Once They Reach the Web Property

Converting interest to action is the heart of linking social tech to the Web properties and the Web properties to sales. Thus the conversion rate—the number of visitors who come from social tech accounts and then complete the desired action at your website—is an extremely important metric that can be provided by simple website analytics. The responsibility of achieving a high conversion rate is partly borne by the website designer, but also by the marketing strategy analysts, the product developers, and the rest of the social tech team. Social tech is about collaboration and information sharing, and if each member of the team is putting forth his or her best effort, it's much easier to achieve the high conversion rates everyone at the company wants to see.

How Can eWord of Mouth Work for You?

eWord of mouth—eWOM for short—refers to the concept of using the Internet to spread good (or bad) opinions of a person, place, or thing. It includes online reviews of movies, music CDs or MP3s, books, professionals, travel destinations, airlines—virtually any product or service on the market. eWOM is the *vox populi,* the voice of the people, and organizations have come to be very wary of its power. eWOM gives the buying public a chance to read authentic reviews and then decide whether a particular product or service is worth the investment. Good reviews from customers can have a powerful positive effect on sales, but organizations wince at the bad reviews, which can taint the perception of potential customers.

eWOM is carried out through blogs, microblogs, posts on product review pages, newsletters, social networking accounts, discussion and community forums, and many other online venues. Reviews of movies, music, restaurants, and shows have been widely available since newspapers became affordable, and the power of the reviewer has traditionally been very much feared; a review could make or break the prospects of an artist. In the case of eWOM, this is still true, except that a firm can now quickly round up paid reviewers to post favorable reviews.

Many services now offer to help companies generate favorable reviews through eWOM. But don't fall into the obvious trap: Although these public relations efforts can create a positive image for a company's products or services, an excessive number of positive reviews can signal to readers that there is something wrong–that they are being lied to. In the Information Age, readers have access to multiple sources of information, and fooling those readers is difficult. Still, there is nothing wrong with bringing favorable reviews to the front, and most customers appreciate reviews that help them sort through their options; otherwise, they might become overwhelmed with the vast number of choices they have while shopping.

How Many Social Tech Accounts Should Your Company Have?

One issue that arises almost as soon as a company decides to take on social tech is the question of how many channels it should use to carry out the initiative. Many want to be present on as many social tech tools as possible, but this quickly becomes difficult to maintain. For a social tech strategy to be effective, each channel must be consistently updated and must match the content and tone of the other channels. Large firms such as IBM, Microsoft, or Kodak might have the time and resources to position themselves in a number of channels; smaller firms—for example, niche stores like HomeGoods or magazines like *Lucky* and *Wired*—might choose to target users of only one or two channels. Some individual entrepreneurs or free-lance operators might decide to start out using only Facebook or LinkedIn. Whether you develop a presence for one channel or mul-tiple channels, focus on your content; it is quality, not quantity, that matters. It's far better to have a strong, stable presence within just one channel than to have a slipshod presence within multiple chan-nels. Ineffectively handling many social tech tools only casts the firm in a bad light.

Let's take a look at how one successful company has optimized its Web presence by integrating social tech with its Web properties.

Specials That Bring Traffic to the Web Properties

The goal of your social tech and Web property integration strategy is to build your brand and increase its visibility. This can be done by introducing specials that draw people to the company's Web prop-erties. You can also offer special social tech applications; there are thousands of such applications, ranging from virtual aquariums to apps that allow users to make Skype calls. Tech Digest offers a list of "killer" Facebook applications that might give you some ideas; you can access it by going to TechDigest.tv and typing "best Facebook applications" into the search box. You could even have a few social tech applications custom developed; there are so many creative possi-bilities, and many developers are available at very competitive prices. Identifying what apps draw people to your page will be an ongo-ing topic of discussion for the social tech team, and a good under-standing of fan demographics is crucial to ROI and to the strategy's overall success.

Case Study: Intel

Intel is the leading manufacturer and distributors of microchips, which are used to power PCs, laptops, handheld devices, gaming devices, and so on. Intel uses a number of strategies to connect its social tech presence to its Web properties; some of the channels used are listed below:

- **Intel Insider program.** Intel Insiders are a group of social media and networking experts who use the Intel site as a place to share their enthusiasm for social technology and sharing over the Internet. Visit Scoop.Intel.com and click "Insiders" at the top of the page to learn more about the program.

- **Corporate blogs.** Intel's corporate blogs are written by expert Intel employees who offer advice and an insider's view of technology and computing. These blogs are available at Blogs.Intel.com.

- **Inside Scoop blog.** This blog gives Intel employees the means to voice their achievements and their thoughts about life at Intel. The blog is available at Scoop.Intel.com.

- **Intel Developer Forum Twitter feed and Facebook fan page.** Intel has created a Twitter feed specifically for its developer forum, a twice-yearly event at which the latest Intel products are discussed. Both outlets regularly link back to the Intel corporate website. You can follow the Intel Developer Forum at Twitter.com/IDF or Facebook.com/IntelDeveloperForum.

- **Intel Inspire Twitter feed and Facebook fan page.** Intel also set up a Twitter account for its Inspire site (InspiredByEducation.com), which is a community of people sharing stories about the importance of global education. You can follow this feed at Twitter.com/IntelInspire; the campaign has a Facebook presence, too (Facebook.com/InspiredByEducation).

- **Intel Software Network TV.** This unique site (Software. Intel.com/en-us/tv) collects on-demand episodes of its weekly Intel Software Network show. The site is also used to cover live Intel events and to give visitors a behind-the-scenes look at the company.

- **Intel news on Digg.** By going to Digg.com and searching "Intel," Internet users can find the latest news about the company and share it with their friends. Many of the news items link back to Intel's website.

- **Intel news on Slashdot.** As with Digg, Slashdot—a technology-related news site—can be searched for the term "Intel" to bring up the latest company news. Because of the nature of Slashdot's content, this page is intended mainly for core application developers.

- **Intel Communities.** Visit the site at Communities.Intel.com is the home page of Intel Communities, which allows visitors to interact with technology and company enthusiasts in a variety of forums.

As you can see from the breadth of this list, Intel makes extensive use of social tech tools to reach discrete audiences. Within each of these channels, the company consistently refers people back to its website for additional resources and offers.

* * *

Now that you're thinking about how your Web presence can bring value to your constituents and drive sales, you're ready to move on to the next chapter, which describes how to harness the vast flow of information provided by the Internet and its users.

⚊ KEY POINTS ════○══════════○═

- It is critical that you have a plan for uniting your social tech strategy with your Web property strategy. Both of these tools decrease in value when operated as stand-alone pieces of the digital marketing puzzle.

- Social tech is a *conversation*, and your Web properties are a *destination*. These two online components serve completely different purposes. Forming a conversational relationship by providing a valuable stream of information via social tech can lock in your target audience. This earns you the right to periodically send them an advertisement or promotion that will take them to your corporate website where you can persuade them to take the desired action that will drive revenue.

- An important goal in bringing together social tech and Web properties is to get people to bring their friends with them when they go from your social tech accounts to your website. Create advertisements and coupons that people will want to send to their friends, family, or coworkers.

- Companies need to be careful to avoid advertising and promoting so much that their streams of information look like spam to Internet users. Set a guideline for how often you will send out offers or direct promotions over social tech channels. A good place to start: Aim to have only one in eight social tech communications be promotional.

- Once you have integrated your companies social tech account(s) and Web properties, you must have a sophisticated system for measuring success. This will allow you to fine tune each component of your Web presence for better results.

 To get a copy of our constituent-based process for building Web properties and tying them to social tech strategy, go to EnterpriseSocialTechnology.com and click on the Resources section.

CHAPTER 5

Building a River of Information

In recent years, social technology has become an integral part of a glorious new era in which information is reliable, available worldwide, delivered in real time, and most important, free. Every activity or hobby, every career path or business plan, every goal or ambition—almost any subject you can think of—has page after page of information and resources written about it, all just waiting to be discovered and utilized by ambitious learners. Smart businesspeople take advantage of social technology to form a constant supply of new information and resources gathered from all across the world every day; this is their "river of information."

People have always built rivers of information for themselves, but in the past it was a laborious process that required determination and discipline. Newspapers, magazines, books, radio, and television were the most accessible forms of media, and storing the information gleaned from these media required detailed cataloguing. Most people who grew up in an age before the Internet still have boxes filled with old magazines and newspapers that they collected. Now, with Web 2.0 and the new information tools that are being developed every day, everything you ever wanted to know is literally at your fingertips. The Internet acts as the eyes, ears, and mouth of just about every organization in operation today, and it offers users a larger, more accessible river of information that can help their companies reach new heights of success.

Of course, business leaders can use the power of the Internet for more than developing their own knowledge base; they can also increase organizational IQ dramatically by helping employees learn how to build their own powerful rivers of information. This will result in better decision making, increased awareness of industry happenings, and the timing advantage you gain when you access information faster than the competition can. In our economy, knowledge is power, yet even though we have an unprecedented amount of information flowing all around us, this is not much use unless we learn to harness it.

Harnessing free-flowing information is probably the most important practice anyone can embrace, and it is an invaluable asset to every business in the world. Everyone wants to work with companies that are informed and well versed on the latest developments in their industry, and the companies that generate the most revenue are those that research, explore, and self-educate endlessly until they know absolutely everything there is to know about what they do.

Using the Internet to seek out information is effortless and completely free; it simply requires self-discipline and consistency. Even with just thirty to forty-five minutes a day of browsing the Web—reading articles, case studies, press releases, news stories, creative work, and reports—you can find torrents of information that will help you succeed. People who work to develop strong and effective rivers of information find themselves making better career and business decisions and seeing much farther down the road. They are filled with knowledge and insight that tell them exactly where they want their career to take them, and their business strategies and solutions are stronger and more effective than those of their less-informed competition.

Developing and using a river of information is crucial to keeping up with younger generations, who have a natural advantage in using technology. They are accustomed to using social tech tools to stay up to date on subjects they care about—it's as natural to them as blinking. They're always seeking out new tools to help them learn, and if you don't do the same, you will quickly fall behind.

Why Do You Need a River?

You don't know enough about your industry. No matter how long you've been working or how much experience you've gathered over the years, there are still thousands of articles and studies you haven't seen that could help you succeed. Most of this information is free, and it's everywhere—all you have to do is click your mouse and type a few words to find it. The business world is dominated by people who constantly research topics relevant to their organizations and by people who are willing to learn, no matter how much they already know. More and more it's becoming evident that the experience of older professionals isn't worth anything unless that knowledge applies to the present day. History is important, but it serves only as a standard by which to measure and understand modern developments. Therefore, if your younger competition has developed strong rivers of information, they will use the resulting knowledge to dominate their fields.

Staying informed and updated on your organization's industry shouldn't be just a personal goal. Every member of your organization should be striving to better both themselves and the company as a whole through information harvesting, and it's the responsibility of the organization to educate its employees on the importance of keeping their rivers of information up to date. Start by creating your own river and documenting how it's helped you. Showing these results to your employees will give them proof that collecting information is worth the effort, and it will inspire them to begin working on their own rivers.

A recent article by E. Chandlee Bryan on QuintCareers.com contained an interesting statistic that shows the relationship between social technology and success:

A recent ExecuNet newsletter reports that "60 percent of wealthy Americans with an average income of $287,000/year and net worth of $2.1 million participate in online social networks, compared to just 27 percent a year ago." These individuals belong to an average 2.8 networks.[26]

So, with this limitless resource waiting for you—at absolutely no cost—what are you waiting for? Almost every area of a business can benefit from proactive information gathering. Here are just a few examples of what having a well-developed river of information can do for different members of an organization.

Executives

Almost every major industry is in a state of constant change, whether it's due to new manufacturing practices, the latest rules and regulations, updated technologies, or innovative branding ideas. For executives, staying informed is the first step in analyzing a business plan and figuring out how to place the business at the cutting edge of the market.

Gathering information on the business models of competing companies can give you profound insights into what works for other businesses in your industry. With countless pages devoted to team-building exercises and successful employee programs, executives can also discover practices that increase employee productivity and encourage teamwork. Ideas for internal and external changes are available all over the Internet, along with tips on how to implement them and advice about the pros and cons that come with them.

Sales

The success of salespeople depends on rapid creativity and invention, and ideas for how to outsell the competition are all over the

---

26 E. Chandlee Bryan, "Five Strategies for Leveraging Your Online Social Networks," QuintCareers.com, accessed September 10, 2010, http://www.quintcareers.com/leveraging_social_networks.html.

Web. Salespeople are always striving to reach that untapped market that constantly eludes them. Having a well-developed river of information can give them instantaneous insight into what products the other companies in their market sell, how those companies sell those products, and what they're doing to attract customers. Salespeople can also find potential customers on Internet communities and discover what these people expect—right from their own mouths. Implementing that knowledge will vastly improve sales techniques within their organization.

There are also many ongoing webcasts and online seminars on effective sales techniques, and forums and blogs contain a tremendous amount of information that can direct salespeople to new customer leads.

Product Engineering

A company's engineering departments are dependent on having the newest and most advanced technology to design the products that keep the organization in business. Without a river of information keeping engineers constantly updated about new developments—including news of the tools their competitors just discovered—these departments can quickly fall behind.

When engineers are active in online communities that include other engineers, they can benefit from discussing the individual projects they are working on. A good engineer and employee, however, will take care not to divulge any trade secrets or confidential product information.

Human Resources

Social technology drastically changed the way companies interact with employment candidates by giving both parties direct access to each other through blogs and social networking sites. Being active in social tech can enable HR personnel to easily push information and updates to both current and potential employees.

HR regulations and policies are always being revised and updated, and the Internet is full of useful data about the latest trends in human resources. There are also many places, including blogs and social networks, where HR workers can exchange ideas and opinions about how to deal with common issues.

Financial

Just like HR departments, financial divisions within companies face constant changes in regulations, most of which are hard to understand unless employees seek out information pertaining to those changes. On top of that, new investment and financing strategies are created and talked about online every day. A financial specialist can save substantial amounts of money and generate tremendous profit by having a river of information that keeps him or her up to speed on how the economy is affecting the company and how the company dollar can go further.

Tip'd (Tipd.com) is an online community designed for the open discussion of financing and investing strategies, and it's only one of the thousands of resources available on this topic. Financial experts and enthusiasts post useful information on Tip'd every day, including advice on successful methods for improving a company's bottom line, hints on where companies can save money, and tips on where they should invest to make money.

How to Build Your River

The first step in developing your personal river of information is to seek out the best sources on whatever topic interests you. An amateur Web designer shouldn't just type "Web design" into the Google search engine and hope to find what he or she is looking for. Take a moment to compile a list of all possible places you could find information relevant to your business. You'll want to watch as many competitors as possible, monitoring both their primary website and any other

Internet presences they maintain. You'll find that you can frequently pick up good ideas from competitors and adapt them for your own purposes. Also be sure to keep up with what your customer base is talking about by visiting the forums or communities in which they are likely to discuss anything relating to your business.

Look for networks that peers and colleagues frequent, and join them to discuss industry news and share resources. Members will share interesting articles, and seasoned experts in your field will often share their hard-won advice. All this content must be filtered to find the most relevant pieces, but these professional networks are a great way to gather information and form your own opinion on hot topics in your industry.

You can also seek out general information on business philosophy and practices, no matter what industry you're in. There are countless articles on ways to better yourself by sharpening your mind and honing your talents through discipline and motivation.

Once you have an exhaustive list of sites and resources that could offer you valuable information, narrow it down to about twenty-five or thirty. You don't want to overwhelm yourself with sites that aren't giving you value, so it's important to weed out those you can do without and focus on the ones that best fit your needs. Once you have prioritized these sources, you can check them all in just a few minutes of surfing.

Even after you have narrowed down your sources, it can still be challenging to organize all the information they contain. This is where aggregators come in. An aggregator is a website or software program that gathers content from across the Web and displays it in one place. Aggregators (also known as "news feeds" or "news readers") can save you huge amounts of time; populate yours with the twenty-five to thirty content sources you've identified, and you'll be able to check them for updates all at once. Examples of aggregators include Google Reader, NetVibes, NewzCrawler, and Onfolio. Many aggregators also allow you to share content by e-mailing posts or articles to friends or by linking to them on social networks. This allows you to support your colleagues by sharing the helpful resources you find.

Once you've got your sources organized, you need an effective method of storing the information you find. Configuring news readers to automatically store information to your e-mail or hard drive is the preferred method, as it saves you time and organizes your content for you. The problem with this method is the potential lack of control in how the aggregator stores content; some professionals prefer to fill whole hard drives manually, with carefully catalogued folders filled with information of their choosing. Either way, be sure to keep the data organized and navigable for ease of use when you need to refer back to it.

How to Tell If Your River Is Working

In the first stages of your information gathering, it can be difficult to discern the results of your efforts. But if you're actively maintaining your river, the knowledge you gain will manifest itself in your own improvement and development.

In order to maintain and benefit from a powerful river of information, you need to keep an eye on what you're seeing from each of your sources. If a website or blog is consistently giving you valuable information that stimulates you and helps you succeed in a former area of weakness, that site is definitely worth keeping. However, if a source continues to offer redundant articles, ill-informed opinions, or information that isn't relevant to your interests, it may be time to drop that source and replace it with another.

You also want to ensure that every aspect of your professional life is covered by your river of information; not having the right sources for information on one or two key facets of your business can leave you with noticeable weaknesses. If a designer wants to know every-thing about Adobe Photoshop, he or she needs to cultivate sources on photo manipulation, painting technique, effects managing, file optimization, and many other aspects of the software. If the designer is missing out on any of this information, that individual will suffer from a nasty handicap that limits his or her effectiveness with Photoshop.

Reviewing the sources of your river should be expedient and hassle-free: You shouldn't have to spend more than forty-five minutes a day on your news feed. Some sites may have a cluttered structure, with article organization that makes you click page after page before you finally find what you're looking for. Other sites may post too much content that you don't care about, forcing you to wade through irrelevant information to find the few nuggets of value to you. Every source in your information river needs to be efficient and well designed, or else it's not worth following routinely. Keep the sources that guide you right to what you need, and drop the ones that are making you do too much work. But don't completely write off a source you drop from your river, even if it's not easy to use. Instead, keep the source on file and check it when you have time—just not as often as your more efficient sources.

Getting the Most Out of Your River

No matter how passionate you may be in your quest for information, it can be hard to form the habits necessary to make the most of your information river. It takes a great deal of diligence, maintenance, patience, and ingenuity to find the success you're looking for through information gathering. Here are some habits you can form to help you optimize your river of information.

Use Web Tools to Help You Find the Best Content

Sites like Blogged.com and Twellow.com take the legwork out of finding sources; they help you narrow your search results to the content providers that are relevant to your interests. Using them it will take only a few minutes for you to find the top ten bloggers and Twitter pages in your market. Industry news feeds that aggregate all the best sources in your particular field are also readily available from the associations that are normally tasked with trumpeting information from an industry. For example, the SIIA (Software & Information Industry Association) newsletter aggregates a number of headline news items from the software industry so you don't have to hunt around for articles on this subject. If you are involved in the franchise industry, the IFA (International Franchise Association) provides a news stream that aggregates news from the franchisor world.

Keep Your River of Information Accessible All Day

It's important to configure your news aggregator so that all your information is condensed into one or two easily accessible screens. Depending on your online habits, your forty-five minutes of research may be spread over an entire day, so it's important to be able to bring up your feed in an instant and bring it down just as quickly. Having news updates sent to your phone or mobile device is another way to keep up with the news—even when you're away from your desk.

Never Stop Looking for New Sources to Add to Your River

There will always be worthwhile new sources out there, and old sources periodically will reach a point at which they are no longer of value. Be prepared to update your source list so you can keep your flow of information fresh. Ask around your organization or an online community to find out what sources other people are using, and jump on the ones that respected informants say are valuable.

One Last Plea

Social technology has introduced a new and *incredibly effective* method for people to stay informed and grow within their industry. By building a powerful flow of content and updating your river of information, you can find that same success. It's no longer enough to have experience that applies only to how the world has worked in the past—even the recent past. Every organization values people who are willing to make an effort to find information that can help themselves and their company. These people are the ones who rise through the ranks by being the best at what they do, and they are always willing to learn something new or seek out a new skill set. Keep proactively learning about your industry and sharing the information you find, and you'll see the rewards in every area of your career. On the other hand, make the decision that you are too busy to build and digest a river of information each day, or that you are already overwhelmed and cannot fit this discipline into your life, and you will soon fall behind others in your industry. Do this for a few months and you might survive; fail to consume a valuable river of information for a year, and your business will become irrelevant.

The concept of a river of information can be applied to benefit any member of your organization. The most visible and potentially lucrative effects, however, may be felt by salespeople. An information river increases the level of industry knowledge, competitor knowledge, and product knowledge that any type of salesperson has at his or her fingertips—all of which help in the closing process. With that said, there are many other beneficial ways that social tech tools can be brought into the process of selling—be it within a B2C or a B2B operation. The winners in your market will be the companies that figure out how to leverage these tools, as discussed in the next chapter.

KEY POINTS

- It is likely that you are accessing less than 5 percent of the information that is available to you on a daily basis—information that can be extremely valuable to your business and your career.

- Building a powerful river of information takes a conscious effort to gather a robust group of information sources, aggregate them, learn to process and review them quickly, and then store and forward the useful parts.

- A valuable river of information harvests many different types of sources and data, including information about competitors and thought leaders, industry news, statistics, and infographics.

- You must learn the skill of processing your river of information in thirty to forty-five minutes a day, and you must be consistent in doing this every day so you do not miss something critical.

- It is helpful to learn how to use websites and software programs to aggregate, filter, store, and forward information quickly and easily.

- You should constantly refresh your river of information by shedding information feeds that lose their value and adding new sources that look promising.

- It helps to continually ask the trusted people around you what information sources they find useful.

 To access a shell document that will help you assemble a river of information through social technology, go to EnterpriseSocialTechnology.com.

CHAPTER 6

Integrating Social Tech Tools into the Sales Process

Whether you're selling commodities or complex products, sales has changed. In fact, a whole new powerful layer was added to the sales process when social technologies forever altered the art of selling.

Take a small, family-run insurance agency in the little city of Henderson, Kentucky, as a case in point. This enterprise sells various types of insurance coverage to small businesses and individuals. Prior to engaging in social technology efforts, this agency focused its sales and marketing efforts on traditional channels such as chambers of commerce meetings, word-of-mouth referrals, newspaper and phone book advertising, and so on. Its website consisted mainly of a Web 1.0–style "About Us" page. Leads were handled offline using repetitive processes that required great effort. These sales processes were long, tiring, and—quite honestly—*boring,* to both the prospect and the agency.

Enter Web 2.0: LinkedIn, Twitter, Facebook, blogs, and an interactive website. Once it employed all these social tech tools, the once-sleepy insurance agency was rejuvenated and energized. Clients and prospects are now more engaged with the local brand than ever. Sales cycles have shrunk, revenues are up, and the agency is building a national reputation within the industry for "doing social the right way."

How are you, the salesperson, doing social? Take a hard look at your most recent sales—or losses. Whether your organization is B2B or B2C, did the buyers check you out online either before they contacted you or after? Through this due-diligence process, what did they find out about you? Have you performed an online search of your organization, your product, your brand, your market, and your competition lately? What information is out there about you, your product, and your brand? Have you thought about how much influence your online presence has had on your recent sales results and your lead volume? Selling has changed dramatically in the past few years; perhaps it's time for you to change your processes in response.

Evolution of the Art of Sales

Before we dive deep into the impact of social technologies on sales and what you can do about it, let's take a few minutes to review the selling paradigms we've seen over the past few decades. You are likely to find that these paradigms have synthesized into an extremely powerful combination—both for the seller and for the buyer.

To start, we might characterize the sales process up until the 1980s or so as "relationship selling." Remember Zig Ziglar and Dale Carnegie and their books *See You at the Top* and *How to Win Friends and Influence People*? The basic strategy was to meet with potential prospects, wine and dine them a bit, impress them with your brand and credentials, and then continue to work on the personal relationship— perhaps by presenting them with tickets to sporting events or expensive meals. Sure, the rep needed to know enough about the products to carry on an intelligent conversation and maintain professional credibility. But the real work of filling the pipeline, closing deals, and getting referrals was primarily based on the relationship. Guys who were great at building relationships and networking—those with a low golf handicap or ex-athletes with compelling professional sports "war stories"—seemed to sell more than those who didn't. (Note that we're not being gender insensitive here; back in those day, most sales-people were men.) The better the brand reputation, and the richer the personal history of the rep, the more effective the salesperson was at pure relationship selling.

IBM, Oracle, Procter & Gamble, Ferrari, Nike—you name it. The reps for the leading brands had a great time wining and dining prospects and clients—and thereby filling their sales funnel. The second-tier brands definitely tried to use relationship-selling strategies, sometimes even boldly pursuing the same prospects as their first-tier counterparts, but often at great expense and with minimal success, usually succeeding only when the first-tier rep made a big mistake (or a long series of small mistakes) that opened the door. More often than not, the second-tier reps had to settle for second-tier accounts.

The relationship-selling days were lucrative for first-tier reps and companies. Margins were high. Sales cycles were short. Buyers had the comfort of buying from a trusted brand. The financial pressures we see today didn't exist. The second-tier reps and brands were grateful for the scraps from the first-tier tables and focused their efforts on the second-tier markets. For the tier-three brands and below, survival depended on strong specialization and niche marketing, low turnover of sales reps, and extremely efficient operations (i.e., low costs and acceptable quality).

But then, in the 1990s, an interesting thing started happening. As competition and selling skills inevitably adapted, the second-tier reps starting playing the game a little smarter. In addition to building relationships, the second-tier reps began to think a little harder about how to beat the first-tier reps at their own game. Savvy sales reps began to level the playing field by focusing their efforts on *educating the prospect* during the sales process. Managers and trainers started to focus on the Miller Heiman techniques of strategic selling and to examine what certain inefficiencies really cost them. They asked themselves how they could educate prospects and clients about the actual savings that stemmed from their distinctive solutions. As always, building relationships was important, but second-tier sales managers and sales reps began to focus on the bottom line and to address the real issue the prospect was trying to solve. By understanding the underlying costs of a situation, these reps could offer solutions that rendered better financial and operational outcomes than those offered by the first-tier brand. They knew that getting the prospect to see things more clearly would give them an edge.

Of course, it didn't take long for the first-tier brands to get wise to this strategy and then improve upon it. Thus we entered the era of "solution-oriented selling," which was layered on top of relationship selling. Remember that all this change occurred when business was done one deal and one client at a time. Very little technology was used, other than printed form letters and business reply cards sent blindly to the sales rep's prospect list.

Meanwhile, the advent of computing started to have an impact in markets of all shapes and sizes. Customer databases became very much in vogue. Rather than reams of paper, filing cabinets, and the costly system of staffers mining customer files for information in the service of clients, powerful mainframe computers and relational databases were installed and loaded with client data to automate and improve customer service. It wasn't long before someone asked the obvious question: "If computers work in the service department, how can we leverage them in the sales department?" In those days, salespeople were still using Rolodexes, manila folders, and stacks of business cards. But now technological evolution was bringing about the convergence of customer service systems and sales processes. New customer relationship management (CRM) systems retained critical data points, reminded the sales reps of appointments and follow-up tasks, and tracked deals through well-defined stages of the sales funnel.

With the advent of "CRM-based selling," you not only had to build the relationship and then identify the solutions to the prospect's problems—you also had to use the new CRM tool to manage the whole process. An interesting phenomenon in the sales department started to emerge, and today we see it in full bloom: The "techies" who grew up with PCs, had great interpersonal skills, *and* had business smarts began to emerge as sales leaders. And they not only led—they shredded the competition and beat all the sales forecasts! With the right tools and training in the hands of a good sales rep, leveraging CRM made selling easier and more efficient, and thus scalable—meaning that salespeople were able to do more deals with the same level of effort.

On the B2C side, we saw a similar evolution. E-commerce began to enhance the sales and marketing efforts of traditional paper-based, direct-mail catalogs like L.L. Bean and big-box shopping stores like Target. Suddenly Amazon.com was a popular alternative to Borders and Barnes & Noble. In direct-to-consumer sales, the same principles were in play for the early adopters of sales technology—they built their brands with advertising and relationship-building sponsorships, established efficiencies for the consumer, and leveraged economies of scale in order to lower prices. It's hard to believe, but there *were* naysayers in those early days of e-commerce—stick-in-the-mud operations that stubbornly refused to see the future intersection of offline and online sales and marketing. But look at all the books (and countless other items) Amazon.com sells today. Where have brick-and-mortar shops like Brentano's, B. Dalton, and Waldenbooks gone? The market for books is thriving, but these retail outlets are gone.

In the mid-2000s, things started to get a bit chaotic. The Internet and e-commerce began to mature. User-generated content started to proliferate with the advent of YouTube and blogs. Search engines like Google began to "disintermediate" salespeople. Some brands, such as Progressive Insurance, even went so far as to pronounce the end of the era of the sales agent. Yet in spite of many claims of ROI and productivity gains, few organizations understood how to use new Web-based technologies for business, let alone sales. Professional online networking within industry forums started to take shape, and many sales reps experienced social tech burnout as they tired of maintaining multiple online profiles. One-to-many communication concepts started to develop, all designed to feed the funnel and get a sales process started. White papers and webinars—free or low-cost forms of communicating with prospects—began to be widely circulated, even though many of them consisted of little but PR drivel. Meanwhile, there was a funny, perhaps unintended consequence to all this: Consumers started getting savvy to all these tools, too—and started using them in their buying process! In a sense, the tables were turned.

Given that today's buyers are facing increasing pressure to find ways to maximize value and stretch dollars as far as possible, when it comes time to make a purchase, won't savvy consumers leverage the Web in the buying process? Won't they seek out existing customers of a potential business partner and look for references, deal points, negotiation tips, and the like? Won't they want to get the inside scoop so that they have as much advantage as possible in negotiating and getting the biggest bang for their buck? You bet they will. Savvy buyers now have more control over the sales process than ever before. Today, this chaos has stabilized and matured into two of the most important concepts in the ongoing evolution of sales: *socially facilitated selling* (B2B) and *socially directed buying* (B2C).

Whether at the high end (with expensive, complex products) or at the low end (with commodities and consumer products), selling has always been about being at the right place at the right time with the right message; and it's always been about communicating information and building trust. Social technology now augments communication and provides new ways to build trust. It is also reorganizing how buyers buy—and thereby forcing sellers to adapt. Social tech helps salespeople be at the right place at the right time on a scale never before attainable, and at a cost never before imagined—essentially nothing! A powerfully constructed blog, integrated with Twitter and LinkedIn, is replacing the premium country club membership.

To best understand the many and varied impacts that social tech has on sales, let's consider the two ends of the product spectrum separately. We'll start on the complex, B2B side of the spectrum and consider the concept of socially facilitated selling before we move on to socially directed buying on the consumer products end.

Socially Facilitated Selling

Whenever salespeople talk about using social tech in their sales processes, they always want to know the *how*—but often they skip the necessary *why*. The *how* is the easy part. But to really be effective at social tech, we need to deeply understand the answers to certain questions: Why is it helpful for the salesperson to join online professional networks like LinkedIn, to update his or her status daily, and to get recommendations from clients? Why is updating a professional blog once a week one of the most important activities for a salesperson? Why is getting a customer to comment on a blog post a huge event in the life of a customer relationship? Why do Facebook and Twitter play such an important role in the sales process? Why are "listening" devices like TweetDeck, Google Alerts, SocialMention, and Addict-o-matic helpful in growing sales? Why is it important to use social tech for making introductions, gaining credibility, building rapport, and understanding the concerns and priorities of a prospect—all before the first direct contact, and certainly before the first sales event?

Once we clearly understand the answers to these questions and are familiar with the real-life facts and figures that back them up, then we will be ready to tackle the execution of social tech. The sales process will continue to change—permanently—over the next few years, and the cost of learning these lessons too late from your competitors will be high.

Understanding the concept of socially facilitated selling is critically important in the new landscape of sales. The basic definition of *socially facilitated selling* is the use of social technologies to facilitate the process of moving a prospect from the position of stranger to that of client—from "Hey, look, I'm on an extremely tight budget" to "I'm so glad you solved that problem for me—of course I'll give you a recommendation!" Yes, it's easier said than done, and there are plenty of landmines to avoid. The question is, how can your organization employ socially facilitated selling without diluting your immediate sales results—or worse, making you look bad?

Creating a Sales Environment

In order to use social tech tools to create an environment that will help salespeople sell, an organization must accomplish three things:

1. It must define a corporate voice.

2. It must team with its salespeople to implement a social strategy.

3. It must promote interaction with its customer base.

Let's take a look at each of these points in further detail.

Defining a Corporate Voice

What is the operation's corporate voice within the social tech landscape? What best captures the spirit and essence of the organization? Some companies use memorable characters like the Geico gecko or Erin Esurance. Some, like Zappos and Apple, use the persona of the CEO to gain online recognition. Others (e.g., Dell, H&M, Whole Foods, JetBlue) take a more straightforward approach to marketing and PR in the social tech realm by using the new tools to deliver coupons and to provide discounts, product information, and company news. Sadly, many more are silent, apparently paralyzed by the explosion of new options and the speed of change away from traditional methods. That, or they are suffering from one or more of the nasty diseases of arrogance, stubbornness, complacency, greed, or fear.

Teaming with Your Salespeople to Implement a Social Strategy

According to a study by PR firm Cone, 85 percent of people who use social networks and social media expect to be able to interact with the brands they do business with, and interacting with customers online takes teamwork.[27] The organization must have a vision for its salespeople embedded within its Web properties and its Web-based tools, and that vision must be primarily social in nature. You can have the greatest sales strategy in the world, but if marketing isn't creating brand identity, or if customer service isn't serving, or if the product is flawed, or if executives are gallivanting around (either virtually or physically) creating a bad reputation, your great new process may drive interest and traffic, but it won't convert that interest into sales. Your organization must work with its salespeople to create a holistic, strategic, and tactical environment in which they can best compete and win. It's worth repeating: The organization must include a vision for its salespeople embedded within its Web properties and Web-based tools, and that vision must be primarily social in nature. Remember, when someone interacts with a website, he or she is more likely to return, more likely to share, and more likely to buy.

Promoting Interaction with Your Customer Base

Let's say we want our clients and prospects—and anyone else in our sphere of influence—to recommend us within their own sphere of influence. That's the goal, the desired action: referrals and word of mouth. Let's look at an example of how social tech can get us there, remembering that user-generated content and online interaction are key components of social tech:

> Step 1. Write a blog post—perhaps a couple of paragraphs about an interesting trend. Be sure to write the post in a way that encourages readers to comment.

---

27 "Cone Finds That Americans Expect Companies to Have a Presence in Social Media," ConeInc.com, accessed September 13, 2010, http://www.coneinc.com/content1182.

Step 2. Select a few LinkedIn connections with whom the post might resonate.

Step 3. Message those connections with a link and a note encouraging them to comment.

Step 4. Moderate the comments and immediately thank the commenters via e-mail. In the e-mail, ask the person for a big favor—to share the story with his or her network.

Step 5. Add your own comments to any comments that invite further discussion.

How does this simple example illustrate how social tech can be leveraged to put prospects into the top of the sales funnel? Does it reinforce existing relationships? Does it establish a dialogue? Does is enhance a value proposition or an industry reputation? Yes, it certainly does. People are far more likely to consume and engage content published by a friend or business associate who asked for their opinion. People are four times more likely to return to a site they have previously engaged with. And people are twice as likely to share a piece of content that they have engaged with (e.g., a blog post they commented on). Therefore, if you want a prospect or client to share something with his or her LinkedIn network, get that person to comment on your blog post and then share it. If the person does share it, he or she is now doing your prospecting and marketing for you. That person is also engaging with your content—and thus, perhaps, *not* your competitors' content. You are pulling him or her into your web, your circle, your center of influence. And you're getting referrals and free publicity in the process.

Monitoring the Social Tech Skill of the Sales Force

As of 2009, more than four out of five American adults with Internet access used social media at least once a month.[28] More than sixty-five

---

[28] Sean Corcoran, "The Broad Reach of Social Technologies," Forrester Research, August 25, 2009, http://www.forrester.com/rb/Research/broad_reach_of_social_technologies/q/id/55132/t/2.

million people now use professional networking site LinkedIn, and—as mentioned previously—85 percent of social tech users expect brands to interact with them through social technology. Clearly, teaching and training salespeople how to leverage electronic connections with customers and prospects as a part of their sales plan is a sound strategy. In fact, it is one of the most effective skills in play today—especially if your salespeople are running up against social tech–savvy competitors. To reward the development of these skills, part of a salesperson's annual review, or perhaps even bonus, might be tied to how many connections he or she has on LinkedIn. Or the organization could consider evaluating how effective the salesperson has become within a few online industry groups—or how well an industry group the salesperson started is doing. The company can also look at how many people are reading and commenting on the salesperson's blog, what his or her Klout score is, and how productive his or her professional Twitter or Facebook presence is.

These are just a few of the ways that social tech can become part of a salesperson's annual review. Of course, all this assumes that the sales manager, sales executive, and CEO have a solid understanding of these tools and are practicing what they preach. (Remember, your company must coordinate its social tech efforts and build a social tech environment in which its salespeople can thrive.)

Once consumers see that a salesperson really "gets" social technology, they start to expect the same skills from all the salespeople they deal with—giving you a great opportunity to get ahead of competitors who don't understand social tech. And if your prospects are expecting to find you in the social tech landscape because your competitors are already there—well, you'd better be there, and your salespeople had better know how to become recognized experts in their fields.

Why "recognized experts"? Buyers have always had an intolerance for salespeople they perceive as "peddlers." A peddler is essentially an arm twister who cares little about the product really helping a customer and just wants to close a sale and move on. Although this is a bit of a harsh term, it captures the spirit of exactly the kind of sales rep from whom people do *not* want to buy, even if the peddling rep has the best product at the best price. Not only does buying from a peddler leave a bad taste in the buyer's mouth, but the relative utility of the relationship ends there. Following the main transaction with the peddler, there are no secondary or tertiary benefits to either the buyer or salesperson—no introductions and referrals either way, no ongoing education or resources, no ways to add value and richness to the relationship. Buying from a recognized expert, however, includes all of the above. In the eyes of the buyer, a transaction with a recognized expert not only will solve the primary objective, it has the best chance of bearing fruit in other ways as well.

A simple example might be the salesperson who makes an effort to understand and communicate a success story through a professional blog. Client A then reads the post and comments with additional insights or questions about the story. Client B might read the post *and* the comment by Client A and then contribute a second comment that makes an impact on Client A—all because the rep took the time to get a blog in place, write a post that would stimulate sharing and conversation, and then promote the blog post as a resource for the online community.

It is critically important for sales managers to motivate salespeople to engage in this kind of behavior. It *does* take time—perhaps an hour or two a week—but it pays off if you do it right. Imagine the ROI of the one-hour blog post, in terms of referral opportunities and additional business. And what if one or both of those clients were prospects, and what if a prospect saw the whole thread? How would that reinforce the sales process?

Learning to Be an Industry Expert

A salesperson blogging might seem like heresy to some executives who see blogging as something only the marketing and corporate communications departments do. Yet we're learning fast that sales-people must be perceived as industry experts if they want to close more sales.

More than ever before, with a few clever Google searches, prospects can learn all sorts of things about the market, the brand, the products, and the rep—whether positive or negative. Take it as a fact of doing business today: Buyers know more than they used to, and in many cases they know it before we ever talk to them. Don't get too excited about that first out-of-the-blue phone call expressing interest in your product. Don't think, "This is going to be a lay-down! Heck, *they're* calling *me!*" Assume the prospects have researched you, your products, your brand, and your competition. Assume they have a fairly mature understanding of the important deal points they might face. They might have already spoken to a couple of your clients and asked them a few straight-up questions about money, time, and potential issues related to your product or service. Assume the prospects have already had an internal meeting to review all these details, perhaps the kind of meeting they used to have *after* they called you. Now, they're doing their research and making high-level decisions *before* they make the first call. But even if they call before doing their research, remember that they will likely start researching you online as soon as they hang up the phone.

With all this in mind, do you see why it's important to become an industry expert and not a peddler? Do you see why a business card should *never* mention sales in any way? Instead, your title should read "Strategic Market Manager" or "Strategic Industry Solutions Director" or "Vice President of Market Solutions" or something similar. People are getting more and more jaded about being sold to. Buyers want to be in charge. They want control. They need excellent, high-quality information—and lots of it. After all, it's their neck on the line. Buyers want to deal with a recognized expert, someone who also has a stake in the game. Make one big mistake and the buyer will mark your scorecard with a triple bogey for the whole world to see. Buyers want to deal with industry specialists, not salespeople who appear to care only about commissions. Remember, it's much harder to push buyers toward a sale in the social tech era; today's buyers would rather be convinced by your expertise than to have their arm twisted.

Socially facilitated selling is all about driving revenue by combining an organizational strategy of big-picture online reputation improvements with a sales force that is trained in social technology interaction. It's not enough to simply encourage salespeople to learn how to use LinkedIn. The entire organization must commit to creating an environment that gives salespeople the easiest possible path to closing sales.

Socially Directed Buying

Now let's shift to the consumer products side of the equation and consider socially directed buying. In this case, we are creating not so much an environment that helps salespeople sell as an environment in which consumers will make purchases on their own when they walk into a retailer or go to an e-commerce site. To get there, however, we have to first understand the consumer and his or her buying behaviors.

Across the economy, and at a high level, there is a prevailing lack of trust in standard advertising, and people have grown tired of interruption marketing. Technologies such as DVRs, caller ID, and spam filers—but a small sampling of the technologies designed to prevent unsolicited interruptions from marketers—have made it possible for consumers to filter out advertising and marketing messages as they consume media. Even with these new tools, people seem to be gravitating toward investing more time in social networking, where the advertising is less intrusive to the flow of "entertainment."

Perhaps this phenomenon in part explains the explosive growth of social networking sites like Facebook, where 50 percent of the active users log on during any given day, and the average user has

130 friends (according to the Facebook Statistics page). Why are people gravitating toward social networking and then making it a part of their daily routine? There are two main reasons:

1. People find satisfaction in expressing their opinions, sharing what's happening in their lives, and talking about their trials and tribulations.

2. People appreciate the opportunity to ask trusted friends and neighbors for advice and help.

Facebook has filled both of these needs. It provides ample opportunity to share pictures, stories, commentaries, travel histories, and any number of details of the user's daily life. Facebook also provides a forum for dialogue with trusted friends about products and about solutions to the wants, needs, and frustrations of our lives.

For example, Chris may be considering the purchase of an iPad, perhaps partly as a result of the status updates of his Facebook friends who also bought the device. On the strength of these impressions, Chris asks questions about the iPad to his entire network so he can get advice on the product's functions and the available customizations. Chris might do the same were he buying any of a variety of products, including movies, firewood, new gutters, a washer or dryer, books, cameras, or food. And Facebook is just one example, just one tool that has been put in the hands of millions and millions of people to help them connect, share, filter, and learn.

Conversely, traditional media advertising revenues are freefalling. The effectiveness of direct response, direct mail, and telemarketing is dwindling, whereas the costs of postage and printing are increasing. Magazine, newspaper, and TV ad revenues are dropping, while online advertising revenues are rising.

Sellers and marketing professionals, especially senior managers, need to dive in and start using new media as consumers. Marketers need to become thoroughly aware of the trends, patterns, and opportunities of social technology. You may be the CEO of a Fortune 500 company, but to understand socially directed buying, it's critically important that you personally get into the fray yourself. Once you do, you will likely discover several interesting characteristics of the environment that you can then apply to your direct-to-consumer sales and marketing strategies. At a bare minimum, you will be able to speak intelligently and from experience about social tech as opposed to blindly repeating a few clichés you got secondhand.

Leveraging Online Influencers

Once you get into the fray, you will notice that in whatever their category of interest, people follow influential communicators. These influencers include expert bloggers and hardcore fans. Whether it's about Harley-Davidson motorcycles, beagles, cell phones, or healthcare services, there are always people blogging or microblogging about their opinions, experiences, and preferences in regard to products, services, and brands. Many have tens of thousands of followers listening to everything they say.

As these influencers share information and opinions, they develop a following, in much the same way the late William F. Buckley generated a following with his writings and TV shows, and later Rush Limbaugh with his radio broadcasts. Successful bloggers generate massive amounts of content and develop significant followings, and they are thus capable of influencing many potential buyers. Savvy sellers will naturally want to engage these influencers as a part of their socially directed buying strategy.

As with any marketing strategy—but especially with social tech strategies—engaging influencers needs to be handled with proper social etiquette. Bloggers will be cautious about turning into pitchmen or pitchwomen and thus potentially alienating their audiences. Readers will want to know about the financial underpinnings of product recommendations—did the blogger receive some benefit from this positive review? Not disclosing any such deals will sabotage both the seller and the blogger. Disclosing them in a diplomatic and artful way, however, will reinforce the reputation of the blogger as an honest person who is capable of providing objective information.

Connecting with Consumers by Creating Online Fans

Savvy marketers will also develop characters and personalities that fans of their products and services can connect with personally. One terrific example previously mentioned is Erin Esurance, the pink-haired sensation created by Kristin Brewe, former director of brand and public relations for Esurance. In an effort to compete with the likes of Progressive and Geico in the commodity-driven auto insurance market, Brewe created a character called Erin Esurance—a hard-nosed, animated crime fighter, a sexy chick, an action hero doing battle against the evil, overpriced auto insurance thugs, who are characterized as giant robots. Appealing to both men and women in the target markets, Erin Esurance first hit the scene in TV commercials, fighting crime and selling insurance in thirty seconds or less. Soon, hardcore fans created a Facebook profile for Erin Esurance, even describing what she was doing each day. This, of course, pleased the brand managers greatly. Esurance then created the "real" Erin Esurance Facebook page and started amassing significant amounts of friends. At one point during the zenith of the campaign, Esurance released the original Erin Esurance media assets to the crowd of hardcore fans on YouTube and announced a contest: Whoever could develop the best thirty-second Esurance video on YouTube would be in the next Esurance TV commercial. The company received more than eight hundred entries in the contest, developed tens of thousands of views and followers, and eventually achieved the goal of becoming the third most popular insurance quoter on the Internet. And note the cost of the YouTube contest—practically nothing.

Of course, this is just one example. Brands are also using the social Web to create a cadre of fans with whom they can interact regularly. But be careful and prudent. Social tech is rife with pitfalls and landmines. While we all have products to sell and revenue goals to hit, disingenuousness and overselling become readily apparent and are immediately dismissed by the fan base. A good rule of thumb, mentioned in chapter 4, is to post between seven and eight useful bits of information before making one offer. Following this rule will make truly connecting with fans (i.e., your prospects and current customers) a more long-term prospect, because they will perceive your content stream as caring more about them than about an advertising platform. Fans create more fans—and when a prospect sees that one or more of his or her connections is already a fan of your brand online, that prospect will be more comfortable about connecting with you directly. Once that connection is made, the door is open to all sorts of revenue potential.

Employing an Effective Online Sales Process

Have you ever noticed the friendly, often elderly ladies in the grocery store cooking up tasty bits of food and handing out samples to shoppers as they pass by? What's going on there? What are they trying to do? Ideally, they want to get someone to smell the cooking food, then draw closer to get a look. Next comes a taste. Then the shopper asks a few questions, perhaps chats for a while, and finally buys the product. Very, very simple.

Let's apply the same process to social technology. Of course, the olfactory senses aren't in play, but visual and auditory ones certainly are. To influence the online buyer, you must follow a series of steps that entices your prospect, by providing *context*, a *draw*, *engagement*, a *sample offering*, *follow-up*, and *sharing*.

Let's briefly define each of the steps in this process.

Context. The initial contact with the prospect must be in the *context* of a place the Internet user is visiting. If you are advertising life insurance on a teen site, you will not have a very good response, since most teens aren't thinking about preparing for the end of their life. The correct context might be a particular blog or Twitter stream related to your product.

The draw. The *draw* is the method you use to encourage the customer to take action. Banners and links from static websites used to be our only tools, but now we can put links in social networking conversations and place banner sponsorships on blogs as well.

Engagement. *Engagement* is the sharing of knowledge with the potential customer. This could be in the form of a video, a Web page, or an online presentation that promotes our offering in some way. Engagement can take place in any type of social media environment (e.g., YouTube, SlideShare, Scribd, Flickr).

Sample offering. In some cases, your organization can use a *sample offering* to gain the trust of the potential customer. Depending on the service or the product, you can share just a little of it with people so they will learn for themselves that it's something they need more of. Samples have always been popular with the public, and it is simple to them share online with thousands of your friends through websites and social technology platforms.

Follow-up. *Follow-up* is the step in which you make the sale. If you have done your job well and demonstrated a true need for your product on behalf of customers, they will follow up your efforts by purchasing the product, whether online or in a brick-and-mortar store.

Sharing. After the sale, you need to encourage customers to *share* the news of what they have purchased with their social networks. This initiates the eWord-of-mouth cycle you so dearly want to leverage.

Now let's apply this process to a specific example. Say you want someone to buy your high-tech light bulb, one of those compact fluorescent lamps (CFLs) that saves energy and lasts longer but looks funny and costs a little more. First, you craft a catchy banner ad and pay to place the product in *context* on the Home Depot website. The banner says, "Win a Chance for a Year's Supply of Light Bulbs—Guaranteed to Cut Your Lighting Cost by HALF! Click Here." This is the *draw*. Once the customer clicks through, he or she sees the landing page, which has a five- or ten-second video that says, "Yep, it looks funny and costs a little more, but does it ever save on utility bills!" This is *engagement*.

The site might then offer a *sample*: "Register for a Chance to Win a Year's Supply of These Money-Saving Light Bulbs." In exchange, you capture the customer's name, e-mail address, cell phone number, and contact preference. After the customer clicks "Submit," he or she sees a thank-you page with yet another beautifully done video showing a customer screwing in the light bulb and flipping the switch, with a voiceover talking about saving energy while cute kids in their jammies run in for a bedtime story. The voiceover may say something like, "Saving energy is important to all of us—especially the next generation. Won't you help by sharing this video with your network? Maybe they'd appreciate knowing what you know—and they'll want *their* chance to win a year's supply for free. Thanks!" The hope is that the customer will *follow up* with a purchase and then *share* the video with his or her networks.

Next, you send an e-mail confirmation of the customer's registration to win the free light bulb supply; you also ask for his or her opinion, or request that he or she "likes" the story on Facebook. Better yet, send a video via e-mail and ask the customer to forward it to his or her friends. As incentive for sharing, liking, or forwarding, you can offer to send a free light bulb, which requires that the customer give you a physical address. Then, about seven days later, you can send an e-mail:

> Did you get the CFL? Did you use it for the stove light that
> you probably leave on all the time? We want to know!

Thirty days later, send another e-mail:

> What do you think about the CFL? Is it still cranking away? Did you share the story with your friends?

Then, another sixty days later, send another e-mail:

> Did you notice a difference, even a small one, on your electric bill? Imagine if you replaced all the light bulbs in your house with these CFLs? You might spend an extra $10 or $20 in the process, but you could save that money on your first utility bill alone, and you'll be doing your part to save energy. Click here to order a supply, and we'll send them right away. And let your social network know that you're doing your part to make the world a better place.

In short, the process of placing our product in the context of the Home Depot site, drawing the customer in with video, engaging the customer, and then offering a sample led to the sale. With the added element of following up about sharing, your campaign could go viral!

Building Revenue-on-Demand Programs

Revenue on demand is a sales process that can help an enterprise create demand during slow times in a way that won't compromise revenue streams during peak times. To illustrate, let's say your business operates in cycles; at certain times of the day, month, or year, you have the problem of staff (and related overhead) sitting idle, waiting for the next wave of customers. You've tried coupons in newspapers and magazines, but people use those discounts on orders they would have placed at full price. *Rats!* Then you tried blackout periods and other fine-print *gotcha!* techniques, but you merely succeeded in irritating your regular customers. If only you could find a way to engage customers and generate revenue during the downtimes—without irritating your customers and at a selling cost low enough to keep the effort at least minimally profitable. Revenue on demand is a form of socially directed buying that can help you achieve this.

For example, during these downtimes, you can issue an instant coupon that is available only to your Twitter followers (or other online connections) and good only for the next two hours. Encourage retweets and other forms of sharing, and *presto!*–you have revenue on demand.

Think about how you might creatively entice prospects to take advantage of specials, discounts, or gifts with purchase, all through the use of social tech. How can you use social technologies to minimize predictable losses that were previously considered a cost of doing business? Consider, for example, these companies that use social tech to issue time-bound incentives for customers:

- Dell frequently has special offers on refurbished computers.
- JetBlue uses social technology to sell unsold seats on flights.
- Many restaurants drive traffic on Monday and Tuesday nights through special offers promoted online.
- Many coffee shops advertise two-for-one beverages between, say, 2 p.m. and 4 p.m. through instant notifications over social networks.

These companies have tested various special offers and learned which ones drive optimal results. Carefully measuring the results of these initiatives is of paramount importance; you don't want to give away the store or dilute revenues during traditional peak times. Revenue on demand helps you drive off-peak traffic while continuing to maximize predictable revenue.

* * *

Socially directed buying is all about using social technology tools for branding and eWord of mouth; it can be useful in engaging consumers in activities that will cause them to look for your products when they have a particular need or desire. It provides an entirely new landscape for the field of advertising, and we are already seeing winners and losers emerge. Using social tech to connect with consumers is not just about creating a Facebook fan page or getting a lot of followers on Twitter; it entails putting together nearly all the concepts discussed in this book in ways that will draw you closer to your customer base and create a more emotional bond between them and your brand.

Final Thoughts on Selling

Socially facilitated selling (B2B) and socially directed buying (B2C) both require tight integration with a company website. As mentioned in chapter 4, the website often serves as a destination for purchasing. Depending on where the prospect or client sits on the relationship continuum, this engagement might start as a conversation on Twitter, LinkedIn, a blog, or some other online location. An interaction on this level draws the visitor into a dialogue, as compared to the more traditional didactic, one-way messaging that is the "About Us" section. Once the relationship is established, you can begin to solve problems and create advantages for the customer with your products and services. As discussed earlier, the website is the destination; the featured social technologies facilitate and direct the ongoing conversation.

That all-important conversation can be created by the marketing department or the sales staff—just make sure the two departments are speaking with one clear voice, even if it is through different employees and channels. We want our salespeople to be industry experts. We want our brand managers to have the ability to talk to their consumers directly. But we don't want the customer to be confused in either case as to where the information is coming from.

As always, *innovate or abdicate!* Organizations that build a new vision for how they can leverage these new tools to sell will prosper.

And organizations that do not? While it's a bit premature to say they will die, I'd be hesitant to predict their prosperity. It's a much safer bet that these operations will soon learn the hard way that social tech is a powerful influencer. To be on the safe side, if you are selling a product or a service, you had better learn how to leverage social tech before your competitors do.

One of the most important concepts to take away from this chapter is that you should not focus on just one specific element in the social tech inventory to grow your revenue next year. To truly ensure results, you must assemble a number of social tech concepts in order to form a socially facilitated selling environment or a socially directed buying model. In combination, the tools you choose can make a huge difference. With either of these models, you will need to manage your online reputation. Regardless of the product or services you are selling, buyers will very likely check online at some point to see what others are saying about you and your products.

For this reason, managing your online reputation is a huge part of successfully using social technology to sell. What people find when they search for you, your company, your employees, or your products will have everything to do with their odds of taking the next step forward in the sales process. Because online reputations are now becoming so critical in people's decision making, we have dedicated the next chapter to learning how to manage your online rep effectively.

═ KEY POINTS ═══════○══════════○═

- The art of sales is changing, and the change taking place is a permanent step in a new direction. We have moved from the relationship-building sale to the solution-oriented sale to the customer relationship management–driven sale. All these approaches are valuable, and they can be even more effective if you wrap the new social technology concepts and tools around them.

- Socially facilitated selling is the process of creating an environment in which salespeople can more effectively close sales. This requires a partnership between the organization, which backs up the salesperson's social tech efforts, and the salesperson, who applies his or her newly learned social tech skills.

- Socially directed buying is the process of supporting sales by more effectively engaging the consumer and improving perception of the brand through social technology.

- Salespeople must become recognized industry experts rather than being perceived as arm-twisting peddlers.

- Salespeople and brands must engage customers in conversations that help the customer remember the brand and trust the products.

- All conversations with consumers must be coordinated so that your company maintains a consistent voice—regardless of who is creating the content.

CHAPTER 7

Online Reputation Management

Ethan Gunderson was just another underemployed young man living in Wisconsin, until the day he discovered his dream job at Obtiva, a custom-software consultancy based in Chicago. That day Gunderson tweeted, "Hmm, I wonder if I could get into Obtiva's software apprentice program."

Gunderson's tweet did not go unnoticed. Dave Hoover, minority owner and chief craftsman of Obtiva, had learned to harness the power of social technology and was listening in when Gunderson broadcasted his desire to get into the program. Because social networking sites such as Twitter make it easy to "listen" for keywords—like Obtiva, in Hoover's case—he found Gunderson's tweet and connected with him almost immediately. After several e-mails and tweets, Gunderson was hired as an apprentice. Eventually he was brought on as a full-time employee, at which point he tweeted, "I got my job at Obtiva today via Twitter. True story."[29]

Ethan Gunderson's true story is just one of the countless tales of men, women, and organizations across the globe that are utilizing the power of social technology. For the first time in the history of communications, the 1.9 billion people who have Internet access can get information and communicate with one another for free, and

---

29 David H. Hoover, E-mail message to the author, April 28, 2010.

that access equals power.[30] Whether you are expanding the reach of your organization or promoting your personal expertise in a particular field, social technology is a vital tool that, if managed properly, can enhance your personal and organizational reputations like never before.

For corporations, the online reputation has become absolutely critical and will continue to grow even more important; your reputation will soon dictate how much you can sell, the caliber of employee you can recruit, and the number of investors you can attract. You must successfully manage your online reputation, and you must begin doing it now.

Take United Airlines, for example. When disgruntled passenger Dave Carroll tried unsuccessfully for months to both call and e-mail United Airlines about baggage handlers breaking his $3,500 guitar, he took his complaint (in song form) to YouTube. In 2009, the infamous "United Breaks Guitars" music video spread like wildfire, receiving more than 1.5 million views in just four days; as of this writing, it has reached more than nine million views, according to the YouTube site. Due to the power of social media, the airline suffered a damaged reputation and great financial loss. The *Times of London* reported in July 2009 that "within four days of the song going online, the gathering thunderclouds of bad PR caused United Airlines' stock price to suffer a mid-flight stall, and it plunged by 10 percent, costing shareholders $180 million." The *Times* went on to say that this amount would have allowed Carroll to purchase 51,000 replacement guitars.[31]

United Airlines is not alone. Pampers, a Procter & Gamble subsidiary, garnered national media attention in April 2010 when mother and customer Rosana Shah tried to complain about a diaper

---

30 Internet Usage Statistics: The Internet Big Picture, www.InternetWorldStats.com, accessed September 13, 2010, http://internetworldstats.com/stats.htm.

31 Chris Ayres, "Revenge Is Best Served Cold—on YouTube," *Times of London*, July 22, 2009, http://www.timesonline.co.uk/tol/comment/columnists/chris_ayres/article6722407.ece.

rash caused by Pampers' new Dry Max technology in two of its diaper lines. When Shah felt that Pampers did not take her complaint seriously, she took her story to Facebook. In a matter of weeks her anti-Pampers site had close to one thousand members, leading the Consumer Product Safety Commission to launch an investigation and causing a backlash among customers nationwide, and even globally in some instances. Mothers everywhere were calling news stations, complaining on Twitter and MySpace, and uploading gut-wrenching videos and pictures of their babies' diaper rashes all over the Internet. Parents far and wide were expressing their outrage about a company that was once the most trusted diaper manufacturer in the world, thereby injuring Pampers' previously positive online reputation. The story became another cautionary tale for companies that ignore their customers. The bottom line is that the poor management of Pampers' online reputation meant the loss of customers and money as the company tried to compensate angry moms from around the world. Pampers' stock plummeted.

On the other end of the spectrum, PepsiCo learned the importance of online reputation when the company changed the look of its Tropicana Pure Premium orange juice, replacing the beloved straw in the orange with a glass of orange juice. Responding quickly to consumers' boycotts and complaints on a variety of social networking sites, PepsiCo—in less than two months—reverted to its traditional packaging, gaining the cola company a positive reputation for knowing how to properly engage with social technology.

PepsiCo recently took another hit when, during an online marketing contest, it reportedly broke its own rules by editing a celebrity's entry, giving her an unfair advantage. Said Nathaniel Whittemore in an article for Change.org, "To Pepsi's credit, though, the company has responded quickly, and with the sort of openness that's essential for success in the new social media sphere."[32]

---

32 Nathaniel Whittemore, "Pepsi Refresh Pulls a Flop, But Also a Fix," www.Change.org, February 26, 2010, http://socialentrepreneurship.change.org/blog/view/pepsi_refresh_pulls_a_flop_but_also_a_fix.

In addition to responding immediately, PepsiCo tried neither to hide the event nor to quiet consumer complaints. Instead the company posted its mistake on Facebook and on its blog, with links to the original complaint, allowing consumers to easily access all the information and enabling them to discuss the event as they desired. It is this sort of online reputation management that will continue to keep investors, customers, and top-list employees interested in Pepsi.

Jason Fitzpatrick, writer for the blog Lifehacker, recently posted the following:

> If you're not actively building your identity and establishing a presence online, you're letting search engines cobble together information, good or bad, and write your public story. You need to establish and maintain a healthy online identity. Your online identity—or lack thereof—becomes more prominent by the day. People rely more and more on search results to help build a picture of you, and you want the picture to be a good one.[33]

The bottom line is this: It is no longer viable for an organization to exist without a solid online presence. However, the key is *balance*. You and your business have a legitimate desire for privacy, which is healthy and necessary. Yet at the same time, you must establish an online reputation if you want to get noticed. The question then is not "Should I create an online social presence?" but rather "How do I maximize and manage my online social reputation?" It's sort of like high school—reputation is everything. Today, a good or bad online reputation can make or break a company.

Social networking sites like Twitter, Facebook, LinkedIn, and a variety of others are particularly powerful for recruiting employees, strengthening relationships, connecting with clients, and exposing others to what your organization is doing. No matter the size of your

---

33 Jason Fitzpatrick, "Establish and Maintain Your Online Identity," *Lifehacker* (blog), May 5, 2010, http://lifehacker.com/5531465/establish-and-maintain-your-online-identity.

business, you have the power to shape and manage your online reputation with a few simple steps.

Whether you realize it or not, you do have an online presence, and it fits into one of three categories: the Good Reputation, the Bad Reputation, and the Nonexistent Reputation. If there is any question in your mind as to how you might rate, pay close attention to the next few pages. Anything other than a good reputation may prove to be very painful to your career in the near future.

The Good Reputation

If your online reputation is good, don that cheerleading uniform and put a smile on your face: You are popular! You have online relevance because you have learned how to utilize blogs and social networking sites to connect to as many consumers as possible. It also means you are producing a lot of information; you're updating those microblogs with regular, fast-paced, and interesting content to keep your customers engaged and encourage them to share with others. If your online reputation is good, others are also saying good things about you on their own blogs, microblogs, and other social networking sites.

Joshua Bingaman, owner of the Austin, Texas, landmark Progress Coffee—a coffee shop and art venue—understands the power of social technology. Progress Coffee has not only a website but also a blog and accounts on Twitter, Facebook, and Foursquare. Bingaman, an artist and entrepreneur, says:

> Constantly being in contact is our most successful online tool. Nobody said [Progress Coffee] would work, and it's now one of the most successful small businesses in Austin, as it spawned Progress Roasting, Owl Tree Roasting, and Progress Ventures (which includes a few other cafés); a management company; and now Helm Handmade Boots, a high-end shoe company and store.[34]

---

34 Joshua Bingaman, Facebook message to the author, May 6, 2010.

Progress's success is due in large part to the fact that Bingaman understands what his clients value: community. His customers interact with, comment on, and post pictures and artwork to Progress's various websites.

Consumers have a sense of ownership when they can make their mark on a business and engage with it online. When that sense of community is developed, consumers are much more likely to spread the word on their own social networking accounts—and that enhances your good online reputation.

The Bad Reputation

If you are in the "bad reputation" category, you have an online presence, but what you publish is poor and not worth sharing or recommending to others. It also means that others are saying negative things about you online. A bad reputation will result in people easily discerning that hiring you or doing business with your company is a big risk. It will be very hard to overcome this perception, and your organization will suffer economically.

Like the rebellious kid who walked the halls of your high school, many organizations have a past to hide, a past in which they behaved badly. Consumers are realizing the powerful fact that with the push of a button, their stories of poor customer service can be read and even watched by millions around the world. These stories are both easily searchable and permanently available.

Organizations are having a harder and harder time protecting their online privacy. If an organization has wronged a customer or group of customers, millions of people can easily find that negative information online. Never before has a company's reputation sat so firmly in the hands of the consumer. With just one click, the consumer can determine whether you are deserving of your current reputation and whether your goods and services are worth his or her time, energy, and money. As in the Pampers and United Airlines stories, at the snap of a consumer's finger, even the smallest faux pas can be posted online for millions to see and judge.

The Nonexistent Reputation

The nonexistent reputation is like being invisible. Think back once again to high school and you may remember the quiet kid, the one who sat alone in the cafeteria, didn't say much in class—the one you never noticed. That person may very well have had great intelligence, humor, and even the potential to add a lot to your life—if only he would have made himself known. If your online reputation is invisible like that kid was, and you have little or no Web presence, you lack social relevance. Consumers who do come across you somehow will assume that you are not an expert in your field and that you are not well connected. Having no reputation at all will not save you. If someone searches your company's name and finds nothing, they will assume you are not valuable; having no online reputation is only slightly better than having a bad one. Invisibility is a big red flag for people who are considering doing business with you.

Beth-Shar Construction, a small company in the Chicago suburbs, has a word-of-mouth reputation for wonderful service, a fabulous work ethic, and reasonable pricing. However, the operation has no online reputation whatsoever. In doing a Web search for this company, you find that it only comes up in a few bare Yellow Pages listings—Beth-Shar does not have a website or a blog, nor does it participate in any other form of social technology. In fact, even in a specific search for contractors in Warrenville, Illinois, Beth-Shar does not appear at all in the list of local businesses. For many organizations, this type of invisibility doesn't just discredit their reputation as a strong and viable company, it also robs potentially wonderful companies of sales and investment opportunities.

These days, even home-based businesses are realizing the importance of joining the social networking community in order to make their brand visible. At-home business owner Jenn Ohlinger recognized the need to promote Sorella Fashions, her jewelry and accessory business, yet she had neither the time nor the resources to do so. Luckily, this stay-at-home mom's husband has a passion for technology; he is the one who finally started promoting her business online. The Ohlingers began using a website (SorellaFashions.com) and a blog and subscribed to Facebook and LinkedIn. Soon, Sorella Fashions began to make an online name for itself, all while allowing Jenn Ohlinger to keep her family the number-one priority in her life. Despite working from home, Ohlinger says, "I am able to get the word out in ways that are manageable, considering my amount of free time and my lifestyle–without spending large amounts of money to promote my business."

Ohlinger explains that Facebook has been her most beneficial form of advertising: "People become fans of Sorella Fashions, which shows up on their homepage. Then others see Sorella Fashions and become fans. I can then market through word of mouth much more easily. Facebook also helps because I can display visuals of my work along with any comments."[35]

The arrival of social technology has ushered in an era in which, no matter how big your business is, you can freely and easily market yourself and your brand. Simply by appropriately utilizing a few online resources and tools, you can move your brand from virtual invisibility or flat-out negativity to online stardom.

Managing Your Social Reputation

Once you have successfully moved your brand's reputation from "invisible" or "bad" to "good," the next step is managing and maintaining your positive online standing. Like no advertising tool has ever done before, social tech can launch nobodies into celebrity and can grow your organization's influence and value in a matter

---

35 Jennifer Ohlinger, interview with the author, May 7, 2010.

of weeks, fueled only by positive comments and feedback posted online by consumers. Even more amazing, social tech ratings tools— for example, Yelp.com (if you are a restaurant) or Angieslist.com (if you are a doctor)—will help you show consumers that they can trust your goods and services. On the flip side, these sites give you unprecedented power to find trustworthy vendors and suppliers for your organization.

Remember, however, that your company's reputation can be sullied in a New York minute by angry consumers out for their money's worth—whether or not they have a right to be upset. Therefore, it is essential to develop a strategy for maintaining a positive online presence.

Recently, *Glee*, a TV program on Fox about a group of students in a glee club, aired an episode called "Bad Reputation." In the episode, the singing and dancing high school students did almost anything, from humiliating themselves to dating people they did not find attractive, in order to gain popularity. All these attempts backfired; the students could not manage their overwhelming desire for attention or undo the bad reputations acquired during their attempts to gain approval. Even though it's just a show, *Glee*'s point is a good one: It's not simply *having* a reputation that matters; the most important thing is to have a sincere and positive one that you nurture and grow. Sincerity and common sense will go far in maintaining that positive online presence for your company.

Infamous Twitter user @theconner, after receiving a job offer from Cisco, tweeted the following: "Cisco just offered me a job! Now I have to weigh the utility of a fatty paycheck against the daily commute to San Jose and hating the work." She never expected to hear back from a channel partner advocate, who tweeted this in response: "Who is the hiring manager? I'm sure they would love to know that you will hate the work. We here at Cisco are versed in the Web."[36]

---

36 Helen A.S. Popkin, "Twitter gets you Fired in 140 characters or less," www.msnbc.com, March 23, 2009, http://www.msnbc.msn.com/id/29796962/.

The story goes that @theconner immediately set her Twitter account to private and deleted all personal information from Facebook—but it was too late. Her reputation had been marred forever. @theconner learned the lesson we all are learning: that there is great tension between privacy and an online reputation. The day and age may come when employers and customers can dismiss such online faux pas as simply that. But for now, you must use common sense and care when you enter the online world of social technology.

Now more than ever it is easy and inexpensive to gain access to a broad and deep understanding of one's online reputation. Although people have always had the ability to do a little research on a company or person, it was traditionally expensive and difficult to discover anything more than shallow information. Today, the Internet is constantly aggregating in-depth information—information we can post about ourselves to boost our reputation and sales, and information others can post about us. In true locker-room fashion, it is now cheap and easy to learn a bucketful of information in a single search. Pampers and United Airlines learned this lesson the hard way when their relatively minor mistreatment of single customers led to the rampant spread of negative information about their brands.

To avoid the pain experienced by Pampers and United and to feel better about providing sincere and helpful information, you must learn to *listen* to your customer base, *engage* consumers effectively, and *measure* your online reputation. Here are some guidelines that will help you and your organization.

Listening to Your Customer Base

First, develop a listening process. This must include multiple methods for listening to what people might be saying about you online, such as Alerts.com, SocialMention.com, Google Alerts, and Yotify (promoted as "Google Alerts on steroids").

Jamie Tallerico is a freelance artist and a senior graphic designer with Abercrombie & Fitch. Tallerico uses social media tools such as online galleries and magazines, and he regularly uses social relevance tools to "listen" for how his name and website (SkullsAndRoses.com) are being mentioned. His client list includes some of the top names in the music industry, and Twitter has given him further reach than any other social networking site because of the large amount of mentions he gets there. "When some of my famous or semifamous friends mention my name or talk to me directly," Tallerico explains, "their fans in turn seek out who I am and what I might do or how I am related."[37] Tallerico can then engage those who seek him out and is thereby able to grow his clientele.

If you are part of a large organization, you might want to consider more sophisticated tools like Radian6 and Viralheat, which perform real-time monitoring on all kinds of microblogging platforms and millions of websites, and then deliver the results directly to your desktop.

Engaging Consumers Effectively

Once you've begun "listening," you must establish an engagement policy, which defines how you will respond to the positive and negative things said about you and your brand. You must determine who will respond, when they will respond, and how they will respond. This is critical because you want to minimize negative mentions or get people to retract them because you have reached out. And you want to capitalize on positive mentions as possible connections and sales opportunities.

Because consumers are giddy with their newfound power to lambast organizations, they sometimes go out of their way to say negative things. Therefore, organizations need to enact a formal response paradigm that includes as the first action reaching out immediately to people by phone. In this day and age of computer-run customer service lines, your company will stand out simply by offering person-to-person contact.

---

37 Jamie Tallerico, Facebook message to the author, April 27, 2010.

Pampers, although it responded late in the game, countered its negative reputation by directing consumers to its hotline. Staff members also commented on the anti-Pampers Facebook page, the company's own Facebook page, and in the media, urging all customers with complaints to call the hotline. Irate and fragile customers did not have to push buttons or wait impatiently while a call was transferred; callers to the hotline were surprised to find that an actual human being answered right away. Pampers knew that angry consumers would get more irritated if pushed to a point of impatience, and so it made sure it had very apologetic and well-trained people on the phone.

Without having to be asked, Procter & Gamble clearly stated its listening policy, apologized for the Pampers debacle, and offered compensation. The company's representatives took reports over the phone for its Quality Health and Safety team, and then followed up via e-mail and letter. As mothers called the hotline and received satisfaction, they began to retract their negative sentiments online. These small seeds of positivity made a world of difference in a forest of negative comments.

You can also use social networking and social relevance tools to curb negative attacks before they get out of hand. Although this is a gray area of social technology, organizations need to learn how to ethically deal with negative comments that appear high in the list of search rankings. Search engine optimization (SEO) tools can help you flush negative comments out of the top search pages, respond to those negative comments, and place positive information above them, so people will see these first and foremost. Furthermore, new online platforms such as Radian6 and Viralheat (mentioned previously) will help you monitor social networking mentions, measure the effectiveness of ad campaigns, determine sales opportunities, and stay connected to all relevant information regarding your online reputation.

Finally, the most profound tool for establishing an engagement policy is to actually engage! Be present within the community of your fans and consumers by interacting with them on blogs, microblogs, and your website, and also by posting on their sites. Having an open dialogue with this community will go a long way toward maintaining a positive online reputation. Although you can never control what people say about you, you can be prepared to deal with it, and by simply listening, you can finesse a nonexistent or marred reputation into one that is powerful and positive.

Measuring Your Online Reputation

Remember slam books—those spiral notebooks that surfaced in the bathroom of almost every high school across America, ranking girls, guys, and even teachers on everything from hotness to body type? Awful, right? Well, you may be dismayed to hear that rating systems are back, and they're in vogue!

The Internet has become a place where we judge everything from doctors to grocery stores. Very soon, this form of rating will not be focused only on businesses; already we are beginning to have the power to rate individuals (see GetUnvarnished.com) and affect their online reputations. These rating systems can show how influential a person is in his or her field or how popular that individual is as a social influencer. And they will only become more important in hiring as time goes on. As these sites and systems become more stable, they will have a dramatic impact on the online reputation of professionals.

In response to this, you must implement a measurement system that gauges how often people are talking about you online and whether the sentiments they express are positive or negative. Your measurement system needs to tell you how many times you were mentioned in a week or month, what the positive/negative sentiment ratio was, and how effective your customer service was in remedying problems (i.e., whether you were able to persuade the dissatisfied users to delete negative mentions or ratings).

Sound overwhelming? Fortunately, tools like Klout and Addict-o-matic can be utilized to create a sort of standardized scoring

system—much like a credit score—for the online relevance of an organization. These scoring systems can be used as another way to measure a person's or an organization's value in the business world. The
formula is built around the following basic variables:

- The amount of content produced online
- The quality of that content (judged by how many people rate
  it or share it with friends)
- The number of connections a person has across social
  networks
- The ratio of positive to negative mentions posted online
  about you or your company

These measurements will come to be viewed as a way to see how
well regarded a brand is and how much value a company brings to its
constituents. Klout, for example, measures numerically the size and
strength of a person's sphere of influence on Twitter. Addict-o-matic
can alert you daily (and free of charge) when your brand, name, or
organization is mentioned online, and it can then begin creating (or
curbing) buzz with that information.

Listening, engaging, and measuring will benefit your personal
and business success tremendously, and furthermore, these skills will
soon be required rather than optional. The faster you get control of
your online relevancy, the sooner you can benefit. Why wait until
you learn that something you were unaware of online costs you a
sale, a new job, or a new relationship?

A Case Study in Managing a Reputation

Liza Ford, owner and founder of AddictedToSaving.com, a couponing blog, knew absolutely nothing about the world of social technology when she inadvertently entered it. A Realtor by trade, Ford
began struggling financially when the market dropped in 2008. In

order to save some money for her family, Ford began doing online research about saving money at grocery stores. After a few months, Ford had cut her family's grocery bill by at least 60 percent and was saving hundreds of dollars each month. Generated by the interest her friends were showing in her couponing expertise, she started a website to get the word out to others.

AddictedToSaving.com exploded almost overnight. Ford had to learn quickly how to utilize social networking and social media tools to her benefit. She says, "Blogging is a world unto itself. I had zero experience blogging before late October 2009. And even now, there are many websites, programs, and affiliate codes I have to figure out on a daily basis. When I first started, all of the computer/blogging/HTML jargon seemed like a foreign language, but with time, it is becoming second nature."[38]

Although new to managing her online reputation, Ford is committed to the tasks of listening, engaging, and measuring. Her site produces practical content several times a day. She gives her readers daily tips on how to save at grocery stores and drugstores and even publishes links to freebies given away by major companies. When the site first started, her rate of Internet traffic was low. However, with the addition of AddictedToSaving's Facebook fan page, YouTube video blogs, and a Twitter account, Ford noticed a huge increase in traffic. Below is a breakdown of each month's visitor numbers thus far:

- November 2009: 650 visits, 190 visitors (busiest day had 45 hits)
- December 2009: 865 visits, 272 visitors (busiest day had 60 hits)
- January 2010: 6,845 visits, 1,416 visitors (busiest day had 392 hits)

- February 2010: 15,526 visits, 7,544 visitors (busiest day had 1,507 hits)
- March 2010: 35,498 visits, 13,787 visitors (busiest day had 2,060 hits)
- April 2010: 45,972 visits, 15,694 visitors (busiest day had 2,637 hits)

As the site grew, Ford realized she could actually make money from it. Now AddictedToSaving is contracted as an affiliate of many companies that pay Ford to post their deals on her site and microblogs. Ford has not only experienced fiscal success, but has also learned the joy of truly reaching people with her organization. Mothers all over the country regularly post comments and e-mail Ford, telling her that they can quit their jobs and stay at home with their children because of the money they are saving on groceries. AddictedToSaving.com also posts stories of those who have lost their jobs but, because of the simple tips the website provides, will not have to go on food stamps. Ford says, "The positive e-mails I receive give me motivation to continue to post new material."

And as the positive comments flow in, her website's good reputation grows. In order to measure her online reputation, Ford keeps track of her competition by watching what they do on their sites and how they use affiliate marketing and innovative website features. She is always trying to get ahead of trends. "The more helpful posts I make," she says, "the more my brand becomes reliable, authentic, and trustworthy. The blogosphere is very fickle and not at all loyal. So, my goal is to become known as a reliable source for deals."

In order to listen to and engage with her consumers, Ford responds to all feedback, both positive and negative. "Even though there are times I don't want to allow negative comments to be posted on my site," she says, "I do post them, because I want to be authentic.

I haven't received much negativity, however. I do respond via e-mail to all negative comments. Positive comments I respond to as well."

If Liza Ford and Ethan Gunderson can each create a powerful online social reputation, so can you! As you emerge from the world of online obscurity and into the world of online popularity, you are joining the ranks of a community of people who have harnessed the power of social technology and moved to the head of the class.

As an organization, you must realize that not learning how to manage your online presence will be disastrous. You will sell less, you will be unable to recruit A-level players, and you will turn off potential investors. By creating a positive online reputation, on the other hand, you will not only develop new sales opportunities but also maintain a presence in the business community that is long-lasting, powerful, and fiscally sound.

KEY POINTS

- Every organization and every professional will have an online reputation whether they choose to or not. It will either be a good reputation, a bad reputation, or a reputation that is so small as to be virtually invisible.

- For many organizations a few bad comments that come up high in the search rankings can be devastating. This bad publicity can have an impact on sales, recruiting, and morale.

- For an executive, a few bad comments online can devastate a career; they can affect his or her ability to be hired, to close deals, or to move up in an organization.

- There are three steps organizations and individuals should take to maintain control of their online reputations: implement a listening process, design an engagement policy, and assemble a measurement system.

- Some people feel that being invisible is OK—at least there is nothing bad for people to find and all your information is private. In reality, consumers and partners will view this as evidence that you or your organization do not really exist or are not to be taken seriously.

 For a list of Web tools that can be used to build a listening campaign or a measurement process, go to EnterpriseSocial-Technology.com and click on the Resources section.

Implementing Crowdsourcing

There are many options for getting work done these days. If you imagine a continuum—at one end is having work done by your own team, and at the other is having work done by anonymous people—you would have the following points along it: insourcing, nearsourcing, outsourcing, and now, crowdsourcing. Harnessing the power of the Internet herd is the latest on the scene—and possibly the most world changing—of all the work-for-hire options.

To understand this, we need to take a step back to gain some perspective on how contracting out work got to be so popular in the first place.

Outsourcing in a Nutshell

In the 1980s, faced with a market environment that held U.S. firms in a very weak position regarding their cost of operations, American businesses began to employ the then-radical strategy of closing domestic operations and moving production to foreign locations. Outsourcing strategies infiltrated a variety of industries, from auto manufacturing and assembly to filmmaking. By the 1990s, the trend had seen the outsourcing of white-collar and service jobs in travel, electronics, and information technology to countries where wages are paltry, even for the highly educated. Virtually any corporation that required call centers or a minimally trained workforce found tremendous savings in placing those operations in Central America or Asia. In countries like India, even highly trained specialists could be found, working for wages that afforded them an above-average lifestyle in their home countries while costing the company a fraction of the expense for a similarly trained employee in the United States.

Today, however, the ability of an American firm to outsource a $70,000-per-year job to Asia and pay $15,000 per year with no loss in quality or administrative control is no longer a unique competitive advantage for a firm. Now that the practice of contracting with outside suppliers of manpower has become the norm, many organizations must seek other approaches for getting noncrucial tasks done that can help them gain and maintain that cutting edge. Firms without the size or structure necessary for outsourcing need cost-cutting solutions if they are to stay in business.

Outsourcing . . . to the Crowd

Crowdsourcing provides a mechanism for organizations of any size to take advantage of outsourcing. Simply defined, crowdsourcing is the act of a company or institution taking a function once performed by employees and outsourcing it to an undefined (and generally large) network of people in the form of an open call. The job can be performed collaboratively, through peer production, but crowdsourced work is also frequently performed by individuals. The defining components of crowdsourcing (Jeff Howe is credited with coining the term in a 2006 blog post) are the use of the open-call format and the large network of potential laborers.

Successful crowdsourcing involves input from a decentralized group of individuals reporting to a corporate management entity that initiates the project, considers its options, and makes a final decision that it believes is in the best interests of the company. Management then rewards the contributing member or members of the crowd either directly, with a payment or prize, or indirectly, by implementing the idea. Crowdsourcing, as a strategic element of a corporate business model, can be applied in conjunction with traditional and nontraditional business operations. Calls for participation can be made over new or existing social media channels. Tasks can be designed to facilitate either competition or cooperation among the members of the crowd. Wiki-style, real-time editing features, as well as voting mechanisms, can be incorporated into the project to ascertain and analyze the "wisdom of the crowd."

Conceptually, the idea of tapping into a large audience to outsource a specific function in bringing a product or service to market predates the Internet. *Reader's Digest* has been inviting readers to submit short, humorous stories and jokes for decades. Political talk radio hosts have built empires around a format that relies on dialogue with everyman callers. It could even be argued that *The Price Is Right* has been crowdsourcing with every "Come on down!" since 1972. ABC's *America's Funniest Home Videos,* too, was an early experiment in crowdsourcing; the show's embarrassing and sometimes painful content was provided by viewers who responded to an open call for video submissions.

In 1995 Mars, one of the most well-known candy makers in the world, sourced the masses for input on a proposed historic product change: Should the company replace the tan M&M? If so, should the new color be blue, purple, or pink? In essence, by encouraging the public to call and vote via a 1-800 hotline, Mars was using the crowd for product development. This kind of idea vetting is a popular task for crowdsourcing and can provide valuable information on products and services much more cheaply than traditional research involving surveys, focus groups, and test markets.

Crowdsourcing and the Internet

Is the Internet a requirement for crowdsourcing? No—we have just seen pre–World Wide Web examples of this practice. Does the Internet play a vital role in unleashing the power of crowdsourcing? You bet! We had the concept all along; we just needed a method of cheap, easy global communication that could match workers with the work that needed to be done. We also needed tasks that could be done by knowledge workers ("creatives"), since the majority of these tasks can be done by any qualified person from anywhere in the world.

More than two out of every five of the people that provide labor in the crowdsourcing market are located in Asia, with the bulk of the remainder scattered across North America and Europe. But let's look forward into the future for a moment: Africa has seen the world's largest growth in both population and Internet usage per capita over the past decade, and the combination of these two factors should help its population join the crowdsourcing workforce soon. The bottom line is that in a knowledge economy, where the work is done between the ears, any country that has a growing low-wage-based workforce and Internet capabilities is primed to provide talent to the crowdsourcing pool.

In an article on National Public Radio's website, MIT professor Eric von Hippel says that "online design is becoming a substitute for in-house research and development while voting is takes the place of conventional market research."[39] And for good reason: Crowdsourcing harnesses the power of the Internet herd without any need for the management structure and the overhead found in traditional outsourcing. Crowdsourcing is easier to implement and is less expensive, with no loss in speed or quality—in fact, both the wisdom and the sheer volume of the crowd are likely to promote more accurate and creative solutions to business problems.

That might lead you to wonder—just who is in this crowd? If you look at crowdSPRING.com, you will likely see a banner on the front page saying that more than 53,000 people have been registered to ply their services on the site—which is only one in a great number of such crowdsourcing sites. So, the first thing to note is that we are talking

39 Wendy Kaufman, "Crowdsourcing Turns Business on Its Head," NPR.org, August 20, 2008, http://www.npr.org/templates/story/story.php?storyId=93495217.

about potentially millions of people who are already experimenting with—or fully earning their living by—using crowdsourcing sites to find work.

If you were to run a contest on LogoTournament.com and have a new logo created by a crowd of designers, you would be impressed to see hundreds of participants post their submissions. You might be even more impressed to see designers from twenty different countries competing. And don't be surprised when your teenager tells you his or her part-time job is finding work on Amazon's Mturk.com crowdsourcing site. (I should warn you, though, that your child may in fact be an expert on this particular site because he or she uses crowdsourcing to get term papers written there.) When crowdsourcing, you are often connecting with a user profile that includes few personal details and so have no idea who is actually doing the work.

As we created this book using crowdsourcing, we were surprised at the mix of ages, locations, and backgrounds we tapped into. The crowd that is out there and willing to work is made up of freelancers, stay-at-home moms, retirees, and workers looking for extra income. It's made up of people from every corner of the world. The crowd is larger than you probably think it is, and it is still in its infancy. Give this concept a few more years, and there will be an explosion of workers—which will also drive an explosion in the amount of work given to the crowd.

Leveraging Crowdsourcing

Organizations of all sizes and types can leverage crowdsourcing—there is no advantage to being either large or small. If you have creative or knowledge work to be done and would like to get it fast and for a competitive price, you have that opportunity. Virtually any need can be packaged and disseminated to the masses using any of a number of up-and-coming websites, each of which acts as a network hub that connects seekers with providers. Massive international corporations, small businesses, sole proprietors, national and local governments, entertainment companies, and nonprofits all take advantage of the speed, low cost, and high quality associated with crowdsourcing.

Here are some of the most popular ways in which organizations use crowdsourcing.

Feedback–Sharing, Voting, and Discussion

Crowdsourcing feedback from the public takes the notion of a suggestion box to an entirely new level. Traditionally, surveys and other research processes could be both time-consuming and costly. Today, companies can utilize crowdsourcing to harness the opinions of their customers and potential customers. MyStarbucksIdea.com is an online forum that invites coffee shop patrons to share any idea that might improve customer relations or product lines at the nation's number-one coffee retailer. To date, more than 92,000 ideas have been shared and nearly five hundred ideas have been reviewed, with many resulting in new product launches, alterations to the in-store experience, and increased community involvement.[40]

Web-based feedback platforms like UserVoice, UserTesting, and Feedback Army give companies a way of connecting with individuals in the crowd and hearing their ideas about products and services. Many platforms invite the crowd members to vote on the feedback comments of their fellow consumers, giving the service provider or manufacturer clear information about the issues that concern its buyers and about the relative importance of those issues. Corporate users can pay a monthly fee to set up specified domains for one or more brands as well as dedicated forums for crowd interaction regarding individual products. The information is compiled and sent back to the corporation to aid in future decisions regarding products and marketing.

---

40 "Powered by Salesforce, My Starbucks Idea Brews Customer Feedback and Community Engagement," Salesforce.com success story, http://www.salesforce.com/customers/ distribution-retail/starbucks.jsp.

Connecting Creatives

All companies large and small are image conscious, and many invest in a certain degree of vanity. That is, most companies have a logo, letterhead, business cards, brochures, and a website. However, many companies don't have a large enough workload or the resources to hire a full-time graphic designer, a copywriter, and a public relations/marketing professional.

Dedicated advertising agencies and design boutiques do impressive work, but they can be prohibitively expensive and may require the client to sacrifice a degree of control over the messages that will be sent to its audience. A brick-and-mortar creative firm can charge well into the thousands for a logo package and can take anywhere from several weeks to several months to produce a final product—with no guarantee that the client will be satisfied with the results. Corporations and especially individual entrepreneurs and small businesses often struggle to afford such an expensive, time-consuming luxury.

And now they don't have to. Dozens of crowdsourcing websites connect freelance designers, writers, and other creative professionals with individuals and corporations that need single-project creative work completed. Sites like 99designs.com (which we used for this book's cover design) allow businesses to advertise an open call for a project and assign a value to that project in the form of a prize. Designers are free to submit ideas, giving the company dozens and sometimes hundreds of options before it has committed a dime to the project. Competition among the members of the crowd encourages high-quality work produced in a very short amount of time, and the company never has to worry about committing more money than originally planned due to extended deadlines or other hidden costs.

At the time of this writing, 99designs.com lists competitions by a crowd of more than seventy-one thousand designers for 594 projects. Most logo projects have prizes that range from $250 to $800. (For a frame of reference, we offered $750 as a bounty to get the cover of this book done, and we received more than three hundred entries.)

Crowdsourcing sites, including crowdSPRING.com, NameThis.com, RedesignMe.com, and Ponoko.com, connect businesses with writers, product and package designers, and other professional and amateur freelancers. Within some platforms, corporate clients shop out creative work to the lowest bidder. Other platforms require the client to post a creative brief with a specified price it is willing to pay. In general, clients are quickly convinced of this model the moment they experiment with their first "contest" online. They normally are surprised not only by the quantity of people who are willing to compete to win a bounty for doing the work you post, but also by the quality of work some of the top providers will supply. In other words, with crowdsourcing, seeing is believing!

Software: Crowdsourcing's First Love

The open source movement, which is particularly prominent in software development, involves a continually evolving project with many contributors; there is some debate about whether the concepts of "open source" and "crowdsourcing" are mutually exclusive. The only difference may be that "open source" refers to a crowd that *administers and grows* a software platform, whereas "crowdsourcing" refers more to leveraging the crowd to complete a specific task. What is certain is that both concepts tap into the crowd in order to produce a product that is more forward-thinking and of higher quality than those produced by traditional employee structures. Innovative software developers like TopCoder have created business models that rely on competition and a potentially lucrative payoff scale to elicit top-notch software development by crowd members.

Crowdsourcing plays a role in software testing as well. uTest offers software developers an on-demand community of professional testers who promise fast, high-quality testing at a low cost. The scope of the crowd ensures that testing occurs across a complete set of operating systems, Web browsers, and service providers;

members of the crowd report their results from all corners of the world. Google, Microsoft, Intuit, and MySpace are a few of uTest's more prominent customers.

Empowering Communities to Drive Innovation

Driving innovation through empowered communities is the motivation behind IdeaScale, a Web-based platform that allows organizations to create online communities and surf the crowd for ideas that pertain to their industries. Brainstorming is a potent area for crowdsourcing as manufacturers and service providers look for more cost-effective ways of determining the most promising next step. Chaordix, Kluster, and other platform designers match organizations with tools that help tap the crowd using idea submissions, voting mechanisms, conversational forums, and even wiki-style, real-time modification of working proposals.

Recently, an IdeaScale client proposed an environmental project that centered on a simple problem—the ridiculous number of coffee cups produced, used, and thrown away each year. A massive call for solutions was launched, giving the crowd an opportunity to submit ideas, comment on the ideas of others, and vote for its favorites. The solution was brilliant, simple, and typical of the kind of thinking that crowdsourcing encourages. Despite a number of solutions that offered design ideas for less wasteful (but still single-use) cups, the winning idea was an incentive-based program designed to alter the behavior of the consumer: The "karma cup" encourages customers to bring their own reusable cups to their local Starbucks for a one-in-ten chance at getting a free drink.

At the end of the twentieth century, despite holding a respected position as a leader in research and development, Procter & Gamble began to note that its R&D productivity had begun to wane while costs were rising. For the company to maintain steady growth, it would need to look outside its 7,500 R&D employees. Procter &

Gamble's leaders noticed that smaller organizations and even individuals were capable of impressive innovation, and that the Internet was making these talented people more accessible than ever before. In a daring move, Procter & Gamble restructured its organization, setting a goal that 50 percent of its new product innovations would come from sources outside the company. The company now maintains its own crowdsourcing hub at PGConnectDevelop.com, where it broadcasts its needs and encourages new ideas. To date, more than one thousand partnerships have been established.[41]

The U.S. government, the Federal Communications Commission, Microsoft, Choice Hotels, and *Wired* magazine are just a few examples of the varied list of entities that crowdsource innovative, high-level projects of this type.

Democratizing (and Funding!) Product Development

Some crowdsourcing applications encourage the crowd to put its money where its mouth is. On Spot.Us, citizens can submit tips on stories they'd like to see reported. Journalists and small news organizations submit pitches for stories in such categories as local politics, the environment, and personal interest. They also list a funding plan for writing the story. The crowd is invited to voice its support for the story by pledging a monetary contribution to that story. When the fee amount is reached, the contributors are charged and the journalist gets to work. The concept counts on contributors' desire to sponsor stories on subjects that ignite their passion or effect positive change in the world.

At FashionStake.com, a new online high-fashion boutique, consumers are invited to criticize (via a voting system) the designs of potential garments submitted by designers. Furthermore, members of the crowd can buy a stake in a designer, helping to fund his or

---

41 Larry Huston and Nabil Sakkab, "Connect and Develop: Inside Procter & Gamble's New Model for Innovation," *Harvard Business Review*, March 2006, http://hbswk.hbs.edu/archive/5258.html.

her work and bring the product to market. Those with "ownership" in a particular designer receive credits toward the purchase of that designer's items.

Threadless.com is a community-based T-shirt company with an ongoing, open call for design submissions. Celebrating its tenth anniversary in 2010, Threadless operates an online system that accepts design ideas and presents them to the voting public for approval, using a five-point rating scale. High-scoring designs or those that display a thought-provoking viewpoint—usually identified by having both very high and very low voting scores—get produced, and the contributing designer is paid up to $2,500 for a first run. At Threadless, crowdsourcing leaves its mark on business operations in several areas, most notably in product development, market testing, and marketing. Says Blake Mycoskie, founder of forward-thinking retailer TOMS Shoes, "When Threadless releases new shirts every week, there is never a doubt that their products will be remarkable, because the tribe has, in fact, already spoken. Every shirt carries with it its own unique story: Somewhere in the world, an artist has been turned into a T-shirt entrepreneur."[42]

Similar sites encourage idea generation, collaborative production, and funding of projects ranging from feature films to business launches to philanthropy to personal fund-raising.

Crowdsourcing Problem Resolution

In late spring of 2010, BP's Deepwater Horizon drilling platform experienced a catastrophic failure, resulting in lost lives and an open well spewing oil into the Gulf of Mexico from a depth of more than a mile. Immediately, several entities, including BP and the Department of Homeland Security, utilized crowdsourcing platforms to create virtual think tanks, calling for solutions to contain the oil spill

---

42 Blake Mycoskie, quote on Threadless.com, accessed September 13, 2010, http://www.threadless.com/book.

and clean up the affected region of the gulf. Tens of thousands of solutions were submitted, and several hundred merited consideration and future research as feasible ideas.

InnoCentive.com is one provider of crowdsourcing platforms. Uniting "seekers" with "solvers," InnoCentive lets visitors browse problems with accompanying rewards of between $5,000 and $1 million. Current examples of seekers include those in need of ideas on microgravity laundry systems (for use in long-distance space travel), reducing fat content in fried snacks, and the design of shower accessories for men; there are numerous calls for high-level chemistry and medicinal solutions as well. This site is essentially performing as an outsource research-and-development function for, as an example, the pharmaceutical industry. It is very likely that InnoCentive will become a powerful facilitator of brokering solutions for years to come. If you have never visited this site, we strongly urge you to take a look at the types of solutions that organizations are seeking and some of the success stories that have been documented.

GasBuddy.com was created to help address the consumer's need for cheap gas. The site operates on a simple, cost-effective principle: It lets the crowd provide raw data on gas prices over the Internet, analyzes and organizes that data, and then disseminates the information back to the crowd in a useful format. Since 2000, founders Dustin Coupal and Jason Toews have managed a real-time forum that compiles gas prices at retail locations as reported by civilian motorists. The system further encourages crowd participation by awarding points and holding weekly drawings for prizes such as $250 gas cards.

Crowdsourcing White-Collar Functions

Feedback, creativity, and innovation are all logical areas for applying outside-the-box tactics—but can a crowd be reliable enough to aid in management or provide workers for white-collar, back-office functions?

The answer seems to be *yes,* at least in the case of the Torrington Titans, a collegiate summer baseball team that is crowdsourcing its management. Our Baseball Haven–the business entity behind the team–states that the Torrington Titans are "the first community-controlled sports franchise in the United States." In this innovative organization, public citizens are invited to purchase a non-owner membership in the franchise. The membership fees go toward operating costs–a.k.a. crowdfunding–and each member receives a vote that he or she can cast in operational decisions. Tasks that would traditionally fall to an employee in charge of marketing or management are decided upon by a popular vote among members. Furthermore, a percentage of the franchise's revenue goes toward community philanthropy. Our Baseball Haven was formed in spring of 2009, and the team played its inaugural game in June 2010.[43]

Guru.com is a Web-based crowdsourcing platform that connects freelance providers in areas like technology, creative arts, and business with the companies that need them. Within the business category, companies can call for assistance in administrative support, legal services, and accounting. Each freelance provider has a profile on the site that includes his or her location, earnings to date, minimum rate, and a feedback rating of up to five stars.

Implementing Crowdsourcing for Your Project or Business

Like any other business tool, crowdsourcing must be managed properly in order to give maximum value to a company. A dedicated manager should be placed in charge of researching the whole gamut of crowdsourcing sites to find services the company needs. Given time, this person–who should be something of a "crowdsourcing

---

43 Our Baseball Haven homepage, http://www.ourbaseballhaven.com/, and About page, http://www.ourbaseballhaven.com/about.html, accessed September 13, 2010.

evangelist"—should become a liaison between Web-based crowd-sourcing platforms and the organization. He or she should be able to explain the exact benefits and the expected costs of implementing a crowdsourcing strategy for a specific project.

A few test projects your company could potentially crowdsource are probably already springing to mind. A product logo or packaging design for a new offering might afford you an excellent opportunity to survey the speed and quality available when you use the crowd-sourcing process. And as mentioned, seeing is believing with this new way of getting things done.

Before you launch your first project, here is a practical, step-by-step guide to successfully crowdsourcing a project.

1. Picking the Right Site

This is a critical step. The field of crowdsourcing is still young, and some websites offer a much bigger workforce than others. These sites are also starting to specialize in various types of work, so you want to find a site that has workers looking for the type of project you have. The easiest way to find the right site is to do a few simple Google searches for keywords relating to the type of work you want done, paired with the word *crowdsource*—for example, you might search for "crowdsource logo design." You can also go to our website, EnterpriseSocialTechnology.com, to see lists of crowdsourcing sites.

2. Picking the Right Bounty Amount

Setting the amount you'll pay for the crowdsourced project is also a key component in receiving quality work. Most sites are beginning to find a balance between the prices providers are willing to work for and the prices seekers are willing to pay. It is wise to provide a bounty that is at least somewhere in the middle of this range, though being on the higher end will ensure that you get the attention of the most talented people. It also helps to guarantee the bounty; understandably, some of the more talented people will not work on projects that do not have a guarantee.

3. Writing the Instructions

Providing thorough instructions will help everyone get to a good outcome. The more detail you can supply as to what you are looking for and what the boundaries of the project are, the less time you will waste having to review submissions that do not meet your requirements. You also will not waste as much of the crowd's time; although each crowd member would love to win the bounty, no one wants to waste time trying to guess at what you might want. When crowdsourcing the cover of this book, for example, we neglected to tell people that we did not want a black background, and 60 percent of the first wave of submissions were black. That wasted lots of our time and the crowd's.

4. Managing the Project While in Progress

Most sites allow you to communicate with the crowd while the work is being done. This gives you the ability to critique submissions along the way so that people can tweak what they are doing. It also shows others in the crowd what you do and do not like, and that helps them improve their offerings. The crowd can get annoyed very quickly if you do not give feedback in a timely manner. Its members are looking for daily—even hourly—opinions on what they have done for you. Be honest, be clear, and be timely with your feedback. This helps the whole process. You should also rank the submissions in order according to which ones you like best; that way, providers can see which styles suit your needs, and competitors for the project know how they should tweak their work.

5. Picking a Winner

Once the contest has ended, you will have a week or so to pick a winner. Be sure to communicate clearly the file formats you need and any final tweaks that might be necessary. Many of the sites will allow you to do a final round of upgrades only after you have picked the winner. It's always a good idea to thank providers who worked hard but didn't win. Remember, these are real human beings on the other side of this transaction, and a kind word goes a long way.

6. Closing Down the Project

Understand that once you have picked a winner, many of the submissions and submitters will disappear almost immediately. If you want to communicate with any of them for any reason, do it before you close down the project. The crowd has a short attention span for projects once they see that they have not won. There is a particular flow to the interest you will receive on these projects, a bell curve in the crowd's attention span, which ends abruptly when the contest closes. So be prepared to get everything you want in place before closing the project.

* * *

Once a crowdsourced project has been completed, consider these questions:

- How much lower was the cost of completion in comparison to traditional methods?
- How fast was the work done?
- How many options did I have to choose from?
- How did the quality compare to traditional methods?

Make sure you plan your project thoroughly, get everything you want out of it, and treat people fairly. It is a smaller world than you would suspect, and if you go back to the crowd for more work, your reputation as a seeker will follow you.

Who's in Your Crowd?

Participants on the provider side of crowdsourcing are varied, ranging from professional freelancers and moonlighters to students and amateur hobbyists. They are often referred to as "solvers," "vendors," or "sources." Because of the global reach of the Internet, they can be located anywhere in the world; they need not work from a brick-and-mortar office or even from their home. Access to the Internet is virtually the only requirement. Sources maintain their own software and other materials needed to perform the jobs that they accept—another overhead-slashing benefit that opens up this option to the masses.

An examination of provider profiles on crowdsourcing sites such as Guru.com and Spot.Us reveals that crowdsourced business opportunities have attracted the attention of small, specialized firms in such disciplines as accounting, legal services, and journalism. Most of these firms focus on more traditional means of generating business; however, they are taking advantage of the growing popularity of crowdsourcing to supplement their revenue and build new contacts.

Some individual freelancers work exclusively as crowdsourcers, generating income comparable to that of an in-house professional. Some crowdsourcing sites list the total revenue each provider has earned as a benchmark of that provider's reliability and the quality of his or her work. One provider on a popular crowdsourcing website has been a member for two years and has participated in at least 1,261 projects, exclusively as a logo designer. His designs have been selected eighty-six times, usually earning between $300 and $800 dollars per job. A look at his profile reveals that he has closed as many as seven deals in one month, though it also shows gaps of several months at a time between projects awarded.

Another vendor profile on a leading website for professional and amateur freelancers provides details about a full-time ghostwriter with all-time earnings topping $170,000, including more than $57,000 in the first half of 2010 alone. In fact, at least twenty writers with varying specialties have earned at least $20,000 during that same six-month time frame, through projects obtained from the same crowd-sourcing website.

Our experience with crowdsourcing this book has shown that the quality of people available is greater than what you might think it would be. We used bounties that were at the high end of what is normally offered for crowdsourcing creative and writing work, though still very inexpensive relative to obtaining this work through traditional avenues. This incentive enabled us to work with a crowd from all over the world and from every walk of life. The end of the story is not written, however—we are also using crowdsourcing to help with publicity efforts for the book, by offering bounties for various means of exposure. If you are interested in seeing the list of these publicity activities, check out EnterpriseSocialTechnology.com to see what has been claimed so far. There might be some task left that you could tackle for us!

Your Internal Crowd

Crowdsourcing can be used with an internal crowd as well as with the Internet herd in general. When Dell and Starbucks built sites that allowed customers to provide their best product ideas and vote other ideas up or down, they were leveraging their internal crowd, made up not of the general public but of established customers of those brands. We will soon see employees of large organizations making up an internal crowd that can also be leveraged in new ways.

Associations, too, can leverage their members as an internal crowd, and governments can tap into the abilities of their constituents. As crowdsourcing sites get more effective and user-friendly, we will see them provide platforms that help organizations mine the potential of these internal crowds.

The Future of Crowdsourcing

The Pew Research Center recently conducted a survey of nearly nine hundred experts from the fields of science, business, technology, and journalism, concerning the future of the Internet. The experts' collaborative effort reveals several predictions that have a direct impact on the future of crowdsourcing. By 2020, advances in bandwidth and software developments will make global connectivity easier than ever before. Seventy-two percent of the experts surveyed expect that innovative forms of online cooperation will result in significantly more efficient and responsive governments, businesses, and nonprofits.[44] Said writer Steve Lohr, "The overarching notion is that the Internet opens the door to a new world of democratic idea generation and collaborative production."[45]

As more and more crowdsourcing sites come online to facilitate new relationships, and as highly visible companies adopt crowdsourcing processes, a greater number of corporate entities will begin to trust that crowdsourcing is not only an effective business strategy but also a secure one. Much like outsourcing once represented a competitive advantage, crowdsourcing will greatly benefit early adopters and those who continually find new ways of leveraging the crowd to fulfill business needs. Crowdsourcing will allow firms access to a quality of work and a quantity of skilled professionals that previously were unattainable and unaffordable.

Crowdsourcing is a new social tech tool that simply cannot be ignored. As the infrastructure for harnessing the Internet herd grows,

44 Lee Rainie, "The Impact of the Internet on Institutions in the Future," Pew Internet & American Life Project, March 31, 2010, http://pewresearch.org/pubs/1543/impact-of-the-internet-on-institutions-in-the-future.

45 Steve Lohr, "The Crowd Is Wise (When It's Focused)," *New York Times*, July 18, 2009, http://www.nytimes.com/2009/07/19/technology/internet/19unboxed.html?_r=2.

it would be foolish to let your competitors figure out how to lower their costs and speed up their development time while you watch from the sidelines. And certainly there is no doubt that corporations will follow Procter & Gamble's lead in developing their own proprietary crowdsourcing website. The future will surely bring a continued move toward verticalization of sites and an explosion of workers looking to find new sources of revenue.

The results of implementing a crowdsourcing strategy are eminently measurable, so you'll be able to immediately determine the strategy's impact on your bottom line. Being able to prove a return on investment in your use of *any* social technology tool is critical—and the next chapter will show you just how to measure that impact so you can ensure ROI for your organization.

KEY POINTS

- Crowdsourcing is the latest, most innovative way to contract work from outside your organization. It is a powerful way for organizations to lower back-office costs, better acquaint themselves with customer's desires, and get work done faster. The volume of crowdsourced work will soon dwarf the volume of work being traditionally outsourced today.

- Global economic dynamics, social tech tools, and the Internet are combining to create a wage scale for crowdsourcing that is very attractive to Western businesses.

- New crowdsourcing sites are currently blossoming in numbers and beginning to specialize in specific types of work.

- There is an art to effectively running a crowdsourcing project, and it pays to choose the sites you will work with carefully, provide the right bounty amount, give very detailed instructions, and stay involved with the process.

- The "crowd" in crowdsourcing can be made up of the general Internet herd, or it could be made up of your employees or customers. Sometimes your constituent crowd can help you much more than the general public could.

 To get a list of well-known crowdsourcing sites, visit EnterpriseSocialTechnology.com. There, you can also learn more about the making of this book—including samples of covers and chapters we didn't use.

CHAPTER 9

The ROI Measurement Process

> "The ROI of social media is that your business
> will still exist in five years."
> —Erik Qualman, author of *Socialnomics: How Social Media
> Transforms the Way We Live and Do Business*

In the world of sports, the score tells us very simply which team or player wins. However, sports managers keep and analyze much more complicated data sets to help teams and players keep winning. Today's baseball managers have laptops in the dugouts so they can predict the effectiveness of a specific pitcher against a specific batter based on historical data. Team owners create convoluted measurement schemes to evaluate players based on ratios and combinations of performance statistics.

Companies are no different. They play a very different game with very different measurements, but in the end the goal of a business, like that of a sports team, is to win.

In the business's case, winning means making a profit, and in theory, all of a business's activities should contribute—whether directly or indirectly—to that goal. You can argue about the usefulness of many expenses (fancy executive suites, for example). You can argue about the responsibility a business has to employees, local communities, and other stakeholders. But in the long run, management must generate a satisfying rate of return on invested capital or risk angry shareholders, loss of market share, and eventual bankruptcy. (If you are in public service, you may not need to make a profit, but what you do is measurable, too. Surely you have analytics that tell you whether you are hitting the mark, even if profit isn't your primary goal.)

Using social technologies to create online conversations, to connect and engage with constituents, and to foster communities—it all sounds nice, right? But do these activities really help organizations reach their goals? Without adequate systems in place to track the results of social technology activities, a company can burn through lots of resources without anything to show for it.

At this point in the process, it's time to start figuring out how to measure the results you get from social tech tools—and how to track whether these tools are helping you achieve your goals. The most important question we need to ask is: What is the return on investment (ROI) of allocating resources for social technology?

A number of organizations that are experimenting with social tech tools have found that the resources spent on them are not generating an adequate return. This can be due to poor implementation, bad timing in the adoption of a social tech strategy, or several other factors. There are also many examples of social technologies, however, that are successfully adding to the bottom line.

Gary Vaynerchuk, author of *Crush It!,* used social technology to grow his family's wine business from a $4 million company to a $50 million company. He found that when he used direct mail, he spent $15,000 to acquire two hundred new customers. Spending $7,500 on billboard advertising got him three hundred new customers. But for just the cost of a little of his own time, he used Twitter to acquire 1,800 new customers.[46]

---

46 Lon Safko, "The Twitter About Twitter," FastCompany.com, June 13, 2009, http://www. fastcompany.com/blog/lon-safko/ten-commandments-social-media/twitter-about-twitter.

A study from Wetpaint and the Altimeter Group found that the companies using social technology the most had an average increase in sales of 18 percent; the companies with the least use of social technology showed a 6 percent drop in sales.[47] Here are a few examples of companies that saw a very clear return on their social tech investments:

- Blendtec's "Will It Blend?" series of YouTube videos multiplied the company's sales volume by five times.[48]

- Dell has used Twitter to sell $6.5 million worth of rebuilt and discontinued models of computers.[49]

- Alan Mulally, CEO of Ford Motor Company (the one American car company that didn't have to be bailed out by the government), attributes his company's success to social technology. Twenty-five percent of its total ad spending is now online.[50]

- When Web host and site builder Moonfruit spent $15,000 on social technology, it saw a 300 percent increase in website traffic and a 20 percent increase in sales.[51]

- Lenovo saw a 20 percent reduction in call center volume, thanks to encouraging customers to visit its website instead.[52]

---

47 "New Study: Deep Brand Engagement Correlates with Financial Performance," Altimeter Group, July 20, 2009, http://www.altimetergroup.com/2009/07/engagementdb.html.

48 Marianne Kolbasuk McGee, "YouTube Videos Stir Up New Sales for 'Will It Blend' Maker," InformationWeek.com, September 27, 2007, http://www.informationweek.com/news/internet/showArticle.jhtml?articleID=202102372.

49 Lionel Menchaca, "Expanding Connections with Customers Through Social Media," Direct2Dell (Dell corporate blog), December 8, 2009, http://en.community.dell.com/dell-blogs/Direct2Dell/b/direct2dell/archive/2009/12/08/expanding-connections-with-customers-through-social-media.aspx.

50 David Kiley, "Ford Spending 25% of Marketing on Digital and Social Media," *The AutoBeat* (Businessweek.com blog), September 1, 2010, http://www.businessweek.com/autos/autobeat/.

51 Daniel Adler, "Twenty-One Top Twitter Tips," Forbes.com, July 31. 2009, http://www.forbes.com/2009/07/31/top-twitter-tips-entrepreneurs-technology-twitter.html.

52 Chiaki Nishino, "Achieving Less Din, More Dialog in Your Social Media Presence," Prophet, June 6, 2010, http://www.prophet.com/thinking/view/461-achieving-less-din-more-dialog-in-your-social-media-presence.

Each of these organizations has found measurable success through the use of social tech, and they are all seeing profit by leveraging social tech in different ways. One thing you can be sure of is that for each of these results, a well-defined set of goals and measurements was put in place. These companies did not just stumble across success by throwing things at the wall and seeing what stuck. They likely started out with a negative ROI and a few issues, then course-corrected multiple times in order to see the positive return.

Measuring Activity and Results

"What gets measured gets done" is a timeless business axiom that applies perfectly to social technology. Tracking activity and results is a vital part of your organization's initial social tech plan, because without this tracking, you will simply wander around in the world of social tech without knowing what you are doing well and what areas need improvement. You will waste time and resources. You will allow some of your people to live in a netherworld of all talk and no action.

Before going any further, let's examine the term *return on investment*. In many cases the math behind calculating whether an investment will actually be returned over a given time period is pretty straightforward. For example, if a company buys a piece of software for $100,000 that will save the company $10,000 a month in direct labor costs, we know the company will see a full return on their investment within a year. Finding the ROI on social technologies can be a bit unclear, however. We often see that social tech tools help improve customer satisfaction or brand preference; this might show up in sales gains, but since sales gains also reflect the impact of many other factors, it can be impossible to discern what value the social tech tools brought to bear. With that said, we must always force ourselves to do the best job possible to figure out whether we are making wise investments with each social concept we put in place. Taking the time and investing the energy to really measure social tech impact is key to determining the ROI of enterprise social technology. Without this due diligence, you will really just be guessing at the value you are getting back.

Let's look at how to measure ROI through the following five-step process:

1. Measure the current impact of your social technologies.

2. Set objectives for ROI.

3. Determine social tech results needed to meet objectives.

4. Source and implement social tech measurement systems.

5. Measure results, compare to objectives, and adapt continuously.

1. Measure the Current Impact of Your Social Technologies

Because social tech has grown organically within some organizations, it is important to figure out where are you now in terms of activity and results. To determine that, you must take an inventory of the social technologies you are now using across the organization and speculate on each one's impact. You must also establish a person within your organization who is responsible for social tech measurement and analysis. Select this person before evaluating your current status; participating in this process will help your analyst get up to speed on what needs to be measured and what level of ROI you are already achieving.

The social tech analyst should be responsible for gathering the measured information, compiling reports, and distributing them to the organization every month. This person can also coordinate the flow of information to anywhere else it needs to go for analysis. Too many companies rely on informal networks of friends and contacts to transmit information; these loose arrangements do grease the organizational wheels, but they are no substitute for clearly defined lines of responsibility and accountability.

The social tech analyst should make the results of the measurements known to as many people as possible. Social technology should not be regarded as just one more department or activity within the organization. It should be thought of as an important, broad mode of contact with customers and clients, who are the most important people to everybody in the organization; after all, they fund each employee's salary.

Once you have established who is going to be responsible for analyzing social tech, take an inventory of all your organization's current social applications. For example, maybe you have a blog nobody has posted to for three months and one video on YouTube of the company president giving a speech. Or you might have a plethora of people working on social tech in an uncoordinated fashion.

In taking this inventory, you should consider the following categories of social tech:

- **Web properties.** Does your Web presence tie into your social tech presence? Does your website promote a blog and a Facebook fan page? Is there a real-time stream of tweets about your firm on the website?

- **Blogs.** Does the company have an official blog, and do any employees have personal blogs in which they discuss company matters? If your company does have a blog or blogs, you'll need to look at how many views and comments each receives.

- **Twitter.** Does the organization have a Twitter feed? Are any employees tweeting company-related content? Measure the number of followers, the number of tweets produced, the number of tweets that are retweeted, the number of times the organization is mentioned on Twitter, and the sentiment ratio of positive to negative mentions.

- **Facebook.** Does the company have a Facebook fan page or group? How is it being used? How many members or fans

does it have? What are the conversations like on the wall?
Is the page being used to drive people to the organization's
website to purchase products? If so, what kind of response do
you see to promotions on the Facebook wall?

- **Videos and other visual media.** Are there company videos
  uploaded to YouTube, Vimeo, or any other video-sharing
  sites? How many views are these videos getting? How many
  comments? Have they been favorited? This same research
  needs to be done for other social media sites, such as Scribd,
  SlideShare, and Flickr.

- **Podcasts.** Is anyone from the organization producing podcasts
  or vodcasts (video podcasts)? If so, for what reasons? What
  are the benefits? How many downloads are they getting?

- **Crowdsourcing.** Is anyone in the organization using a crowdsourcing site to complete tasks? If so, are these efforts saving
  resources? What problems are they solving?

- **Online reputation.** Is anyone using listening tools to monitor when the organization, its products, or its executives are
  mentioned online? If so, how many mentions are you getting
  and on what channels do they happen most often? What is
  the sentiment ratio?

- **LinkedIn.** How many of the company's employees are on
  LinkedIn? How many of them have more than two hundred
  connections? Do these employees know how to use all of the
  site's features? If so, how have they leveraged LinkedIn to
  help them professionally?

Obviously, there are many more social tech tools that can be
researched. If you are part of a small organization, this process won't
take long, but if you belong to a large firm, it could be a month before
you know what everyone is doing. It's an important step, though; to
accurately measure your success with using social tech, you must get

a good idea of how it is being used before you implement a new strategy. For many leaders, the state of the company's social tech efforts is shocking—these tools are often implemented by individuals without any coordination, strategy, or approval.

Once you have made an inventory of your social technology usage, consider also measuring these more specific metrics:

- Number of comments posted to your blog posts (on average)
- Number of blog page views
- Number of RSS feed subscribers
- Number of mentions in blogs, tweets, videos, Facebook pages, etc.
- Number of Twitter followers
- Number of Twitter retweets
- Number of Facebook friends
- Number of Facebook fans
- Number of Diggs, and number of mentions on other social bookmarking sites
- Number of YouTube channel subscribers
- Number of YouTube friends
- Number of comments posted to your videos on YouTube and other video-sharing sites
- Number of podcasts downloaded or played
- Number of podcast subscribers
- Number of downloads of free content (such as white papers and free reports)
- Number of customer reviews on Amazon and other consumer sites
- Total number of monthly conversations

- Number of brand evangelists
- Number of brand detractors
- Number of key influencers discovered
- Number of sales leads generated through social tech
- Number of website visitors referred from social tech links
- Amount of time visitors spend on website and social tech pages
- Number of social technology connections who become sales leads
- Ratio of social technology connections who convert into sales
- Total number of connections across social tech sites

There may also be social sites specific to your industry, and you should be monitoring your presence on these as well. You'll have to customize measurements for each one based on how it is set up.

When looking at the big picture, you also need to know where your brand or organization stands in terms of the conversations occurring online, as discussed in chapter 7. There is a list of tools to monitor these conversations at the end of this chapter, but don't rely on them—especially to measure sentiment ratios. You need a human being with common sense to read and evaluate the actual posts, comments, and tweets. Don't expect software to understand the full meaning of human communication.

When measuring your mentions online, you must also remember that a lot of people are trying to game social technologies. There are numerous software programs, for example, that scrape content from various sites and use it to create "autoblogs." These are value-less as social technologies, but your tracking software may not understand that. It may count an autoblog post as a valid mention of your brand or organization—even though the actual content was copied from your own website.

If your organization or brand is big enough to garner thousands of mentions, you may be humanly able to read only a statistically significant sample of posts or tweets, but do try to read as many as you can. You want to have an accurate and meaningful understanding of their content.

If a large number of your prospects and customers are outside the United States, find out which social technologies they participate in and quantify your mentions there, too. Twitter and Facebook cover the globe but they have localized social technology competitors in countries other than the U.S. For example, if you're marketing to Chinese consumers, you need to participate on QQ and Renren.

In time, consider tracking more sophisticated metrics, such as the following:

- Ratio of comments to blog posts
- Ratio of tweets to retweets
- Month-over-month growth velocity rate of Twitter followers
- Month-over-month growth velocity rate of Facebook fans
- Month-over-month growth velocity rate of RSS feed subscribers
- Month-over-month growth velocity rate of YouTube channel subscribers
- Number of average followers of your Twitter followers

Your goal here is to get as complete a picture as possible of the size of your organization's presence in the marketplace. Many metrics can be presumed to be inherently positive (your number of Twitter followers or RSS feed subscribers, for example). Other indicators, such as user comments and scores, must be evaluated by human eyes and brains.

Once you have measured your current social tech presence, you will have established a good baseline for the further development of your social tech analytics.

2. Set Objectives for ROI

Remember, the goal of all this activity is not to win a "feel good" contest; it's to increase your bottom line. Therefore, you must also use standard organizational analytics in order to set a baseline for where you stand at the time you begin implementing social technology strategies. You'll want to look at the following:

- Gross sales
- Number of sales transactions per month
- Rate of sales growth
- Amount of average sale
- Number of new customers per month
- Amount of new customer revenue per month
- Length of sales cycle
- Lifetime value of a customer
- Cost of each sales lead
- Sales lead conversion percentage
- Cost to acquire a new customer using established marketing channels (TV ads, search engine marketing, ads in Yellow Pages, etc.)
- Your brand's market share
- Percentage of customer satisfaction
- Percentage of customer retention
- Refund rate
- Number of customer referrals

Most organizations track these standard metrics, so your goal here is to simply take a snapshot of these numbers before you get too deeply into using social technology tools. Then you can review them in the future to see whether your social tech projects are making a difference.

If you're implementing a social tech strategy with the goal of reducing expenses, measure the current costs you hope to decrease. For example, if you plan to use Twitter for customer service, record your current cost per call. This will allow you to see whether the costs of customer contact have come down as a result of your social tech strategy.

In order to calculate ROI, management must be able to accurately record the costs of social technology investments. This includes the cost of employee hours, outsourcing fees, work station(s), software, and video production, plus an allocation of total overhead. Knowing these expenses will help you keep your eyes on the real prize: net profit.

Once you have compiled this data, management can set its ROI objectives. Be specific in every category, and tie that specific number to a particular social technology. For example, if the organization is going to use a Twitter account to build a continual conversation with its customer base, there will be an investment of time in finding and generating valuable content to share. This investment can be quantified and a cost can be calculated on a per-hour basis, which makes the expense side of the ROI equation very measurable.

To calculate the value side, you must take into account the revenue that comes directly from tweeting links to discounts and new products. This can be measured by tracking the click-through rates on the specific links and tying them to sales. A less concrete benefit of the Twitter stream is the branding and eWord of mouth that online conversation generates. The value of this is always an estimate. In some cases, progress can be measured by taking comprehensive baseline sales numbers from before the Twitter stream and comparing them to sales numbers after the campaign has been in play for six months. If you see a sales gain, some of it can normally be attributed to your activity on Twitter.

Your overall objectives in using social technology may vary—you may use it to do anything from reducing customer service expenses to generating new sales leads to managing your brand's reputation to driving more traffic to your main website. The social tech toolbox is so varied that each firm will apply the tools in a unique way. This means that calculating ROI is a very different process for every organization. Eventually, your organization should expect to see some bottom-line results, even if your social tech pilot projects run negative in the early days.

What your organization reaps should reflect the original goals you set up in the first step. Using social technologies can both reduce back-office expenses and increase sales by maximizing customer satisfaction and attracting new customers. In other words, social tech can affect the bottom line from both ends.

Measuring ROI is the most hotly debated topic among social technology experts; some even claim it's impossible. According to an August 2009 survey by Mzinga and Babson Executive Education, 84 percent of respondents said they don't currently measure the ROI of their social technology programs.[53] That's appalling, but it reveals an opportunity for your organization to take the lead.

Although your estimates cannot be quite as precise as the final numbers seem, it's important for all businesses to have a handle on the bottom-line impact of their social tech activities. One method is to compare the exposure your social technology activities bring you to the equivalent CPM (cost per one thousand impressions) of a banner ad. For example, Burger King determined that it spent under $50,000 on its "Whopper Sacrifice" Facebook application to obtain $400,000 of publicity. (In fairness, your organization must understand that matching advertising expenses to precise revenues has never been an exact science.)

One way of setting your objectives is to look at your competition. Examine every major company in your industry; these firms' social technology data will be available to anyone who wants to see it. Take

---

53 "Social Media Measurement Lags Adoption," *eMarketer*, September 22, 2009, http:// www.emarketer.com/Article.aspx?R=1007286.

advantage of this! Remember, even if you don't look at what your competition is doing, they're probably looking at what you're doing.

User sentiment is especially important here. You may not mind if your competition is mentioned twice as often as you—so long as everybody is bad-mouthing your competition. Still, you may want to set objectives in relation to competitors. If you're behind in online sentiment, you need to catch up. If you're currently ahead, you'll want to increase your lead, especially if you can see they're already implementing a strong social tech strategy.

3. Determine Social Tech Results Needed to Meet Objectives

Let's assume that you have identified a number of pilot projects you want to test, and that you have locked in the goals you want to achieve with them. The next step is to identify the velocity necessary to meet those goals. For example, if you want to have one hundred thousand people reading your blog by the end of the year, it is a pretty simple thing to figure out the rate at which you will need to add people in order to get there. If you then determine that for every thousand readers, you generate an additional X amount of sales, you'll see how much revenue you can drive from blogging.

You will need to record your social tech conversion ratios separately from revenue driven by other channels. Theoretically, social tech traffic should convert better than "cold" traffic. It should be comparable to traffic driven by mailings to any e-mail lists of clients and prospects with whom the owner has cultivated a close personal relationship.

If you put an online reputation management process in place, you should see an increase in positive sentiment expressed by customers online. This is especially true if you proactively engage every dissatisfied customer. Such an approach almost always has an impact on your customer retention rate, and if it does, that will show you a specific gain in revenue. Once you establish the online sentiment ratio as a predictable indicator of revenue saved, you can determine when you will achieve the goals you set for customer satisfaction, customer retention, and saved revenue.

As much as possible, account for the time spent on each type of activity. For example, if you decide to focus on getting Facebook friends, you want to know how much that effort cost you. You can't accomplish this if your time on Facebook is mixed in with time spent reading industry blogs. Once you've tested the value of adding Facebook friends, do the same test with Twitter followers to see which site is worth more to your organization—perhaps Twitter followers are cheaper to acquire than Facebook friends, but Facebook friends convert to sales more often and therefore are worth more. Perhaps there'll be no difference. The only way to know is to test and track. The resulting analytics will help you decide where to focus your efforts to reach your goals.

In order to get to an awesome ROI using social tech tools, you must understand the results that can be gained with leveraging each of the concepts that could be put into play. There are many ways that social tech tools can help a sales force, and some will be much more effective than others. Because increasing sales volume is so critical to most organizations, knowing which tools will drive general customer satisfaction (retention) versus new revenue (new customers) is an important distinction. It is not just a matter of using social technology tools to make progress; it is a matter of *where* you need to make progress right now.

4. Source and Implement Social Tech Measurement Systems

There are many tools available—both fee-based and free—that will help you analyze the results of your social tech pilot projects and other social tech efforts. Before you spend a lot of time and effort devising complicated measuring systems that take up staff time, make sure to investigate the sites listed next. ROI measurement for social tech tools is a fast-growing field, and every day new measurement tools come on the market. By the time this book hits the streets, there will be new sites that may be even better than those listed here, so keep your eyes open.

If you are part of a larger organization (or a smaller one that doesn't have much time to devote to social tech), you may be considering the fact that social tech evaluation can be outsourced. There are many companies now providing contract services, and many individuals that can help with various pieces of the social tech strategy. Just be careful to be sure you know how to use these tools internally before you contract out the work. Absent this capability, you will be completely dependent on a contractor to make the right moves and provide quality work, because you will have no idea how to judge either one.

If you do take this route, make sure that an internal team member is monitoring the outsourced work and clearly conveying the organization's perspective so that outsourcers are working within an agreed-upon, defined scope. It's one thing for an outside consultant to help you set up your Facebook page, but it is something else entirely for that individual to provide in-depth analytics on how social tech tools are performing. You must also consider that this person may be offering a slanted approach; he or she probably wouldn't want to tell you that your social tech tools are failing, for fear of not being retained.

Here is a list of some of the tools that can help you gather the basic information on how your organization is doing in the social tech landscape.

Social Mention (socialmention.com)

This is a free online tool that aggregates your social technologies mentions. It draws from more than one hundred social technology sites, including all the major ones. It computes values for Reach (range of influence), Passion (repetitive mentions), Strength (the likelihood that your brand is being discussed in social media), and Sentiment (the ratio of positive to negative mentions). Social Mention is a good place to start, but it has its limits. Don't take its measurements as gospel. Use your own judgment. Examine its findings manually to screen out your company's own videos and blog posts, as well as any autoblogs that might be scraping content from your website.

Klout (klout.com)

This tool measures your overall online influence on Twitter. It uses twenty-five variables to determine this score and breaks the number down into three categories: True Reach, Amplification Probability, and Network Influence. Klout screens out spam and inactive accounts.

Radian6 (radian6.com)

Radian6 is a comprehensive social tech tracking and measurement software program. For a fee, it crawls over one hundred million social technology sites, including blogs, blog comments, microblogs, video- and photo-sharing sites, forums and discussion boards, and all other major social tech sites searching for mentions of your organization. It delivers results in real time.

Alterian SM2 (socialmedia.alterian.com)

This is another fee-based tool for monitoring your brand in the social technology sphere. Alterian also has other tools in addition to SM2, such as a content manager, that can help you become a valued member of online communities through social engagement.

Google Alerts (google.com/alerts)

Provide Google keywords related to you or your business, and this tool will send you e-mails every time it finds those keywords used on another site. Keep them specific or you'll have to screen out a lot of junk. This is an extremely useful tool, and it's free.

Better Google Analytics (vkistudios.com/tools/firefox/betterga/index.cfm)

This Firefox extension adds social technology–related data to your Google Analytics dashboard.

Viralheat (viralheat.com)

Viralheat is a fee-based but affordable social technology monitoring service that includes a sentiment ratio for Twitter mentions.

TweetFeel (tweetfeel.com)

TweetFeel is a real-time Twitter sentiments search engine.

Crimson Hexagon (crimsonhexagon.com)

This opinion analysis platform is an enterprise-level social technology tracking tool. Crimson Hexagon's VoxTrot Opinion Monitor uses a sophisticated algorithm to evaluate consumer sentiment toward your brand, based on social technology mentions. It does a lot more than merely count keywords as some other of these other tools do. Its value to your organization will depend a lot on your size. If you're not mentioned often, you can stick with manual sentiment monitoring, but if you're already being mentioned online twenty thousand times a month, this tool will be useful.

Sentiment Metrics (sentimentmetrics.com)

Sentiment Metrics is another sentiment-measuring tool for larger businesses.

Xinu Returns (xinureturns.com)

This tool allows you to enter a URL and receive data on its Google page rank, Alexa ranking backlinks, social bookmarking mentions, and much more (see more about this in chapter 10).

YouTube Insight

Log in to your YouTube account and click on the "Insight" button to locate this dashboard that comes with every YouTube account. Once you have enough volume, YouTube Insight provides demographic data on the people who've viewed your videos.

Tubemogul (tubemogul.com)

This video syndication platform allows you to upload videos to many video-sharing sites at once. It comes with an analytics panel for following views and comments on all your video campaigns.

LookingGlass (advertising.microsoft.com/LookingGlass]

This social technology dashboard program developed by Microsoft is still in beta testing, but it will no doubt be worth checking out. It is being advertised as a platform that can integrate various data sources to allow you to listen, engage, and measure social mentions all from one place.

Of course, no organization can or should attempt to use all these measurement tools. Some are more suitable for larger organizations than others. You must look over the entire range of features, capabilities, and prices to determine which are most suitable for you.

5. Measure Results, Compare to Objectives, and Adapt Continuously

It may be difficult to get any type of meaningful measurement in the early days of a pilot project; however, after the initial three-to-six-month period, you should start to see some results. This is the time to revisit all the financial metrics (such as net profit, sales volume, and rate of sales growth) and compare them to your initial benchmark figures. Hopefully, you will see positive growth.

Remember that your organization must evaluate those figures in light of other factors as well. You can't assume that all growth came from your social tech activities. You also can't assume that a lack of growth indicates that your social tech activities have failed. If sales remained steady but the economy went through a recession, it may indicate social technology success. Perhaps your market share has increased because your competition's sales have fallen—just as your sales would have fallen had you not adopted social technology.

Once you've determined that your social technology activities are bringing you a positive return, you'll want to analyze them in greater detail. Use your Web analytics to learn where most of your traffic is coming from and how well it converts. Perhaps you need separate landing pages on your site for Facebook fans, Twitter followers, and visitors from other sites. This approach can be especially helpful if you're running separate campaigns.

It's important to never stop testing. You should always test common marketing elements such as the headlines, offers, copy, and graphics you use online. You should also test your broader message with real prospects, not a focus group; perhaps your market would react more positively to a different wording of your organization's mission. Use social tech to test customer service results, too: would unhappy customers rather have a refund now or a free item with their next order?

Keep in mind that as much as we love to preach about measurements, some social technology strategies are invaluable even though they are unquantifiable. For example, what is the value of using social technology to prevent bad publicity? In 2009 Sears Hometown Stores responded quickly to a public relations crisis: One of its drivers had run over a family's dog. When the local store manager blamed the family for failing to tie up its dog, the owners put up the site SearsKilledMyDog.com. It soon attracted a lot of attention. A Sears social media monitor alerted the company to the website, and Sears quickly contacted the owners, sincerely apologized for the loss of their pet, and generally attempted to make it up to them, offering to reimburse the cost of their dog and to refund the price of the freezer they had purchased. The customers graciously accepted the offers and took down the site.

Although most cases aren't so dramatic, modern companies understand the necessity of satisfying angry shoppers. In the past, companies knew that unhappy shoppers often told ten to twenty friends and family members of their grievance. But online, their unhappiness can be seen by hundreds, thousands, or even millions of people, and the record of the complaint will remain for many years to come. Aside from the obvious importance of avoiding these situations in the first place, the value of preventing them from becoming disastrous through effective use of social technology can never be accurately measured.

What If the ROI Is Negative?

If after six months you can find no evidence that using social technologies has positively affected your organization's bottom line, you must seriously evaluate why this is the case. Perhaps you are spending too much time and effort on social technology; if you're a three-person company, you can't afford to have two people devoted solely to Twitter.

Or maybe you're not doing enough. Writing a few blog posts a week isn't going to have much impact. Maybe you're using social technology to interrupt people's lives rather than bring them value. People resent this, especially in the online areas they consider personal—which includes most of their social tech sphere. Although consumers are used to conventional marketing in many media, they are increasingly desirous of escaping it by using tools like Tivo or purchasing services like satellite radio. Avoid bombarding them with unwanted messages in precisely the spot—their personal Twitter feed or Facebook account—where they expect to be left in peace.

Are you truly listening to your prospects and the conversations they're having about the problems your organization addresses? Your social tech activity must be integrated with your website analytics, so visitors from social technology properties are tracked and measured. This must include the sales conversion ratio and other relevant metrics (such as size of purchase and, over time, their reorder rate).

If your ROI is negative, you may also need to consider positive aspects that are hard to quantify. For example, say your social technology team discovers a blog post written by a happy customer. They alert the sales force to this, and salespeople in turn leverage this blog post during discussions with prospects. Unsolicited blog posts such as these are more valuable than a company-quoted testimonial, since prospects are likely to give the unsolicited feedback more weight. Yet it may be difficult to gauge the extent to which the post directly increases sales.

To achieve positive ROI, there must be a well-thought-out plan to make sure information flows from the people performing the social technology activities to other parts of your organization—and then back to the social tech people. The social tech team must understand what the marketing department needs, and it must know the company's policy on handling customer complaints. The team should also be on the lookout for new situations and topics of conversation. Prospects may be talking about something that your company needs to know but doesn't yet have a clue about.

Extending ROI: Going the Extra Mile to Get Measurable Results

Once you are achieving a clear ROI from a social tech project, take what you have learned and push even harder with social tech tools— whether that means daily blog posts, regular tweets, crowdsourcing, or the production and uploading of humorous or compelling videos. Take the knowledge you've gathered from your analysis and apply it to the areas that are a success. For example, if you have mastered how to use an online reputation plan to find and engage customers who comment on your products, apply that knowledge in new and creative ways.

Have the customer service department become socially proactive—seeking out complaints and questions other than those that came in on the 1-800 number. That means fixing problems and complaints in real time if possible and keeping the community informed of what you're doing to improve service. People notice when you react to legitimate concerns.

A reporter for the *Boston Globe* wrote an article praising Kodak's Zi8 pocket video camera but complaining about its meaningless name. When Kodak brought out a new model, they held an online contest to name it and received thousands of entries. Two winning customers got a paid trip to Las Vegas, and the reporter was blown away that somebody in corporate America had actually paid attention to what he wrote.

In fact, Kodak is a good example of a company using social technology to shape the world's perception of its brand. Not too long ago, Kodak was considered nearly extinct. Everyone associated its brand name with film and so assumed that digital photography would kill it. Kodak, however, knew it had invented the digital camera back in 1976. The company decided to use blogs, Twitter, Facebook, and YouTube to get its story out. Its proprietary blog, called A Thousand Words (1000Words.Kodak.com), helps dramatize the appeal and potential of digital photography and video using Kodak cameras.

Your organization must give social technology experiments time to gather momentum, at least three to six months. Too many organizations start sending out tweets and promoting their Facebook page, only to give up when they don't see immediate results. Remember, you're strengthening customer relations, often one customer at a time. This process takes time and has a way of teaching you lessons as you go along, so you can constantly improve.

If you use Twitter or other sites to push out the same old "interruption advertising" messages, it will backfire on you. You must build trust. You can't expect people in one day or one week to go immediately from seeing you as just one more uncaring, faceless company to regarding you as a trusted friend who helps them solve problems. If you give up too early, you damage your credibility and show prospects that you had not really become customer-centered—you were just jumping on the latest fad.

As time goes by, and as your social technology team gains experience, their benchmarks for online interaction should be increased so that they are engaging with as many people as possible. Too many businesspeople still see social technology as just another one-way channel they can use to cram their marketing messages down the throats of unwilling consumers. They fail to see the value of a bidirectional conversation that incorporates as many people as possible. To them, social technology is just a new electronic billboard.

These businesspeople must come to understand that using social technology is actually a two-way street. Before it can expect the consumer to change and buy more products, the company may have to adapt to the consumer and his or her needs and desires. Social technology tools come with responsibility; your organization must act on behalf of its customers and prospects. It takes willingness and ability on the part of your organization to put itself into the shoes of those who belong to your market and figure out what types of content will meaningfully engage them.

Measurements and analytics are the key to rapidly getting a profitable social strategy in place. The process is really pretty simple: You must set clear goals, learn how to use the new tools and concepts, find specific areas in which to pilot your ideas, and then build a measurement system that will show you where you can reap value and where you need to back off. Once you achieve positive results and prove the value of social tech to your organization's bottom line, you must then make these pilot projects full-fledged pieces of your overall strategy. If you skip the step of moving your social tech efforts to scientifically handled pilot projects, your strategy will remain vague and amorphous and may take years to show results. But by working hard to measure results and understand analytics, you will beat your competition to the improvements that will make a powerful difference in your future!

KEY POINTS

- As the saying goes, what gets measured gets done, so the discipline of putting analytics in place not only gives you a view into performance, it also drives that performance.

- Assign one person to be responsible for generating and communicating measurements and analytics for anything having to do with social tech in your company.

- Create a dashboard of social program results, and publish it to a wide audience consistently. This will create buy-in for what you are doing and will generate interest in the use of these new tools.

- Investigate tools that can help you provide the foundational measurements you will need to analyze your future progress. Choose a handful of the most constructive ones that you will use regularly.

- Do not outsource the measurement or analysis of your social strategy until you know for sure that someone in-house has a deep understanding of the measurements that will be taken by the third party. It is preferable to keep this analysis internal, in fact, since you are in the best position to compare and integrate internal metrics. Only outsource as a last resort.

- Once you see a positive pattern in the use of a new social tech tool, push hard to fully integrate it into your normal process and leverage it as much as you can. You are in a race with your competitors, and when you find you can use a new tool successfully, take advantage of it before others in your market do.

For more resources addressing measurements and analytics, see the presentations and infographics at our Flickr (www.flickr. com/photos/enterprise-social-technology/) and Slideshare (www.slideshare.net/socialtech) sites.

CHAPTER 10

Assembling the Organization's Social Technology Tools

In this chapter, we'll take a look at how several categories of social technology tools can be put to work for your organization. Since different teams are in various stages of adopting social tech tools, we will start with the basics and then expand. There are still operations that don't have any such tools in place at all! One reasonable excuse for having done nothing yet is that the volume of tools and options available can be pretty overwhelming; it takes time to sort through the large number of options available to find the right ones that will provide a benefit to your organization. There are just too many social technology tools to count, and brand-new ones become available every day; some people are simply flummoxed as to where to start.

Don't be overwhelmed. Stay focused on your goals while keeping updated on the social technologies that might improve your business. These tools can be put into several groups, which we will explore a little later.

But first let's talk about costs. It's quite possible to assemble a package of tools that will bring you success yet cost very little to acquire and use. Free social tech tools are everywhere you look. To many people, "free" may imply that there's a catch somewhere, and businesses don't like that. But most of these tools and sites *are* indeed completely complimentary to users—they thrive on advertising. The more people that use the site or platform, the more money it earns in ad revenue. This model is nothing new, yet many tend to forget it.

In some cases, however, these free tools will collect demographic information about their users, so check the terms and privacy policy of any tools you may want to integrate into your social program. Many of the free tools also come in fee-based versions that give you access to even more robust features and functionality not available in the free or "lite" versions. You can also take advantage of tools that offer free trial periods, which usually last thirty days and allow unrestricted use of the service, giving you ample time to determine whether a particular tool fits your needs.

As you may recall from this book's introduction, the three categories of social technology are social media, social networking, and social relevance. The tools covered in the current chapter will help your organization develop in all three areas as you use them to network, distribute information, and gauge reaction to your company, its products, and its message. Don't make the common mistake of focusing too heavily on social networking as a sales enhancer; there is huge value to be gained from the other two areas as well. Too many companies focus solely on Facebook, Twitter, and blogs while overlooking many social media and social relevance tools.

Before considering which tools are best for your business, you have to gauge the overall potential of using social tech to market your products or services. What value does word of mouth have in your industry? Are people talking about your products or services? What sparks conversation about the type of product or service you sell?

The days of propagating annoying and obtrusive banner ads and spam messages are nearing their end. Today, in the social age, businesses are expected to actively engage their customer base. By doing things like taking part in online conversations and presenting educational videos to online groups, your organization brings value to the community. That community, in turn, will become very valuable to your business.

Being Social, Made Easy

Being social is what it's all about. Providing information. Announcing news. Showing off something new. We use social technology tools every day of our lives to share all sorts of information with friends and family. We announce births, engagements, and even deaths in the family. We post photos of our new car or the family pet. When we do this, it strikes others' interest because they know us. They trust us. They want to hear what we have to say, so they click the photo or status message and dig deeper. As a business, if you were to post a photo of your new product, complete with an enticing headline, it wouldn't quite have the same effect. Something is missing. It lacks personality. To most of us, it's just another unattractive banner ad.

To be successful in the social realm, a business must engage others. Social communities won't stand for spam or blatant advertising—that's not why people are there. People use social sites to explore their own personal world, not your company's latest product line. You want to become a *part of the user's world;* it's pointless to try to bring people into yours. Engage in conversation. Engage in relationships. Engage in sharing. This type of approach builds confidence in you and your business, and that leads to sales!

Starting discussions is the easiest step you can take to engage your audience. Make it a topic that's not directly related to your business, but be sure you have plenty to say and offer on the subject—the better the discussion, the longer it will go on, and longer conversations are better for business. Posting discussion-starters on several social sites is a great way to begin. Try these popular ones, if you haven't already.

Social Sites Designed for Connecting with People

One of the most common classes of sites is the type that connects people through an e-community format or through networking or communication channels. The goal is to facilitate either faster, better, or more robust forms of communicating, and/or an ability to self-select into a group of shared interests. Some of these sites are designed to target specific demographics or to lean more or less toward a user's business or personal life.

Twitter (twitter.com)

One of the most popular and fastest-growing social applications, Twitter lets you follow friends, celebrities, or anyone you may find interesting, receiving their "tweets"—140-character messages—in real time via the home page, e-mail, or text message. You can, of course, send out your own tweets and start building a following of your own. Create a Twitter account for your company, and post daily on topics related to your product or service. To interest and capture an audience, be sure to not limit your tweets to pitches for your products; sharing interesting and valuable content is mandatory for engaging the community.

Facebook (facebook.com)

Facebook has become a household name, and is the largest social networking site in the world. It can often become a part of your company's social tech program if you have a need to create a community location. Have each of your team members create a user account and start engaging with your constituents. It's also a good idea to create Facebook fan pages for your company, brand, or products. This gives your customers the chance to start conversations with you and comment on content you share.

Google Buzz (google.com/buzz)

Google has a tool for everything, so it's no surprise that Google Buzz is a very well-designed social application. Like Facebook, it's based on the idea of sharing: conversation, photos, videos, and websites. Consider what your company has to share, and start buzzing!

Ning (ning.com)

Ning takes the concept of social networking full throttle and allows you to create your own custom online community. Its platform is great for serious buzz generators and is super-easy to use. Having a Ning network is a great supplement to your company's social program, giving it a self-controlled community of its own.

Social Sites Designed for Business Professionals

As this new world of social tools has begun to mature, application builders are more consciously targeting either the personal or the business user. This trend is likely to continue as software companies look to stake out their territory with specific audiences that can bring them fast uptake and a profitable constituency as a target for their marketing efforts. The following sites are becoming associated more with the enterprise world than the personal.

LinkedIn (linkedin.com)

The value of social networking takes center stage with LinkedIn, which is all about building professional and business relationships. Each member of your organization should create a LinkedIn account. On this site, it's not considered shameless self-promotion to discuss and market your business, though you should still be very cautious of how much you talk about your products and services. LinkedIn is also a great place to post job openings and vet prospective employees.

Plaxo (plaxo.com)

This social networking platform touts itself as a "smart, socially connected address book"—and that's the truth. Many social networking sites will import contacts from your various e-mail and website accounts; Plaxo does this in its own Web application, bringing all your contacts and connections together into one universal, online address book.

Blogging and Expertise-Sharing Sites

Blogger (blogger.com)

Blogs are basically online diaries presented as websites in an organized fashion, with navigation, multimedia, and interactivity built in. Your company should have its own blog, and Blogger.com is a great place to start. Consider assigning a blog to each team leader who can offer his or her expertise in a given subject related to your business. If the blog content is updated regularly and offers some value or interest to the visitor, it can create a strong following.

Google Knol (google.com/knoll)

The definition of a *knol,* according to Google, is "a unit of knowledge." Google Knol is like a blog site, but with very specific and thorough topic pages. And so, as with a blog site, several team leaders should be elected to create and maintain a knol on a subject about which they possess a wealth of knowledge that can be shared.

Wordpress (wordpress.com)

Wordpress, the most popular blogging platform, has now extended into providing a full content management system that is open sourced. This means there are thousands of templates and add-in applications that can be downloaded for free or purchased. If you are looking to make a serious run at building a blog that will be a critical piece of your customer/client communications going forward, this is a great place to start.

TypePad (typepad.com)

This well-known blogging platform makes it easy for you to choose a look and feel for your blog, produce the blog, and then maximize the SEO benefits so you can be found by the search engines. If you are looking for a simple way to get started blogging, TypePad makes it easy.

Squidoo (squidoo.com)

This popular publishing platform and community makes it easy for you to create "lenses" online. A lens is a page, kind of like a flyer or an overview article, that collects all sorts of information about your topic of interest and archives these thoughts into a format that is searchable and shareable. This is a great tool for thought leaders to document random concepts in one place for others to find.

* * *

Don't let the word *social* cause you to think of these tools as being more for personal use than for business. Each is focused on connecting people, and that is just as important in the enterprise space as it is in our personal lives. We might have been better off leaving in place the umbrella term *Web 2.0,* so the perceived meaning of *social* would not be mistaken as something that organizations should fear and control instead of embrace and leverage.

Don't Aggravate—Aggregate

Developing relationships and keeping them fresh and exciting can be a daunting task, to say the least. Wouldn't it be nice to have a tool that would make managing online relationships easier and less time-consuming? After all, how many conversations can one person have in a day and still be productive? There are many tools that aggregate social networking sites into one platform in an attempt to streamline the process of tending to each one. We described earlier how aggregation tools could be used to streamline a river of information. At the same time, they can be used to centralize postings so you only have to enter new content or comments one time, and distribute across multiple platforms.

Aggregators save lots of time, but they have one drawback: Posting the same exact message to fifty different social networks all at the same time is considered by some to be close to spamming, so don't let the aggregators do all the work for you. Use automated submission features like this conservatively, and their benefits will be much greater.

Here are some aggregators, software programs, and business tools to help you save time and stay organized.

Ping.fm

Using this aggregator is as easy as it gets. Ping.fm lets you simultaneously post an update to many major social networking sites. It also offers the ability to send your updates via text message, e-mail, instant message, and the website itself.

OnlyWire (onlywire.com)

Similar to Ping.fm, OnlyWire can post your updates, articles, links, and more to nearly forty social networking sites with one click. OnlyWire's setup is very intuitive, and it works from within your browser, blog, or website.

Profilactic (profilactic.com)

The main function of Profilactic is to bring social networks, content, and relationships together in one place. It supports more than 190 sites, essentially providing users with a quick overview of their entire social program.

TweetDeck (tweetdeck.com)

Originally designed as a platform for Twitter only, this application is now a great all-around aggregator that allows you to post updates to multiple sites. It also provides a great overview of the major social networks of your choosing.

Radian6's Engagement Console (radian6.com/products/engagement/)

Engagement Console is an application that takes aggregation and site reporting to a new level. It locates conversations and comments about your company in near real time, bringing it all together in one place for easy overview.

Listen Quietly

Using social tech tools to find online discussions about certain products or services is becoming increasingly useful to businesses. Because people are most honest in a casual atmosphere, they tend to be more open in these social, nonbusiness settings. The most valuable feedback doesn't always come from asking a client or customer for a testimonial. And as you listen to online conversations, be prepared to hear negative things as well; you'll probably find that there is a lot more to be learned from negative feedback than from positive feedback. Mining this information from social networking sites and blogs is a relatively simple process if you have the right tools. Not only can you find, follow, and participate in conversations about your own products or services, but you can also listen to online talk about your whole industry or even a specific competitor. This is an effective way to look at what your competition is doing—and then do it better!

The information available on social networks is quickly becoming integrated into other parts of the Web and therefore should be viewed as very important to your business; you never know where it may show up. There are specific search engines that dig into social sites, and even mainstream engines like Google and Yahoo! are integrating social data into their search results.

Using the right tools to research, listen to, and observe all those conversations and comments is paramount to success. Here are a few tools to get you started.

Google Alerts (google.com/alerts)

As discussed in chapter 9, simply enter specific keywords and search criteria (such as your name or the name of your top-selling product), and set how many results the search should send you and how often. Google Alerts can save you a lot of time and keep you on top of the latest conversations, news, and comments related to your defined search.

Technorati (technorati.com)

This great research tool digs deep into the social world. It pulls relevant news stories and articles, but that's just the beginning. Technorati's best feature is its social search engine, which allows you to conduct searches of blogs, social networks, and news feeds.

ReputationDefender (reputationdefender.com)

This tool does just what its name implies. Like similar sites and services, ReputationDefender monitors discussions, comments, blogs, and more for defined topics and keywords, but it also lets you interact with these findings in ways that other services don't. Your online reputation is extremely important, and this software could be your best way to keep it tarnish-free!

Pipes (pipes.yahoo.com)

This tool from Yahoo! takes a slightly different approach to social tech monitoring than search-based tools do. Yahoo! Search isn't a search engine but rather a catalog site, and Pipes defines itself with a similar distinction: Rather than presenting you with an ordered and sorted list of ranked results, Pipes presents the content in the manner of a catalog or newspaper, using what it calls "a powerful composition tool to aggregate, manipulate, and mash up content from around the Web."

* * *

We have now passed into a time where neither you nor your organization can afford to allow your name to be mentioned online without your knowledge. A listening program is not a luxury; it is a mandatory process that will protect you from nasty surprises and will give you a heads-up when people say pleasant or unpleasant things about you.

Measuring Your Success

As discussed in the last chapter, measuring the success of your social tech efforts is a vital aspect of your company's social tech program. As you compare your most recent results with those of prior periods, you will see patterns emerge. Set up reports to run at weekly or monthly intervals, and analyze the results in detail. Some measurement tools do not store and analyze these reports, so prepare a spreadsheet or database in which to save each period's measurements for comparison and trend-spotting. Some measurement tools have features that set them apart from their competitors, giving you particularly useful statistics such as average time between mentions and number of unique Internet users who mention you. Other tools help you manage the process of engaging with users who mention you.

We have addressed the importance of social tech measurements in at least three of the previous chapters. The following measurement tools are some of the ones you should consider incorporating into your strategy.

Viralheat (viralheat.com)

Get valuable guidance and insight into your social program's success rate by using Viralheat. This tool's charts and graphs provide the analytics and resources needed to identify the next steps your company should take in its social tech strategy.

Social Mention (socialmention.com)

This site combines some popular features of other social tech tools, providing the user with a social search engine, a media alert service, and social analytic tools all in one.

Webtrends Social Measurement (webtrends.com/Products/SocialMeasurement)

Webtrends, one of the oldest Web analytics companies, is now helping you optimize your social technology presence. Its Social Measurement tool provides highly detailed reports and graphs depicting when and where conversations relevant to your brand are taking place.

Social SEO

All the conversations about your brand that are floating around on the Web will eventually be indexed by the major search engines. This is good news because the more people that talk about you and then refer to you in a link, the more your search engine listings, page ranks, and general online discoverability will improve. The reason: Such mentions often include inbound links that will be measured by the search engines. For this reason it is important to use tools that will help you monitor and create as many links for social conversations to your Web properties as possible. Keep this in mind when creating new content to broadcast to the social networks.

SWIX (www.swixhq.com)

SWIX identifies itself as a "social web index." It has numerous widgets that you can build and connect to the various social tech sites you would like to monitor. Each time you log in, not only will you see the usual analytics on your social tech presence—number of friends, number of posts, and so on—but SWIX utilizes an archive of your statistics to highlight changes and trends in these metrics, giving you an excellent indication of the effectiveness of your SEO and social campaigns.

Raven Tools (raventools.com)

Packaged as a suite of SEO and social media tools, Raven offers a set of powerful services that are a great addition to a corporate social tech strategy. Raven Tools includes modules for SEO analytics, custom reporting, link building, keyword research, competitor tracking, and social media management.

* * *

As elsewhere in this book, we are just scratching the surface of what is available, providing sample sites that might help you get started. It is always a good idea to run a search on the description of the tools you are looking to work with. In addition, new tools are released constantly, so in just the time between when we wrote this book, and when you might read it, a host of new options will appear.

The Social Media Channels

Social tech is not exclusively about social networking. Social media platforms provide users with content-sharing tools that many people already use in their daily lives as they keep up with news and entertain themselves. Social media sites allow us to effortlessly put photos, video, and audio in front of our users. Creating and distributing instructional videos, entertaining low-budget commercials, or informative slideshows are all great ways of engaging your customers.

Here are some of the best tools for sharing media.

Flickr (flickr.com)

Photo sharing can be a powerful tool for your business. Realtors and travel agencies, for example, often make great use of digital photos. Creating a Flickr account rather than sending images through e-mail is the best way to share photos: Search engines index Flickr images that are set as accessible to the public (and you avoid sending large files to someone's in-box). With your photos tagged and publicly accessible on Flickr, a user's search for, say, "Miami vacation homes" could bring up the image you just posted of a client's property for sale.

SlideShare (slideshare.net)

SlideShare has created a presentation-sharing site where users can post PowerPoint and Keynote presentations, Word and PDF documents, and audio and video clips. It provides tools that let users tie all these media together into an online webinar and share their creations with the social world.

YouTube (youtube.com)

Video is very entertaining, and it can also be educational and informative. Use YouTube to create product demonstrations, service or maintenance instructional videos, or an enticing video tour of your company's offices. It's like having a company television channel—for free.

Scribd (scribd.com)

This site is often described as YouTube for documents. You can upload any type of document and index so it can be found easily. Examples include a white paper, a case study, or instructions for operating a product. You can build custom channels much as you can on other social media sites.

Vimeo and Other Video-Sharing Sites (vimeo.com)

Vimeo is one of dozens of YouTube imitators. Consider checking this site and others to see whether they have special features that interest you or an interface and appearance that you find appealing.

* * *

As mentioned at the beginning of the book, social media channels use a form of media—video, presentations, pictures, graphics, documents—to communicate a message. We have listed only a few of the general social media sites. There are many more that we have not mentioned, and depending on your market, you might find there are verticalized sites that target your specific audience.

Pass It On!

"Link sharing" used to mean that if you owned a website, and so did I, we could exchange links—I'd put a link to your site on my Links page, and you would do the same for me. Search engines (and site visitors, for that matter) don't pay much attention to these types of link exchanges these days. Now, social bookmarking is the dominant form of sharing links. In fact, the majority of sites and tools that fall into the social technology category involve some form of social bookmarking. Adding a link to an interesting site or a YouTube video on Facebook—or clicking a "like" button—is essentially social bookmarking.

Social bookmarking has become increasingly important in search engine rankings. The idea is that the more people who bookmark your site, the more relevant and important it must be, so it gets a better ranking. Add a handful of social bookmarking sites to your social tech program to get your company's most interesting and relevant pages out there. Here are a few to get you started.

Delicious (delicious.com)

This social bookmarking service lets you set up an account and start bookmarking sites that are relevant to or affiliated with your company's products or services. Delicious is one of the original social bookmarking sites, and should definitely be a part of your social program.

Digg (digg.com)

This content bookmarking system is also one of the originals and today still creates a whole new way to view news. It allows the crowd to "digg" news articles, so readers can see what seems to be relevant to the crowd. In some ways this eliminates our need to scan headlines, looking for something that might seem important. You can simply go to the Digg site and read the top-rated stories as chosen by the crowd.

StumbleUpon (stumbleupon.com)

StumbleUpon adds a button to your browser, making building your social bookmarks intuitive and fast. StumbleUpon is quickly becoming one of the more popular social tech tools, with more than ten million members currently sharing links.

Reddit (reddit.com)

Bookmarks are handy for quickly finding new, interesting content online, but how do you know just how good the content is? Reddit goes a step further than plain old social bookmarking; it allows members to cast votes on other people's bookmarks and then ranks them accordingly. Create a high-quality blog article related to your business and bookmark it; if people like it, they'll vote on it!

* * *

We have learned that one of the really valuable aspects of the Internet is the ability to share, whether it's an opinion, a file, or a simple document. Sharing is a type of voting, in that the crowd vets good content by sharing it with others. The more content is shared, the more we can assume it has value. For this reason, we can assume that as time goes on, we will find more sophisticated ways to share and digest content we find valuable.

Search and Research

In addition to building prospects and customer relationships, social networks can also provide your business with the means to research new employees, secure new vendors or suppliers, and develop new partnerships and affiliations. Here are a few of these research tools.

Jigsaw (jigsaw.com)

As part of the SalesForce.com arsenal, Jigsaw gives you access to an immense database of corporate information and contacts. One of the great services that Jigsaw offers is called Data Fusion, which provides tools to integrate Jigsaw's database of more than twenty million contacts into your CRM system, helping you clean your existing contact information and populate your system with new data.

Spokeo (spokeo.com)

Finding anyone's contact information is quick and easy with Spokeo. Just enter the person's name, and Spokeo will return a list of all the matches it finds, aggregating all the information available about that person from social networking sites and the Web in general.

BackType (backtype.com)

This service takes the concept of research a step further by integrating social tech listening. Enter any URL, and BackType will return a graph showing how people are engaging with the site, what conversations are taking place, who is in the audience, and what social tech platform these users originate from. This is a great tool for monitoring your competition!

Addict-o-matic (addictomatic.com)

Enter a keyword or keywords into Addict-o-matic, and within seconds it returns a custom portal page full of news and information on that topic from nearly thirty top social-tech sites and tools. You can't save these pages, but you can bookmark them or share them on other social sites, which gives you quick access to this data at any time.

* * *

One of the amazing but often overlooked aspects of the Internet is the fact that we can run a search of billions of pages of information from anywhere on Earth in one second or less. This instant access to information has continued to improve as social tools have integrated conversations and opinions into the search results. So not only do we gain product and feature information on a specific camera when we perform a search for that model, but we will also get many opinions straight from the users who have purchased it. This is having a dramatic impact on the online reputations of many products, services, people, and organizations.

At the same time, the integration of social connections with static websites is allowing salespeople to learn about specific people within a large organization, in ways that were impossible in the past.

Building Your Own Tools

Many social technology tools and sites offer an API (application programming interface) or other toolkit that allows software developers to write applications that directly integrate or interface with the main service. Some allow tight integration with the parent site or service; others give third-party access, allowing for the creation of stand-alone software applications and websites. This is how many social tech applications get their power—by connecting to larger services and sometimes directly interfacing with the data.

If you decide to create a custom application, remember that it doesn't have to be Web-based. Between the two biggest mobile-device operating systems, Apple and Android, there are hundreds of new mobile apps created every day. At the time of this writing, Apple has approximately 225,000 apps available on its iPhone and another 23,000 for the iPad. And AndroLib.com reports more than 100,000 apps available for Google Android phones.[54] Just as Web-based tools can be custom-built to support and grow your online social program, you could also have a mobile application developed for your company.

Social communities, too, make extensive use of custom applications. On Facebook, for example, more than 70 percent of users

---

54 "Crossing the 100,000 Application Mark," *AndroLibBlog*, July 30, 2010, http://blog. androlib.com/2010/07/30/CrossingThe100000ApplicationsMark.aspx.

engage with applications, and there are currently 550,000 active applications.[55] More than one hundred thousand applications and websites use Twitter's API.[56] Tens of thousands of other websites directly integrate, feed, or receive social data from Facebook and Twitter.

Here are two ways to create custom applications that interact with two of the most prominent social networks.

SocialGO (socialgo.com)

Running your own social network can bring more finite control over your company's social program and can help promote and generate your social circles. SocialGO gives you the tools to build and maintain a social network website that you can call your own. Offering all the standard features and tools of the popular social sites, you can build a cool networking site and be online right away.

Facebook Developer Network (developers.facebook.com)

Facebook offers one of the most robust application-development interfaces available from a social networking site. Using the tools and services provided by the Facebook Developer Network, you can build applications within Facebook itself or integrate the social technologies of Facebook into your own website—with simple share buttons or full integration with Facebook Connect.

Twitter API (dev.twitter.com/)

Creating applications that run on the desktop, a website, or mobile devices are all possible with Twitter's application interface. Twitter is all about communication and building relationships. Using its API, you can create your own tools to support your social program with seamless integration of other social technology tools.

---

55 "Press Room: Statistics," Facebook.com, accessed September 14, 2009, http://www.facebook.com/press/info.php?statistics.

56 "Enduring Value," Twitter blog, May 24, 2010, http://blog.twitter.com/2010/05/twitter-platform.html.

* * *

Building your own application may sound daunting if you are a small organization without an IT staff. If this is the case, take heart: There is a growing pool of developers and contract firms that are pumping out custom applications for a reasonable fee. It may be worth your while to get a few quotes for that custom application you've been thinking about.

Picking Social Tech Tools Is a Team Sport

As discussed thoroughly in chapter 2, the team approach to implementing social tech tools is very important. Picking what social tech tools will be used and how they will be selected is just another example of how involving multiple people can really improve the inventory of capabilities at your disposal. Having a team of at least three people assures that you will have multiple perspectives on what's available. In the situations where you really can dedicate only a single person to doing the research into new tools, please be aware that this person will make decisions based on his or her personal biases—and that is sometimes a real problem. A perfect example of this: Have a programmer in the IT department pick your social tech tools, and you will most likely end up with a collection of applications that many regular civilians will never figure out.

One of the people on this selection team should lead the effort to discover and evaluate new tools and services as they become available. There are many sites dedicated to listing the latest tools and trends, and they can help the team sort through some of the clutter and bring the more popular and useful tools to the forefront. These sites can be immense time-savers by providing recommendations and reviews of social tech tools that have been put through rigorous tests.

You will still want to conduct your own research and testing with any tool that seems interesting and useful to you, but the following sites can be a great starting point.

Social Web Tools (socialwebtools.info)

Updated almost every day, the Social Web Tools blog is a great resource for reviews and articles on the latest and greatest social technologies available. Here you'll find lots of information that will help you decide which tools are best for your company's social tech program.

Socialbrite (socialbrite.org)

This is another wonderfully useful site that aggregates the latest news on social technologies and posts original articles and reviews by industry experts. Socialbrite's mission statement says, "We're here to share insights about the tools and best practices that advance the social good."

Alexa (alexa.com)

To check on how popular a tool or website is, a team member should view its ranking at Alexa.com. The Alexa ranking more or less tells you how important a site is on the Internet as a whole. The ranking is calculated based largely on the number of other sites that link back to it, which usually demonstrates the overall level of interest in a site. If a tool or website has a ranking below 250,000, it's probably best to scratch it off the list. Sites ranking between 1 and 10,000 are the cream of the crop. Take a wild guess as to what the number one Alexa-ranked site is; that's right, Google.com. And Facebook.com is number two—a strong indication that social networks are consuming the Internet.

* * *

Every person on the team should share the responsibility of being actively social. This is the heart and soul of your business's social program. This is where your content and ideas get pushed out to your target social sites, sparking conversations and generating even more content within the social networks. This is how the word about your new product or service spreads. The more people are talking about you, the more successful your social program will be.

Start by selecting a reasonable number of target sites that pertain to your business, and have the team members create accounts at each of them. Depending on how many team members there are and how many social communities and blogs are on your list, it may be tempting to divide up the list evenly among the members and have each person check out one-third of the options—avoid this approach! Making connections within a social site is what will get momentum going for your business and will show the people testing the sites how others can interact within them. With multiple people seeding your organization's social circle, you are at least one step forward on the track to fast growth if you choose later to fully utilize the new tool.

When it comes to choosing listening tools, have a team member or two assigned to the responsibilities outlined in chapter 7 regarding online reputation. A heavy influencer of your ability to do CRM well will be the tools you choose to discover the mentions you are looking for and to measure the sentiment ratio. The information these people collect will be critical to the success of every business from now on.

Have your listening team perform keyword searches using your social technology tools; this can reveal trends within topics related to your business. Using these trends and your key performance indicators, you can strengthen the weak areas of your social program and gain even higher levels of saturation within social networks. Assign specific team members to the task of resolving any weak areas found during these searches; put multiple members on the job in the weakest areas.

Be sure the team is employing more than one listening tool. Many listening tools let you set up an automated news feed based on a keyword or URL. These feeds are then delivered to you on a regular basis, alleviating the mundane task of revisiting a site over and over again. It's best to set up very specific terms and topics, however, or you may be flooded with more information than you want. When we use search engines like Google or Yahoo!, our search terms tend to be broad and consist of few words. With social searching, try the opposite: Begin by being very exact in your query, and then loosen it up as necessary to receive the right amount of manageable results.

When it comes to the listening process, it is important to have a team approach mixed with a solid process for picking the right tools to use. One without the other will lower your chances of success dramatically.

Miscellaneous Social Tech Tools

Now that you're familiar with the largest categories of social tech tools, here are a few miscellaneous sites and applications that can be extremely useful to a company's social technology efforts.

SocialOomph (socialoomph.com)

Automating mundane tasks is one of the things that technology does best. SocialOomph effectively took some of the mundane tasks of managing a social tech program and developed tools to schedule and automate them. A huge time-saver, SocialOomph can help you schedule tweets and Facebook status updates, send automatic direct messages to new Twitter followers, mute annoying or irrelevant Twitter users, and much more.

CNW's Social Media Release (smr.newswire.ca)

Putting a social tech spin on the traditional press release, the CNW Group offers what it calls a "Social Media Release," which gives your audience a place to get multimedia content related to the release and to engage in discussions about it.

WebEx (webex.com)

This tool provides an interactive solution for online presentations, whiteboard sessions, and sales meetings, using audio- and videoconferencing, instant messaging, real-time remote control of computer desktops, and more.

Trendrr (trendrr.com)

Trendrr aggregates data and statistics from more than fifty social networking platforms and presents a number of interesting graphs that show trends related to certain keywords. Its Scratch Pad feature can be used to compare multiple data inputs in one graph.

Namechk (namechk.com)

This site offers a great way to help an organization lock up its name or its product names as the username to be used across social sites. There is a large grid of social sites provided on its home page, and a place for you to enter any name you choose as a possible username. Namechk then shows you with a green or red color-coding system on which sites your chosen username is still available.

* * *

There are so many sites now doing very specific and helpful tasks that it is difficult to provide only a few samples. By allowing some flexibility in the number and expertise of the people you have out looking for social tools, and by creating a great river of information, you can make sure nothing new and useful slips through your net.

Getting Started!

By now, you can see that there are many different types of social tech tools and techniques you can use to create brand awareness, promote your organization's products or services, and communicate with your customers and prospects. In fact, we have not listed even 10 percent of the possible sites you could use, only the more popular ones.

When it comes time to assemble your organization's social tech tools, there are a few things that are really important to remember. Simply selecting a bunch of tools and posting content would not be effective enough to make this undertaking worth the time and effort. It cannot be stressed enough that choosing the right tool for the right job is very important. Set up a research and development process for maintaining your arsenal of social tech tools and tactics. Put together a financial budget and a timeline to support and reach your company's social tech goals. Create guidelines for employees to follow regarding the use of social technology tools and websites. And most important, gather the right people—those who are either technologically savvy, have personal experience using social networking sites and tools, or have thorough knowledge and a great understanding of your company's products or services. Personnel from marketing, IT, and sales—and especially executives—are prime candidates to participate in the company's social tech program.

With all that covered, and with your tools chosen and ready to go, it's time to start implementing pilot projects that will help you develop a disciplined approach to applying these tools and learning the best practices that will bring you outstanding results.

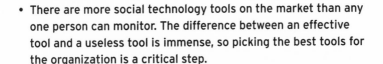 **KEY POINTS**

- There are more social technology tools on the market than any one person can monitor. The difference between an effective tool and a useless tool is immense, so picking the best tools for the organization is a critical step.

- Standardizing on a written set of tools helps employees support one another and lowers the support burden on IT staff. This written list should be provided to every existing team member and to any new people when they come on board.

- There are many free tools available, and using these tools as the standard choices is a seductive option. Depending on the size of the organization and the nature of the social application, however, it might be wise to use an enterprise-level tool, even if it requires a fee. For a few dollars a month, the difference in performance can be substantial.

- It is best to use a team approach to finding new options for social tech tools. This ensures that you will not miss an important announcement for a specific tool that you might find essential. Plus, there are too many new tools coming on the market for any one person to monitor and examine, much less put in practice. As we mentioned earlier, it might make sense to have one gatekeeper who makes the decision about what tools get standardized, but it takes a team to keep up with all the options.

- Once you've chosen your basic set of tools, provide sufficient training so that no one in the organization has to struggle to learn them on his or her own.

 To access a longer list of social tools that includes new additions since the writing of this book, go to EnterpriseSocialTechnology. com and click on the Resources section.

CHAPTER 11

Developing Pilot Projects

Many of you may have put off testing your social technology ideas until you could be more confident that they would work. And we're not talking about starting a blog or a Facebook fan page—those are the basics, and developing either of them generally isn't too intimidating a process. The projects you may have put off are sophisticated, socially facilitated sales programs, online reputation management programs, and crowdsourcing efforts. But the time has come to get started, to really use this new technology to grow your operation.

Developing your first pilot projects may be the most important step in your social tech strategy; it's where you refine your ideas, narrowing them down to a handful of specific efforts. The fastest way to test these ideas is to put together several initial projects, gather feedback, and see whether your assumptions are correct. With no formalized process for doing this, an organization will either learn best practices too late from its competitors or stumble forward in a chaotic manner that will slow it down significantly. Note the word *formalized*; as mentioned earlier, testing social concepts by throwing them against the wall and seeing what sticks could actually do you more harm than good. You must be scientific in your approach to testing concepts through pilot projects. An effort that involves anything less may end up being a big waste of resources.

All the social concepts we have discussed, with the addition of all the basics we skipped over, contain value you have yet to realize. The wealth of information, both implicit and explicit, that flows through these social channels is interesting to observe, but it remains unprofitable unless the masses of chatter can be directed to achieve one's own objectives—to test the feasibility of one's mission.

A well-thought-out program for the design, implementation, and analysis of new concepts and ideas will allow you to shape strategies in ways that maximize positive results and point the way to the achievement of long-term goals. In other words, it makes sense to have a process in place that will help you vet ideas and distinguish the good ones from the bad. And while learning these lessons, you must also be thinking about all the potential impacts a pilot project test might have on your organization. This requires a specific ability to understand the consequences of the test before you get the chance to reap them.

Consequential Thinking

Intelligent, ongoing management of pilot projects is a discipline that requires a specific mind-set called "consequential thinking." Consequential thinking describes the way military minds work. Every military decision can end up being a life-or-death one. Therefore, commanders study every possible path and try to determine where each one leads before they take any action. After World War II, the concept was adopted by many business leaders and innovators. They used this method to identify all possible risks of any proposed operation, especially risks that, while unseen at the onset of the project, could pop up after a project had begun.

A key element of consequential thinking is that every step of a project must be considered before any action is taken. Strategic thinkers must ask themselves, "What are the best and worst things that could happen if I do this? Could my actions have any unintended consequences?" Asking these questions is particularly necessary for you as a business leader when you develop any type of pilot project.

There are stages to social tech adoption, the first one being the "We're excited about the possibility" level. From there, organizations want to learn everything they can about the field of social tech. Then they start narrowing down the possibilities to a handful of uses that look promising—and this is where they come to a fork in the road. Some companies are disciplined and come to an agreement on the three to five pilot projects they want to put in place. They think carefully about the consequences of success and failure and then speculate on the best ways to find positive outcomes. They assign the pilot projects to specific people, document them fully, and then carry them out.

Unfortunately, other companies get to this fork in the road and become overly excited about just one idea or, perhaps worse, thrash around with a handful of ideas. This only wastes time. These organizations are sold on the possibilities of social tech but will take way too long to actually put something solid in place. We have to push hard to get them to focus and lock in on pilot projects, and sometimes even have to resort to a little arm-twisting to get them there.

A well-designed pilot program is developed at the final planning level—it wraps up the strategic planning process. A pilot program is the vehicle for accomplishing all of a company's, a brand's, or a person's objectives and long-term goals. Pilot programs have been used effectively by many different organizations to test new procedures or products before initiating comprehensive investments. This is a common way of learning from the market quickly.

Here is an example of a typical pilot program: a project jointly designed, implemented, and monitored by the North Dakota Beef Cattle Improvement Association, the U.S. Department of Agriculture under CalfAID, and the North Dakota State University Dickinson Research Extension Center. The goal of the project was to involve ten thousand calves in the testing of a high-frequency electronic identification tag that verifies the source and age of the animal. The tags make it possible to identify–immediately and correctly–cattle as they move through chutes and onto trucks. Research specialists were involved in the selection of the test area for this pilot project, and extensive documentation was prepared for all the entities participating in the project. The team members spent lots of time thinking about all the potential outcomes of the test, including the consequences of both success and failure and the potential issues facing every step and each participant. The team was specific about what it was testing and the results it hoped to see from the test.

Advertising agencies run pilot projects to test consumer reaction to ads. Marketing firms run pilot projects to test new products and new packaging. Food companies run pilot projects in certain geographic markets to test consumer uptake. The government uses pilot projects to test new ways of communicating with constituents. Politicians use pilot projects to test new messaging before they go public with it in speeches. In all these cases, running a pilot project is an effective way to learn.

So what does this all have to do with social tech? Nothing specific–and that's exactly the point. To show you how to run a mature pilot project, in this case it's easier to refer to examples from other arenas; there are barely any solid examples of companies applying well-thought-out pilot projects to their social tech programs! There are simply too many people not testing at all or blindly throwing efforts out into the social tech landscape to see what happens. Both of these approaches are doomed to bring failure.

How Pilot Programs Can Help You Avoid Disaster

Many leaders have seen it happen: What seemed like a feasible idea is shot down as a result of poor performance in a pilot project, and what seemed likely to fail somehow passed muster as a pilot project, perhaps even with flying colors. Some pilot projects have saved national brands from disaster. If a decision is made to go national with a new idea, without the precaution of putting a pilot project in place to observe the results of implementation in a much smaller area, major problems can ensue.

Don't underestimate the importance of testing and monitoring product alterations for safety and performance. Consider this example that is well remembered in marketing circles: A pilot program introduced a new bar soap in a small area of the Deep South during what turned out to be a record-breaking heat spell. Previous lab tests had not revealed a dermatological problem that surfaced when the user was exposed to extreme heat. As a result of the pilot program, the germicidal product idea was discarded. A national embarrassment, and a potentially devastating corporate blunder, was avoided.

The Planning and Control of Pilot Programs

Has this discussion gotten you excited about putting together your own social tech pilot projects? Good. So what do you do next?

Although you must consider all possible deviations from the expected path as you design pilot projects, the format for setting up and documenting them is very straightforward:

- Assign each project a name that is as clear and descriptive as possible. Each project should also be assigned a number; start each year with pilot project 1. Also, make sure the title will still have meaning a year or two down the road. If a specific brand is involved, identify it in the name of the project.

- Appoint one person to be in charge of the project—someone who will be able to answer management queries during any phase of the test.

- Describe the strategic reason for the project and the financial and/or volumetric objectives and goals that management hopes to attain through it. An *objective* can be stated in broad terms (e.g., to increase repeat purchases of a product); a *goal* is more specific and requires concrete targets (e.g., to increase repeat purchases by 15 percent for the second half of 2011).

- Give a detailed description of the tactics to be employed—that is, which social channels will you use (Twitter, Facebook, crowdSPRING, etc.)?

- Spell out how results will be measured within specific time periods.

- In a narrative description, lay out everything you expect to learn from the pilot project.

- Provide a detailed schedule, listing due dates for various tasks that will occur during the test. Adherence to scheduled reporting is critical to the maintenance and control of the pilot project. For projects with several steps, critical path management (CPM) should be used. This is the identification and specific handling of the elements of a project that will most impact your ability to stay on schedule or even to complete it at all. Using this system will protect against failure as a result of unexpected delays.

- For a phased introduction of a new product or service, CPM is particularly invaluable. The Dove Beauty Bar was introduced in several waves over a two-year period, and CPM kept the process under strict control. Management was able to quickly reschedule any dependent tasks that were affected by delays.

- Include a section in the project's documentation for a summary statement and other remarks. Record quotes and comments, during and at the completion of a project, as they can provide insight into whether the project was a total success or even a not-so-successful enterprise from which much was unexpectedly learned.

Getting Started with Pilot Project Development

By now you've become familiar with the many intriguing facets of the social technology world; you are intimately knowledgeable concerning your company's websites; you have developed brand profile "bibles" for each of your products and services; and you are eager to design and put in place a pilot project. What shall it be? What would be a wise choice for the first one? Well, naturally this depends on specifically what your organization is trying to achieve. It's tough to go wrong, however, if you pick a spread of pilot projects across the three branches of social tech.

Social Media Pilot Project

Put together a SlideShare channel, and upload a dozen or so presentations on your products or services. Make sure they come up whenever anyone types in a keyword that is relevant to your company. Monitor the traffic and other results that come from the SlideShare channel.

Social Networking Pilot Project

Put together a plan to identify a handful of areas in your organization where crowdsourcing can be used to get work done. Pick a couple of sites to test out, and spend a few months getting work done by leveraging the Internet herd. Then determine whether you have met your financial, timeline, and quality goals.

Social Relevance Pilot Project

Put together a pilot project to implement a formalized online reputation management system that has the goal of finding every mention of the name of your product, organization, or CEO. Then put the analytics in place to measure your sentiment ratio, number of mentions, and the velocity of the growth of those mentions.

* * *

These are just examples of pilot projects you can implement across the various social tech categories to learn a broad set of lessons that will help the organization move forward. In some cases it's also good to look at what *not* to do. Let's reach back to one of the more famous stories of a misstep that could have been avoided with better pilot testing. If you are old enough, you will remember this for sure.

A "Classic" Pilot Project Example: Asking Targeted Questions and Interpreting Results Correctly

In July 1985, Coca-Cola attempted to reformulate its brand by introducing "New Coke"; the company expected the consumer to accept the change without any problems. It didn't work out that way. The whole episode garnered lots of ink in advertising periodicals; *Advertising Age* wrote about the "missing ingredients in 'new' Coke's research."[57] The missing ingredient turned out to be that the company had neglected to ask the right questions, ones that might have clued the company in to the strong degree of loyalty its brand drew from consumers. Coca-Cola didn't recognize that consumers had an emotional relationship with the old formula and regarded it as an integral piece of Americana; consumers strongly believed that this "classic" recipe should not be replaced.

And it wasn't that the folks at Coca-Cola failed to test-market this concept before they changed decades of tradition. In fact, the company did about 180,000 to 200,000 blind taste tests of New Coke recipes against the "old" version. Specially equipped vans located around major markets were used for the taste tests, which were highly publicized. Every effort was made to access hard-to-reach populations.

---

57 Jack J. Honomichl (1985), "Missing Ingredients in 'New' Coke's Research," *Advertising Age*, (July), 1.

According to senior marketing research management, however, only thirty thousand to forty thousand of these tests involved the formula that was eventually introduced to the public. The result of this very expensive Coca-Cola fiasco was that the company dumped the new continued to market its classic formula.

Many marketers still refer to the New Coke fiasco whenever major product changes are considered. Although it is important to do the research and set up the pilot projects, it is even more important to ask the right questions and interpret the results correctly. Consumer attitude is a force to be reckoned with when it comes to making changes to the formulation or packaging of any product. If consequential thinking had been applied to the New Coke project, perhaps someone might have asked, in true ad agency lingo, "What if the dogs don't like it?"

From Coca-Cola's experience, we see that it makes sense to leverage the social community by designing a pilot project with the goal of finding out why people buy your product or service and what elements of it make them loyal customers. What are the specific attributes that keep them coming back to your organization, even when your competitors offer hefty deals? If your business is experiencing tough times, ask the hard questions. Be prepared to flinch at some of the answers; this generation of social tech consumers doesn't pull punches. It can be a brutally honest world online—and that's a good thing.

Pilot Project Example:
Selective Coding of Consumer Response

Still, for all the importance of correct understanding and interpretation, it pays to go about things in a scientific way.

Traditionally, the use of selective coupon coding in the design of a pilot project is an example of how the important information about the target customers—in this case, their geographic location—can be gathered and analyzed. The project design should include some brief form for the respondent to fill out and submit in order to be cleared to download a coupon. Included on this form should be an area for the consumer's zip code. *This is the most important piece of information for a marketer to obtain.* It will allow for summarization of zip code information into company sales districts, cities/states, or any other limited grouping.

Two separate files can be constructed from the zip codes. First, information on the reach and scope of a pilot project can be determined by the initial response. Then, the redemption information that follows can be monitored as the program continues. Pilot projects, other than couponing tests, would also require the consumer to provide zip code information.

In this new world of technology, we have an easier way to accomplish the same goal; we simply provide electronic coupons, which allows us the flexibility to gather demographic data on the redeemer before we even "hand them" the coupon electronically. Going one step further, we should keep in mind what location-based social networking sites like Foursquare are doing. They allow a retailer or any other member location to create a place on the service where consumers can "check in" just by being at the location. In return, the retailer can provide points, bonuses, or rewards based on the number of times the user checks in. This motivates users to check in as often as possible, and that normally entails the added benefit of telling all their friends where they are at that moment. This, of course, helps with branding and subtle eWord-of-mouth marketing for the retailer.

By its very nature, Foursquare provides a way to perform selective coding of the users that are visiting a business—an updated method to include in pilot projects for the social tech era.

Structuring Pilot Projects

Newcomers to the social technology world should select three to five pilot projects, with the principal goal of teaching the organization how successful–or unsuccessful–these concepts might be. A planning and control outline for each of these projects will document exactly what facts the project is seeking and for what reasons. The measurement systems to be used in any analyses should be described as clearly as possible.

When you prepare the planning and control outline for any pilot project, be very explicit when you describe what action may be taken as a result of your conclusions. The person to whom the project has been assigned must be able to provide post-analysis in a timely fashion.

Your pilot programs will have the best chance of yielding profitable results if you answer the following questions for each one:

1. Overall, was the pilot project a success? What worked well and what didn't?

2. Did you learn what you wanted to learn from this project?

3. If there were any failures, were they due to poor execution? Or did this project highlight an unsolvable problem that indicates this path is not the right one for your organization?

4. Should the pilot project be rerun with certain elements altered?

5. If the pilot project seems viable for expansion, can it be turned into a regular practice?

6. How important to the success or failure of this pilot project were the people who were running it?

The mistake that we see too many clients make is this: They work hard to define a pilot project, invest a good amount of energy in the early days when people are excited about possibilities, and then finish weakly. Avoid this trap by ensuring that there is accountability for the owner of the project, and have him or her report their findings at the closure of the timeframe. If you start strong and then just fizzle in the end, you have actually wasted resources, because you have invested time that will yield little useful information.

An Example from the Social Tech Space

Marketing challenges not only come from competition but often grow out of ignorance of one's own brand, its limitations, and its capabilities. A pilot project can find out what makes your brand acceptable (or unacceptable) to consumers and why, and it will generate a flood of ideas for other pilot projects.

Dove Beauty Bar and Dove Deodorant marketers appear to be strong advocates of the effectiveness of social tech in gauging consumer feelings on their products. The Dove product management team uses Twitter, Facebook, and other social networks to reach out to consumers and gather their most recent experiences with Dove, their buying habits, their degree of satisfaction with their purchase choices, and any other feedback that can suggest fertile areas for pilot testing of marketing and sales ideas.

A 2008–2009 Dove Beauty Bar contest, part of a campaign to highlight the product's ability to get rid of soap scum, created a lot of chatter on Twitter, resulting in hundreds of responses from Dove users across the country. Another Dove pilot project on Twitter, intended to spread awareness of the need for early detection of ovarian cancer, has drawn over one thousand followers. The project, based in Montreal, set new standards for using social technology to spread awareness of societal needs throughout the world.

The Dove brand is also prominent on Facebook. Beauty and style experts who are spokespeople for the Dove brand are frequent guests on Dove's Facebook page. Many short demonstration videos on YouTube.com and ExpoTV.com demonstrate the quality of Dove products.

Social networks are natural viaducts for the public to reach across vast territories and alert friends and family to coupons and other freebies that are available on the Internet. This eWOM advertising is a valuable asset to any pilot project. This is what Dove is trying to leverage, and why the company is testing the methods described.

A Few Scenarios That Call for Pilot Projects

Situations that plant "How can we . . . ?" and "What if . . . ?" questions in managers' minds arise in every marketplace niche. Pilot projects can answer questions like "What if we tried using socially facilitated selling to increase revenue this year?" and "How can we improve our overall customer service ratings with an operational risk management process?" and "How could we improve the quality of our new employees by using social tech in the recruiting process?" Once you understand how to construct a social tech pilot project that will answer these types of questions, you can shine light on any problem and gain a better understanding of what's taking place at the grassroots level.

Listed below are several scenarios that call for a pilot project.

Scenario 1: Cannibalization of an Old Product by a New Product

Your new star entry in Category X is exceeding all expectations. Unfortunately, sales of your other brand in the same category have trended down ever since the new brand was introduced. Are you cannibalizing your old brand? Additionally, the new brand requires advertising support; the old brand gets promotion dollars only. If this continues, at what point will such cannibalization cancel out any new product gains? Are consumers switching, and if they are, what attributes are most attractive about the new brand? Which are missing in the old–is it price or quality? Answers are needed immediately.

Management decision: A crowdsourced market-research pilot project is required.

Scenario 2: A New Type of Medical Practice

A young doctor has completed his residency and will join his father's medical practice, but he doesn't want to get involved with all the nonmedical business responsibilities. He believes these chores are overwhelming the "doctoring side" of medicine. He wants to attract young people, perhaps twenty-five to fifty years of age, who aren't covered by medical insurance, and to provide a service to them that includes house calls (one of the best practice offerings from the past). He will have computerized patient files and will carry his computer database with him (the best of the present). He will also be available for face-to-face visits on Skype (the best of the future). For this new kind of medical service, a patient would pay a yearly retainer plus a fee for any office visits, which would take place (rarely, he hopes) at his father's office.

This situation calls for a pilot test in which the doctor would use Facebook to publicize his idea and see if he can recruit ten people to participate in a trial. He could also establish a presence on Twitter to see how many people are interested in his approach to practicing medicine. The pilot test will determine whether young, uninsured people comprise a viable market and will show him how many patients he can handle if he makes house calls. He can then calculate the level of income he should expect from such an arrangement.

Scenario 3: A Possible Secondary Market

An astute forecaster noticed that your product—a cleansing tissue for infants—is doing extremely well in Florida. The Sunshine State is not noted for its infant population—rather, the reverse is true. So just who is buying your product, and why? The answer to this question could open up a whole new market segment. A pilot project in a small area of Florida might show that elderly women are using the wipes to remove makeup from sensitive skin. If this can be validated, perhaps alternative packaging and copy should be tested to see if this secondary use can be encouraged nationally.

The company could use an eWOM pilot project to survey the market's interest in a repackaged product specifically marketed for this new purpose and to build anticipation for its release.

Scenario 4: Facebook Popularity

A brand management team has noted that more and more young mothers are posting comments on Facebook walls. Many of them are sharing product usage experiences, resulting in both positive and negative comments.

An online reputation pilot project is needed here. In order to maximize the good and counteract the bad, the project could monitor markets with a strong population of young parents, and this would give early warning of the adverse postings but would also allow for early response to the good ones.

Scenario 5: Internet Coupon Versus Direct Mail Coupon

With selective coding that enables identification of coupons that are distributed over the Internet versus those distributed through direct mail, a company can evaluate the relative effectiveness of both types of coupon. The costs to deliver the Internet coupon are almost negligible—clearly a cost savings—but will the effectiveness really provide a stronger ROI?

A pilot project could test the redeem rates of the exact same coupon delivered through these two different sources. In addition, giving the coupon out through specific channels with unique coding could test the response rate among different demographics.

* * *

Once you have an eye for using pilot projects to test concepts, you will frequently see possible applications. That said, you must always be concerned with the effective use of your budget and staff time, so it is very important to pick projects from across the spectrum and not just in one category. In other words, don't dig for gold in only one mine.

Remember to employ consequential thinking in every phase of a pilot project and to build adversarial questions into the design process. If you fail to think consequentially, you could end up in a lot of trouble and suffer from a lot of unforeseen difficulties.

Another social tech area in which consequential thinking is absolutely crucial is security. Failure to foresee consequences here can give rise to a massive penalty, yet too many people focus on what social tech tools can do to drive sales while neglecting what they can do to open up your systems to attack. The last step of any good social tech program is looking at how to help each member of your organization become a safer technology citizen—not only for his or her own good, but also for the good of the company.

═ KEY POINTS ═════○════════════○═

- Because social technology is such a new and fast-growing field, organizations need formal pilot projects for quickly identifying possible applications of social tech.

- Consequential thinking must be applied during the development of pilot projects. This includes considering the consequences of doing the pilot and the consequences of certain variables on the rest of the project.

- Organizations should run multiple social-tech pilot projects at the same time and should vary the concepts being tested. This will help the team compare the relative value of various concepts.

- Pilot projects must be structured scientifically. You must determine what you are trying to learn from them and what the major drivers of success or failure might be.

- A document describing the pilot project must be created and made available to all team members.

- Progress should be reviewed monthly, and a summary report should be written at the end of the pilot project to document the lessons learned.

- Once a pilot project is completed, a clear decision should be made between rerunning it with a different set of variables, integrating it into the normal course of business, or closing it out completely.

 To access samples of pilot project management documents, go to EnterpriseSocialTechnology.com.

CHAPTER 12

Security and Regulations

In the preceding chapters, we covered how social tech can be leveraged to change the way organizations operate. There is no doubt that technology has tremendously advanced the business world over the past few years, but alas, there is a flip side: When we become accustomed to using these great tools, we inevitably become dependent on them.

Once a business is dependent on certain technologies, it becomes utterly vulnerable should those technologies be suddenly compromised or unavailable. This vulnerability is further magnified with technologies that are based in a purely virtual environment, as there is no readily accessible hands-on component that can be fixed through conventional means. Social tech in particular is greatly dependent on the agents outside your own organization who provide the digital framework (Internet providers, server hosts, and so forth). The virtual nature of these tools further magnifies dependency and broadens the spectrum of possible threats well beyond what businesses had to contend with just a few years ago.

This brings us to the essential topic of security and regulations in the use of social technology. Do not be fooled by this chapter's position near the end of the book; its importance should be by no means underestimated. Security considerations will have a significant impact on how your organization uses social tech, and in extreme cases might make the difference between going out of business and staying in it! It is critical that, while you invest lots of energy into finding ways to increase sales, tighten customer relationships, and cut costs, you also invest resources into training people about the safe use of social technology. Your IT department cannot protect the organization on its own. It needs the users of social technologies to practice safe computing, and that is more of a challenge than you might expect. Most IT departments struggle simply to keep their head above water without the added hassle of social tech—and that's why some of them just recommend blocking all usage!

For example, take what used to be the IT firm Verus: The company's system administrators temporarily disabled security protections to swap around data on its network and then neglected to re-enable them, putting the sensitive personal financial data of some ninety-one thousand hospital patients at risk. When the roughly sixty affected hospitals caught wind of the breach, beginning in May 2007, they all canceled their contracts, and by August 2007 Verus was out of business—suffering a shocking turnaround from being a thriving medical bill-paying services company to being no company at all.[58]

Always keep in mind that all these great new tools are globally available to nearly anyone with an Internet connection—friend or foe. For every legitimate and legal use of a technology application, there is always a corresponding dark side; every tool that can be used effectively for business can also be abused for unlawful and unethical activities that can harm businesses—including yours. With the same blinding speed at which information can be distributed for the good of your cause and your bottom line, evildoers can use these lightning-fast digital tools to bring your life's work to the ground with the mere push of a button.

There is a dark, worldwide guild of Internet miscreants who are determined to enrich themselves at your expense or to simply

---

[58] http://www.computerworld.com.au/article/224911/stupid_user_tricks_it_admin_follies/?pp=6

cause general havoc. Although in the past a local business "only" had to contend with mostly physical security threats that occurred in its immediate surroundings, today, thanks to advanced technology, you and your organization are susceptible to attack from literally anyone, anywhere in the world. A global cybercrime group can descend on your systems suddenly and without warning if you are not cautious. Although you might wonder what you've gotten yourself into when you think about the potential harm that could befall your organization through attacks like this, the majority of security issues are still rather easy to address, and most typical problems can be avoided with proper regulation, simple education, and some good, old-fashioned common sense.

It would be foolish to embrace these new social technology tools without heeding the many warnings about security risks associated with their use, and without devoting the needed resources to educate staff members on the most effective strategies for keeping a secure environment online. Technology changes quickly, and the "bad guys" always seem to have a leg up when it comes to finding new ways to exploit systems before the "good guys" get around to fixing the security loopholes. It is during this lag time—between the emergence of new security hazards and the dissemination of remedies to them—that you are on your own in policing and protecting your digital environment.

While social tech security is a global problem that concerns millions of users, keeping your organization safe is your responsibility—and no one else's. This is why you need a clearly planned-out set of measures for security hazard prevention, as well as an action plan in case things actually go awry. To date, most security hazards can still be prevented through educating your staff to use basic common sense and stick to certain essential usage rules. However, as you will see, there are other potential risks beyond your control that also warrant addressing, depending on your type of organization.

Generally speaking, your business may face security threats in three broad categories:

1. Attacks directed specifically against your business from competitors or ill-wishers

2. Random attacks from unknown cybercriminals

3. Attacks directed against the actual fabric of the Internet itself and its networking tools (cyberterrorism)

Let's take a brief look at each, as you need to be aware of all these risk factors and seriously think about how to minimize their impact on your organization.

1. Attacks Directed Specifically Against Your Business

These are attacks aimed directly at your business, with the goal of giving the attacker a competitive advantage or disrupting your operation in some way. Also in this category are security risks created by your own team members, whether deliberate or simply through careless use of social tech. Direct attacks against your company can take one of a few forms.

System Invasion

System invasion occurs when competitors or ill-wishers gain access to your systems by obtaining or hacking passwords, or through the use of viruses and other invasive programs. Imagine the havoc your competitors could cause if they had access to all your confidential files, documents, billing and tax data, client contact information, and internal memos.

System invasion can include anything from the use of keystroke monitors and programs that take screenshots (passive methods) to actual system access that allows for direct manipulation of information on your machines (active methods). With the use of social tech, system invasion reaches a whole new dimension, as not only your in-house systems but also your outside social tech tools can be compromised. Someone who steals your Facebook or Twitter account password can wreak almost as much havoc as someone with direct access to your business computers. Furthermore, these same tools can become the very delivery mechanism for invasive attacks.

Identity Cloning

Identity cloning is the stealing or illegal reuse of avatars, logos, names, or other information associated with your organization. The perpetrator passes off him- or herself as you in order to gain access to your clients, finances, or other resources. People tend to let their guards down when they deal with familiar names and images, so someone pretending to be you may well be able to take advantage of your business partners, clients, vendors, industry regulators, or even your employees. Thus it is very important to independently verify all communication involving sensitive information, such as credit card numbers, personal and medical data, and so forth. This holds true for both incoming and outgoing communication.

Intellectual Property Theft and Breaches of Confidentiality

Social tech can also provide a means for others to use your ideas, images, writings, data, or contacts for their own purposes, without regard for copyright, intellectual property law, corporate ethics, or confidentiality rights. This often occurs when too much information is posted by your own team, either by mistake or due to a lack of understanding of corporate confidentiality guidelines. An example would be information posted about a project your firm is bidding on, possibly even with details about bid terms; through your very own channels, your competitors may be alerted that the project is up for bid, giving them opportunity to submit a competing bid with better terms and possibly snatch the deal away from you.

Another extreme example may be a prematurely or accidentally published idea or concept developed by your company that is then promptly copied and patented by your competitor. Other unwanted attention to your organization's projects, products, or procedures can be generated through too much information released on social tech platforms. One organization posted photographs of its newly renovated conference room on a company profile, only to have someone tip off the fire marshal that the room's secondary exit was blocked by a room divider that was clearly visible in one of the posted photos.

Remember that everything you post or send is available to the public, whether you want it to be or not, once you hit that "Send" or "Post" button. Even though most social tech tools allow you to edit and delete content, once something has been posted, you have no real control over its distribution. Electronic information can easily be duplicated within seconds and could already be archived somewhere for all eternity by the time you delete it. Needless to say, once you send an e-mail or instant message to a direct recipient, there is no way to get it back!

The "Burglars Welcome!" Problem

Another facet of sharing too much information through social tech tools is releasing facts about yourself, your employer, your employees, or your coworkers—including marital status, whereabouts, and personal lives—as well as facts about the physical office environment. For example, you might be inadvertently letting the whole world know that you will be overseas for two weeks and your house will be empty. One classic example is the following incident: An office manager means to alert employees that the office security system will be offline for twenty-four hours due to maintenance. Instead of sending out an internal memo, she accidentally cc's several outside recipients, basically informing the world that the office will be unprotected for a day!

Accidental or Thoughtless Communication

Unintentional distribution of information through the wrong channels or to the wrong recipients can be harmful as well, to a degree that can range from the embarrassing to the outright damaging. One example is "pocket calls," which happen to nearly everyone who owns a cell phone and can be very awkward, depending on who was called and what may have been overheard.

This category can include the unintended distribution of personal messages. Imagine participating in an online role-playing game, pretending to be the despotic ruler of a fictional nation. Having composed a threatening diplomatic e-mail to one of your in-game friends and fellow planetary rulers, you accidentally send it to your entire address book—including all your business contacts—instead of to the game's mailing list. This could be very embarrassing, and your boss would not be at all amused.

Needless to say, most opinions about your customers, clients, managers, or bosses do not belong on any public form of social media, whether posted intentionally or not. One much-publicized story about such a social tech post gone wrong is that of James Andrews, vice president of Ketchum, a PR and marketing agency. Upon arriving in Memphis, Tennessee, on a business trip, Andrews tweeted the following: "True confession but I'm in one of those towns where I scratch my head and say 'I would die if I had to live here!'" The problem was, Andrews was on his way to make a presentation to executives at FedEx, which is based in Memphis. Needless to say, his clients at FedEx were less than impressed with Andrews' assessment of their hometown, and embarrassment and apologies followed.[59] This is how 140 characters or less can cost you an important business account!

---

59 Jim Edwards, "Worst Twitter Post Ever: Ketchum Exec Insults Fedex Client on Mini-Blog," BNET.com, January 20, 2009, http://industry.bnet.com/advertising/1000525/worst-twitter-post-ever-ketchum-exec-insults-fedex-client-on-mini-blog/.

Online Reputation Fraud and Cyber-Racketeering

It is very easy to create anonymous or false online identities and leave negative feedback about an individual or organization. There are many avenues, increasingly cross-linked, for rating and reviewing businesses, organizations, and even individuals. An example is Google Maps, where you can search for a Korean restaurant in your area and instantly get links to a dozen reviews of the place from sites like UrbanSpoon.com, VirtualTourist.com, and TripAdvisor.com. If most of the reviews are bad, you are more likely to choose another eatery, even though it would be impossible to know whether these reviews are accurate—or even posted by actual consumers. It's an unpleasant reality that some bad guys attempt to extort money from organizations in return for guarding their online reputations and not filling the Internet with negative posts, which essentially amounts to a company making "protection payments" against crimes the black-mailers would instigate themselves if not paid.

A Mole or a Disgruntled Employee

It may sound like the stuff of movies, but your company could be subject to internal espionage. One or more of your employees who have access to your social tech devices could be working for a competitor, either channeling information to that entity or sabotaging your own channels from within. Disgruntled employees can do the same without actually working for your rivals. They might simply sabotage the system or create deliberate security hazards to get back at the company, undermine a supervisor, or vent their various on-the-job frustrations.

2. Random Attacks from Unknown Cybercriminals

Some security hazards are created by unknown criminals who make a living attacking individuals and organizations more or less at random. These are probably the most common types of security hazards, and you will face them on a daily basis, as they constantly affect everyone connected to the Internet. Although attacks directly against your business may be rare, these indiscriminate breaches can happen to anyone at any time. They are perpetrated by cybercriminals who often operate on a grand scale, sending their bait to millions of Internet users at once. Even a tiny success rate can make for spectacular profitability.

These types of attacks become more sophisticated all the time, and although they generally follow the same basic patterns for many years, their creators frequently find new channels through which to deliver them. Such hazards could potentially beset anybody using the Internet and can include attacks by the following entities.

Spammers

Even though you may think of spam as more of a nuisance than a security hazard, in extreme cases communication channels can become flooded by so much junk that they become essentially unusable for their intended purposes. When the noise of unwanted spam messages begins to drown out relevant information, important messages can be missed, and that can cost you real opportunities and money. Similarly, spam filters have been known to filter out messages you actually want to receive, resulting in the same problem—important messages lost. Spam can also be used as an intentional weapon by attackers to swamp a system. As such, it can be a serious problem and can impede the way your organization conducts vital communication. Always take great care not to expose your e-mail addresses and other communication channels to spammers.

Scammers

Almost everybody connected to the Internet sooner or later gets hit with scam messages. The classics are messages claiming you won a foreign lottery, or e-mails from complete strangers who urgently need your confidential help in transferring large amounts of money from overseas. Scams like these have been around for decades, and had their beginnings in regular snail mail. Later they graduated to e-mail, and now they are making the rounds on all kinds of other social communication channels. Scammers will usually give elaborate promises of cash or other riches, asking you to remit a comparatively small "processing fee" or "tax payment" up front before they can wire you the promised millions. Of course, once you send the funds, the scammer disappears, and your imaginary millions go up in smoke—as do the hundreds or thousands of real dollars you already sent.

Phishers

Phishers are entities who attempt to extract sensitive personal or financial information through fraudulent means. As with spam, such attacks have become familiar to almost every Internet user, first through e-mail and now through other social channels as well. The ready availability and "clonability" of electronic information and graphics such as corporate logos have made it possible for users with even very modest skills to perpetrate scams, misleading well-intentioned individuals and organizations and causing great financial and operational harm.

One example you may have personally experienced comes in the form of neatly formatted messages from, say, "Bank of America" (showing what appears to be the official logo and even the usual legal disclaimers at the bottom of the message), asking you to "confirm the authenticity" of your identity to ascertain that your "account has not been stolen, hacked, suspended, or frozen." The message prompts you to click on a provided link, which takes you to another neatly branded and formatted page, where you are asked to confirm your date of birth, Social Security number, account number, and so forth. The link address contains "bankofamerica" somewhere in the URL, but the site to which it redirects you is a fraudulent facsimile of the real thing. For those who fall for this con, all their confidential information is then sent straight into the underworld! These kinds of messages come from all sorts of fraudsters masquerading as companies, and they are sent randomly; nearly identical messages claim to be from Chase, Wachovia, Citibank, PayPal–all fake, of course. Even sites like Facebook are being used for phishing purposes, with unsolicited messages from phishers prompting users to enter their personal information to avoid "Facebook usage charges" or closure of their account.

Another effective phishing approach is a fake message claiming that your unspecified credit card has been charged a certain amount for some product you obviously did not order. The message goes on to state that if you wish to dispute the charges, you must again provide sensitive data, such as your credit card number, billing address, and card's expiration date. Many people are so flustered by the unexpected charge, they will rush to dispute it without stopping to think or to check their real credit accounts first.

Hackers

Hackers are good, old-fashioned computer-savvy bad guys who figure out your passwords and invade your accounts, or who step through your system's back door and make themselves comfortable at your expense. It doesn't happen just in the movies! And if you think it's difficult to hack simple passwords, think again! Anyone can download freely available tools that almost instantly run millions of password combinations on any account–particularly words found in the dictionary (so "secret" and "password" are not good options, no matter how clever you think you are) and names of people and places (so don't use "Detroit," "Julie," or "Wyoming").

Your social tech accounts can be vulnerable to hijacking if you employ lax password standards. Even high-profile Twitter accounts belonging to people like Britney Spears, CNN's Rick Sanchez, and then-Senator Barack Obama–as well as those of organizations such as Fox News–have been hacked, and they were used to send out malicious and embarrassing tweets before their rightful owners were able to regain control over them.[60]

Hoaxers

Hoaxers are similar to scammers, but instead of promising you information or money, they often use heart-wrenching but false stories about a sick child in need or an injured soldier—any sort of human interest story to solicit donations or support. Although you may think you are contributing to a good cause, don't let your guard down while you're teary-eyed, or your resources may go straight down the drain.

A less harmful, albeit no less annoying, type of hoax includes messages such as "If you forward this e-mail, Microsoft will send you a free laptop" or "Don't add John Smith to your friends list, he's a hacker and will delete your hard drive!" While these types of hoaxes do no actual harm to your privacy or wallet, every year businesses lose millions in productivity due to team members forwarding billions of hoax messages through various channels of communication.

Fake Online Businesses

With the relative ease of composing professional-looking websites these days, it has also become easier to set up fake virtual storefronts to trick people and organizations into doing business with phony companies. A recent example is the emergence of health care fraud sites, companies that claim to be legitimate health insurance businesses, invoking the "Obamacare" reform bill and harvesting your sensitive personal and medical data. Once you send them your information and the supposed insurance premium payments, they stop responding to inquiries and eventually disappear without trace.

Whereas in the past a professional looking website and a 1-800 number was a decent test of a company's legitimacy, in today's

---

60 Gregg Keizer, "Hackers Hijack Obama's, Britney's Twitter Accounts," NetworkWorld. com, January 6, 2009, http://www.networkworld.com/news/2009/010609-hackers-hijack-obamas-britneys-twitter.html.

world you need much more to confirm that you are really dealing with a trustworthy organization. You can waste a lot of time and resources doing business with what you falsely believe to be a legitimate company.

Viruses

Viruses fall into two main categories: They can be purpose-driven viruses created to harvest sensitive information from your profiles or systems and then forward it to their creators, or they can be vanity and cybervandalism viruses that deface your social tech content with useless information or simply destroy your infrastructure. The former often operates quietly in the background so as not to tip off the victim that his or her sensitive information is compromised; the latter blatantly renders your tools largely useless.

Viruses have found many avenues through which to make their way into your systems; e-mail attachments are just one of these. They can arrive as Facebook applications that promise one thing but do another. So when one of your friends appears to be posting a comment with a link on your Facebook wall, perhaps something about her alleged weight loss success, it may be nothing more than a viruslike marketing application that sends itself to all the contacts on your friends list once you allow it access.

Viruses also can be transmitted through pop-up messages on Skype, Yahoo! Messenger, and many other similar channels. Some of your instant messenger contacts might be regularly infected with viruses without even knowing it—that's why you sometimes receive pop-up messages from them with a silly smiling emoticon and a link, saying things like "My Photo," "Look at this!" or "Can you beat me in an IQ test?" If you are temporarily off guard, you might click on the link, believing that one of these messages really came from a friend or a business contact—but beware! Your friends will probably be completely surprised when you tell them they have such a virus, as the virus operates stealthily without any real trace visible on the infected computer.

It can be especially embarrassing if such messages originate from your business account. After all, if you can't get your social tech security in order, what kind of company are you?

3. Attacks Against the Fabric of the Internet

Though this may not seem like a huge problem at present, you need to spare a thought on how your organization will operate as it becomes increasingly dependent on social tech applications, especially should the digital framework of the Internet itself suddenly become unavailable due to a cyberterrorism attack, remote security breaches, or other unforeseen outages. Massive global attacks on the very fabric of the Internet and on large individual sites such as Google, MySpace, or MSN.com have been limited in their success so far; chances are, however, that sooner or later someone will figure out how to create more effective and longer-lasting disruptions.

If your business relies on essential services from social tech providers, and these providers are shut down for some time, then so are you. Major sites have been temporarily disabled in the past through various types of attacks, and although they were able to rebound quickly and without great loss of usability, you need to have a plan in place for when the (as of yet) unthinkable happens and parts of the Internet or individual social tech providers go down for longer periods of time. Should this happen, it not only will affect the way you communicate and make transactions but may also restrict access to your own data.

With the increasing popularity of cloud computing as a major component of social tech applications, more and more data is stored and secured off-site by remote providers. Think about it—if your vital business data is hosted by an outside entity, you do not have absolute control over your organization's information. You need to have plans in place to access and store this vital data through other means. Unless you have a backup plan, in a critical situation you may be left marooned.

Scared Yet? Let's Get a Plan Together

What, then, can be done to combat this vast array of security threats your organization faces every day? The list of risks may seem intimidating and may make you wonder whether you should be using social tech applications for business at all, let alone increasing your dependence them. Relax. This list has not been created to scare you, but to make you aware of certain risks and thus enable you to neutralize them. Technology keeps changing, and businesses are constantly adapting to utilize new tools to their fullest, so if you want to stay competitive in the global marketplace, taking an ostrich's approach will not serve you well in the long run.

Restricting or even blocking social tech as a means of security is not wise. This deprives you of great tools that, sooner or later, might emerge as your industry standard, and it tends to make your organization look archaic. Furthermore, employees will find ways around the ban, which creates an even bigger risk, as you will have less oversight of their social tech use. Since burying your head in the sand—keeping everything private and everyone away from networking online—is not an option, you are going to have to use new methods of protection.

What follows are specific measures your organization can take to keep your social tech environment as secure as possible. In general, more than 90 percent of all security threats you face as a small or medium-size organization can be eliminated through simple, commonsense policies and inexpensive training of your team. Larger organizations face more complex security challenges, but the same commonsense rules apply. Organizations that do not invest in proper training will inevitably open themselves up to employees' mistakes and will have a much higher probability of compromising the organization's security. They are essentially facilitating an open door into their networks.

Attacks are becoming more sophisticated each day, and you and your team members need to stay on top of this fast-changing world of risks. The battle between the bad guys and the good guys is not being won by either party, but because technology moves so fast, the bad guys generally devise their latest exploits before the good guys can anticipate them—leaving the good guys to forever play catch-up. There is also a good possibility that as the use of social tech expands further, the dangers associated with its use will increase as well. That is why it is paramount to stay current. Do not fall behind when it comes to security.

The Do's and Don'ts of Social Tech Security

The simplest format for helping you understand the actions necessary to stay safe is a list of activities to make sure you do and activities to avoid. Some of these may seem basic, and others are geekier. Remember, it only takes one sloppy security mistake for you to find out how expensive breaches can be.

DO pay attention to password security and the sophistication level of your passwords. Simple names, words that can be found in a dictionary, and common combinations like "123456789" or "qwerty" will not do. Make sure you use different passwords for different applications, so that if one of your passwords is compromised, at least not all your accounts are vulnerable at the same time. Contrary to popular belief, changing your password frequently does nothing to enhance security, but it does waste time and create staff confusion and resentment. Pick a different "strong" password for each application and stick to it. Although a password such as "sM5TvgX2" may be exceptionally strong, it is also exceptionally difficult to remember.

Make sure a master list of passwords is stored in a secure place and kept up to date. A forgotten password can cause a lot of headaches.

However, **DO** remind your team members not to write themselves little sticky notes with passwords and keep them affixed to their computer screens! A classic story is that of the well-meaning secretary who collected all staff members' passwords and posted the comprehensive list in the lunchroom in case anyone forgot theirs.[61]

Moreover, remind everyone to disable password-storing features and to log out when they're finished using an outside computer. How many times have you sat down at a public machine to enter your own log-in information, only to find someone else still logged in or another person's password "remembered" as an auto-complete option? One story tells of a person who left a piece of stationery—scribbled with complete log-in instructions, passwords, and other sensitive information—in a hotel lobby after using a public computer terminal there.[62] Make sure this does not happen to you or your team members.

Another thing: If a staff member leaves your organization, it is definitely time to change all passwords that individual knew, as a matter of standard procedure. Another story describes an employee, formerly in charge of the company's website content and e-mail account management, who is laid off—and finds to her great amusement, over a year later, that no one had thought about changing the master password! The employee still had access to all the company's e-mail in-boxes, account control panels, and FTP and Web servers. Don't rely on luck—not everyone is one of the good guys, especially after being laid off!

DO require your telecommuting and traveling staff members to secure their systems whenever unattended, even at home. While

---

61 http://www.computerworld.com.au/article/155396/stupid_user_tricks_eleven_it_
horror_stories/

62 Wayne Rash, "Stupid User Tricks," InfoWorld.com, January 24, 2003, http://www.
infoworld.com/d/security-central/stupid-user-tricks-264.

Daddy is out having a bite to eat, his teenage offspring may be surfing the Web or playing games on the machine—compromising the company laptop, unbeknownst to all. Once the compromised laptop is back at the office and reconnected to your network, the entire company infrastructure is at risk.

DO remind your team members to always keep up their guard about opening attachments, clicking on links, or authorizing applications on social tech sites. Unless you are expecting a specific file attachment from a specific source at a specific time, these potentially risky actions should always be treated with utmost caution. Make everyone is aware that the list of file extensions that usually can be considered safe is very short (.gif, .jpg, .tif, .mpg, .mp3, and .wav) and that all others are best left unopened. Use great caution with .zip and .rar file extensions, and do not click on any unknown links unless first verifying them with the sender. Certain file extensions such as .exe, .scr, and .bat, as well as URLs ending in .php, should raise automatic warning flags and should never be opened. Make sure everybody knows what the safe and unsafe extensions are, and have them follow the policy religiously. People clicking on unfamiliar links or opening unknown attachments is still by far the largest source of electronic security problems, despite repeated and consistent warnings from many sources.

DO have weekly or biweekly information sessions, whether they be staff briefings, meetings of department heads or memos to all employees, informing them of the latest security risks, hoaxes, and false alarms going around. Education is absolutely key to keeping your organization safe. It may get repetitive at times, but it takes only one lapse from a staff member to potentially create a large problem for the entire organization. Your company becomes more vulnerable if you have a greater rate of staff turnover, but even longtime employees tend to get lax or just plain forget. Remind them about security issues constantly. There are many helpful tools out there you can use to enhance e-safety, including a myriad of websites every Internet user should know, such as the following:

Scambusters.org
scamdex.com
usa.gov/Citizen/Topics/Internet_Fraud.shtml
ic3.gov/crimeschemes.aspx
snopes.com

Make sure your team members are aware of them and have the relevant links bookmarked for ready use before they take action.

DO designate a person to be in charge of browsing through your various social tech channels (if possible, from off-site) to keep an eye on your reputation and your published content. Have him or her go through various sites that provide ratings, reviews, and references, to check for false or damaging entries. Let the monitor judge whether your content looks as it is intended to look on various types of hardware and different software clients. In some cases it is difficult to contact customer support and get answers when you need help, so it is useful to keep a listing of proper methods of contact should your monitor find false claims or reviews you want removed. If possible, open up and maintain a direct line of communication with support personnel for all the tools you are using to ensure a quicker response time when needed.

DO be very skeptical about who is on the other end of unsolicited communication. It's very easy to fall victim to a spoof profile or fake identity, especially if you believe it to be someone you already know. Always verify the source independently through other channels before responding with sensitive information, even if the communication appears to come from someone familiar. Likewise, be aware of who may be out there using your avatar, logo, or ripped-off profile, pretending to be you to gain through fraudulent means.

DO be very careful of anyone asking for money over social tech tools. Bad guys are stealing identities and sending out requests to the stolen identities' entire friends lists, with compelling messages asking for help. Don't ever send money or banking information without verifying with the actual person in a live and secure way.

DO control access to your social technology accounts. Not everyone in your organization needs to have the ability to post, communicate, edit, and delete information on every social tech platform your company uses. Not everyone outside your organization needs to have access to the same information that comes from you (for example, clients may have greater access to your information than vendors do). Most social tech tools have settings that let you control the type of access your various contacts are allowed. Use them sensibly.

Also be aware of people who may be outside your organization but personally connected to your team members; some of them could compromise your security. There's a great little story concerning the director of the British Secret Intelligence Service (MI6), Sir John Sawers, whose cover was essentially blown by his own wife, Lady Shelley, when she posted confidential information and photographs about their location, workplace, and friends—and her husband's promotion to MI6 chief—on her Facebook profile, which was potentially visible to more than two hundred million users worldwide. Even though the Foreign Office quickly scrambled to remove the information from public view, the breach almost cost Sawers the appointment and caused embarrassment to an organization that is supposedly all about security and secrecy.[63]

DO have a backup plan in place. This means not only backing up information on your computers on a regular basis but also backing up information stored on your various outside social tech tools.

---

63 Nadia Gilani, "Wife Blows MI6 Chief's Cover on Facebook," *Times of London*, July 5, 2009, http://www.timesonline.co.uk/tol/news/uk/article6639521.ece.

It's too easy to get used to uploading and accessing files and information on remote sites without considering what happens if those sites go down. Social tech profiles and content on networking sites can take lots of time and labor to assemble, often months or even years; if yours is accidentally deleted, you will have to painstakingly start over from scratch. If it is an essential business tool, you need to have backup, a mirror profile, or other means through which you can quickly restore what was lost. You should also avoid putting all your eggs in one basket. It may be unlikely that any of the large global social tech tools you depend on will be compromised for an extended period of time—but what if they are?

DO spend enough money on e-security. Amazingly, individuals and organizations often skimp on security while spending lavishly in other departments. There's no point spending $2,000 on a top-of-the-line laptop if you're too cheap to pay the annual $30 fee to renew your antivirus subscription; this is essentially putting a high-dollar investment at great risk because you're unwilling to pay a miniscule percentage of that system's purchase price. There are some great security tools out there; some are even free. But don't be afraid to spend essential money on the tools you need to stay secure, especially when it comes to antivirus and antispyware tools, firewalls, and data backup systems. Get advice from industry security experts, or even bring one onto your permanent staff—it is usually money well spent and will save you cash in the long run. If you have an in-house e-security department, ascertain whether it has the tools and funding it needs. Make sure your systems have the necessary security software installed and updated, so even if your training efforts fall short and one of your team members slips up, the security software will prevent the worst. It is better to be safe than sorry—especially if these are the lifelines of your business.

DO inform your clients and contacts of your social tech regulations and procedures. Let them know what types of interactions you will use these tools for, and even more important, tell them what your company will never do via social tech (for example, send out invoices or payment requests, send unsolicited files and links, and so forth). When your clients understand the way you operate your social tech tools, they will be better equipped to detect attack attempts from third parties. Feel free to include your business contacts in some of the training memos you distribute to your employees, or make these general memos part of your corporate newsletter. This way, the people you do business with will also stay updated on the latest security threats going around and will be less likely to fall victim; their systems will be less likely to pose a potential security risk when interacting with your own. Your clients and contacts will appreciate your efforts to maintain a secure environment as part of running a professional organization. Of course, use great caution as to which memos are public and which are for internal use only.

DON'T provide too much information. Have clearly assigned procedures in place for who may post what information at what time, or have everything go through a central clearinghouse or "social tech content czar" before it is published. You also need to respect your team members' privacy. It is surprising how much personal information is publicly posted by companies about their employees, including names and ages of their family members, dates of birth, license numbers, home and cell phone numbers, and more. Also, do not post too much information about your own intellectual property or internal confidential information. Everything should be run by the social tech czar for final approval, and someone else should be in charge of browsing through all content created by your team once it has been posted. It is too easy to post something and forget about it, only to find a glaring problem weeks later—or worse yet, to be informed of the problem by someone from the outside!

Once, a system administrator at Downingtown West High School in Chester County, Pennsylvania, managed to accidentally post highly sensitive personal data concerning students and

parents—including Social Security numbers—into a completely unprotected directory to which all students had access through the school
network. Ironically, when a fifteen-year-old student copied this freely
available information, it was the student who was charged with a
criminal offense, while the administrator got away without punish-
ment. The charges against the teenager were eventually dropped,
but it was nevertheless a major security breach that generated much
negative publicity and created a real mess.[64] Situations like this one
can be prevented if posted information is continually checked and
rechecked with fresh eyes.

DON'T assume that electronic communication always reaches
its intended target. Although reliability has increased manyfold since
the early days, issues still exist with e-mail reception—for example,
your provider's automated systems might suddenly decide to black-
list your domain name and no longer send e-mail to that domain.
Only after noticing the eerie quiet of your in-box would you be
prompted to follow up with clients using different means and thus
find out that you had not received some important messages. So
don't drop the ball when it comes to essential communication over
the Internet, as no technology is 100 percent reliable. Whoever is
in charge of monitoring your content from the outside should also
regularly test all your avenues of communication to be sure things
are working as they should be and that information is being sent and
received properly.

DON'T forget that once you hit the "Send," "Post," or "Submit" button, the information becomes public and can theoretically
be forwarded to anyone within seconds. One of the pitfalls of instant
communication is that, in the heat of the moment, people might
send messages containing information they later regret distributing.
According to a 2010 survey of one thousand social networking users,

64 Andrew Brandt, "Stupid User Tricks: IT Admin Follies," *Computerworld*, June 17, 2008,
http://www.computerworld.com.au/article/224911/stupid_user_tricks_it_admin_
follies/?pp=3.

more than 33 percent admitted that they have experienced "poster's remorse" about a message they had published without proper consideration on Facebook, Twitter, or another similar social tech channel. The percentage was even higher for users of mobile devices. More than one-third of those who regretted a comment stated that it caused them serious problems in a personal or professional relationship.[65] Always triple-check your recipient list, and think before you send!

* * *

Are you feeling any better? Good! But consider this chapter only as a starting point for your organization's security and regulations policies. Some of the most common threats have been outlined along with the approaches to combating them, but your organization's particular security requirements may vary greatly depending on its type, size, and core business. This discussion is simply meant to get you moving in the right direction and to encourage you to do your own due diligence based on your company's specific security needs.

Also, as with all things technology, the information in this chapter will already be outdated by the time you read it, as there may well be brand-new types of security hazards that have emerged in the days, weeks, and months since the writing of this book. The one thing you can always count on in the world of social tech is constant change! We live in exciting times with almost unlimited opportunities, but they do come with responsibilities. Therefore, always stay proactive when it comes to your organization's security matters, and never let complacency set in.

---

65 Lance Whitney, "Poster's Remorse Common for Social-Network Users," CNET.com, May 18, 2010, http://news.cnet.com/8301-1023_3-20005264-93.html.

KEY POINTS

- Social technologies have opened up organizations to a whole new set of attacks. Although social tech can be a powerful tool for good, it can also represent large holes in an organization's security defenses.

- User training is the best defense against employees unwittingly allowing attacks that compromise the company's security.

- As fast as we improve security measures, bad guys figure out ways around them. Don't be fooled into thinking that your security department will make your network bulletproof.

- The highest percentage of successful security breaches comes from current or former employees.

- The fact that social technologies allow employees to publicly converse with people creates a serious danger for organizations that do not obtain control of social tech usage. These conversations are permanent and searchable by anyone.

- Don't skimp on applying resources to security. Many organizations put all their energy into trying to use technology to drive the top-line revenue without considering the possible downside of its use.

- Be aware of any social tech regulations that may be implemented in your industry. In some industries, governing bodies are working on specific guidelines for the use of social technology.

CHAPTER 13

Implementation Strategies for the Twelve-Step Process

As explained at the beginning of this book, each of the previous twelve chapters describes one of the twelve steps in the process of implementing social technology into an organization in a holistic way. I have been using this process with clients and teaching it at my boot camps for a while now, and so I can offer a few observations that might be helpful to you as you apply social technology to your own organization.

The first and foremost is that any well-thought-out process will help you move from a state of social tech chaos (where most organizations reside today) to a more systematic strategy. The twelve-step process goes one step further by incorporating existing structures with new concepts and putting them in an order that makes sense for a holistic approach. This will not only help you organize, but will also help you try out new ideas that can have a powerful impact on your success.

Following are a few, more specific social tech implementation best practices we have learned along the way.

Packaging Your Social Technology Effort

Give your social tech effort a name, and build some excitement around its execution. Sometimes packaging makes a difference, so giving this effort a name that has a cool technological slant to it can be a good first step in gaining buy-in. A second step is to have a high-ranking executive present an overview of the program to the team, making it clear that the effort has high-level support. Stir up some anticipation and describe what a great opportunity this is, and people will pay much more attention to it. If employees know the social tech process will now be institutionalized, they will be much more committed to it.

Committing to a Concise Implementation Timeframe

When we coach organizations through social tech implementation, we shoot for a ninety-day time frame. We have found that this is fast enough to get it going quickly, yet it still allows people the time to do a good job with each step. A ninety-day window should be enough time to get all these steps either completed or at least in a pilot stage; a shorter period does not give enough time to plan and organize effectively. If you don't pick a specific time frame, or if you choose one that is much too long (a year, for example) you will find that people simply put off doing steps that could be bringing value today. You will be learning new ways to leverage social technology tools for years to come, but this does not mean that it should take years to get these initial steps completed.

The Order of Implementation

The twelve steps do not need to be done sequentially; any set of them can be done at the same time. That said, there is a natural order to the steps in the process, in that it makes sense to set your goals first and get your governance policies in place early. It also makes sense to lock in pilot projects and deal with security late in the process. Within that framework, however, many of the steps will be assigned to different people, so there is no reason to do them one at a time when they can be accomplished simultaneously.

Social Tech Should Live Within Your Overall Strategy

Tie this twelve-step process to your organization's core strategy by making sure that the benefits you get from social tech actually affect your company's core goals. This is critical because these tools cover many different areas and can provide many different benefits, but if you do not have a clear path between those benefits and why they matter to the organization, you are just treading water while you play with a new toy. If one core goal is to generate revenue in a specific market, then one of the pilot projects for social technology needs to be trying to facilitate that revenue generation.

Understanding Where You Are Versus Your Competitors

Set a goal of outpacing your competitors in their use of social technology. Of course, this means you need to understand where they are in the process of implementing social tech. It is unwise to engage in implementation without having benchmarks for what needs to be accomplished, and one critical goal should be staying in front of your competition. Depending on your level of aggressiveness, you can decide how far in front of them you want to move. As mentioned before, either you will show your competitors the best practices in your industry, or they will show you. The price for learning from them could be steep.

This Is Not "One and Done"

Look at this as a long-term effort—it is a marathon, not a sprint. This process is just the beginning; once you have finished your initial push, you need to continue to develop new pilot projects and refine your governance policies and lists of tools. The implementation process is simply meant to jump-start the organization and create velocity toward your goals in the marketplace. Once the process is done, you must find ways to mainstream social tech in the organization.

The Reward Is Commensurate with the Investment

My final observation from watching clients implement this process is that *you get out of it what you put into it*—there is no magic here. If you assemble a motivated team, give team members some room to be creative, and then measure the results, you will find many ways that social technology can make a positive impact on your organization. If you assemble the wrong people, make a weak attempt at testing new concepts, and hold no one accountable for the outcome, you will find little value and will have wasted lots of time.

CHAPTER 14

The Future of Social Technologies

It seems appropriate to end this book by painting a picture of where the ever-changing world of social tech is headed. I have been in the technology field for a long time, and I have seen over and over the value of having an accurate picture of the future in your mind. This vision gives you the ability to make investments that can really pay off down the road. I call this "high-beam leadership." If you're interested in learning more about high-beam leadership, which helps executive teams see more accurately into the future, visit FuturePointOfView.com.

So, with high beams glaring down the road, here are my ten predictions of how social technology will soon change our world even more.

1. Social Tech Standards Will Improve Ease of Use

Over the years, we have found that everyone's lives improve when we can all agree on standard formats for files, hardware devices, software mechanics, and so forth. When new technologies emerge, there are usually no standards at first, then a few large entities fight to set the standards based on their proprietary products, and then eventually the market agrees on one or two. The rest drop their efforts and join the crowd, creating a standard that benefits all.

In the social tech world, we are at the point where a few of the large entities are now proposing and fighting for their own standards (Google, Microsoft, and Facebook, for example). To create an account with any of these entities, we currently have to sign up and provide a username and password; then we have to fill out a profile and upload a photo; and then we have to connect to friends and tell them we are using this new service. We then have to look through a list of preferences and make several decisions. (I have done this so many times, I want to stick a pencil in my eye every time I have to sign up for a new service.) Lately, you might have noticed that some new sites are allowing you to log in to the site by providing your Facebook or Twitter credentials. This is an example of a standard being born.

One day we will live in an improved state of social tech where this is the norm—the seeds are already planted and have begun sprouting. Our friends list will come in a standardized and portable format that is completely accepted by every new site. Just by signing up, we'll automatically be telling friends that we are using a new service. We will not need to provide a new profile, because we'll have one standard profile somewhere that will just be hooked up to any new service we implement. We will have made standard setup decisions in our profile so that each new service will already see what privacy levels we want and what communication methods we use. We will have one authentication method that we can use with every site instead of creating lots of different passwords and usernames, and this one authentication system will be much more secure than the ones we are using today. In other words, authentication, friends lists, profiles, and preferences will all become modules that we create once and are accepted everywhere.

Just writing this section makes me drool in anticipation of standards that the social tech arena should have already agreed on. (Please, God, do not make me fill out yet another profile . . .)

2. Usage Rates Will Soar

I know this prediction sounds obvious, and that is why I have to make it. Much like cell phones and e-mail before, we will see the penetration rate of social tech continue to grow quickly and consistently for the next five years at least. I have not seen a research firm yet that says anything different. Globally, we will see faster penetration rates in countries that traditionally have been thought of as third-world nations due to the fact that they can use mobile devices—not just personal computers to connect with people using social tech tools. In addition, the citizens of these countries have an economic incentive to learn to use social tech tools like crowdsourcing to improve their economic position.

3. "Connection Addiction" Will Seem Normal

Today, there are still many people who do not understand why a young person sits at a restaurant and sends text messages the entire meal. Or why a spouse checks his or her Facebook page before bed and then again first thing in the morning. Let's be honest: Many of us are becoming addicted to being connected. These social connections are much more extensive than just having an Internet connection and e-mail; it's now about staying current on our work life and our social life in real time. Being out of the know is not cool, and it can even be uncomfortable for some people. That is, not everyone wants to be "cool"; they're just, well, addicted. To be disconnected is to be missing out on information that we may never be able to catch up on later. There would be a gaping hole in our knowledge base—and that simply will not do!

4. A Centralized Communications Control System Will Emerge

A big piece of functionality is missing from our communication capabilities today: There is nothing that tells other people our current state and how we prefer to be communicated with. If a person wants to get in touch with me *right now,* he or she has to guess what I'm doing and how I want to be reached. Based only on his or her preferences—rather than on my own convenience—the person might call me, text me, contact me through Facebook, or e-mail me.

If you really think about this, you'll see that it's a huge problem, and the current attempts to solve it are headed in the wrong direction. Many companies are trying to unify the ways to connect so that someone can call one number and be routed to the recipient based on some set of rules. That won't be meaningful in the future, though, because we don't need just one method of being contacted—we need multiple methods that we can advertise depending on our status at the moment. For example, right now I am in a hotel with a great Internet connection and no cell service. There may be people trying to call or text me who are not getting through. If only I had a way to tell them that I'm best reached by e-mail at the moment, they would get what we both want—to communicate now.

Very soon, someone is going to wake up and smell the coffee. Someone will create a standard profile (see point one, above) that includes a list of all the ways someone can communicate with us. There will be a way for us to rank the methods so that people can see what we prefer. Then, we can choose a set of status rankings—available, not available, emergency only, text only, and so on. We will be able to show where we are geographically, if we choose, so our contacts know what city or part of the city we are in. When this is all bundled up, someone who wants to get in touch with me can look at my profile, check my status and communication preference, and then follow the directions to reach me. It will be much better for them and much better for me.

Look for this kind of communications control to come soon. No longer will people wonder how best to connect with you at any given moment. No longer will you have to deal with people trying to connect with you in so many ways: phone, text, e-mail, Facebook, Twitter, LinkedIn, and in person. (Right now, I would be fine with just the e-mail method—I'm busy trying to write.)

5. Location-Based Connections Will Change How We Network

One huge change in the future will be the simple fact that we can choose to let people know where we are geographically at any time. This may sound scary to a lot of people, but the benefits will drive many people to advertise where they are. We are now starting to see the first applications that allow us to look at a map and see which friends or contacts are close to us at any given moment. Very soon, we will have an application that simply checks our entire contact list for everyone who has location capability turned on. Once that happens, we will then have notification systems that chime any time one of our contacts is within a hundred yards. You can probably see that every trip out of your house will be a different experience in this kind of world.

I'm not that good at networking face to face because I am an introvert. However, even I think this is a *very* cool capability. I cannot wait to be lying on a beach in Hawaii and look around the island to see whether I have any friends or acquaintances there. My wife will probably make me leave my phone in the room, and she will definitely not let us go to dinner with the business contact who's staying in the hotel next to ours—but at least I will know he or she is there!

6. Immersive, Real-Time Information Flow Will Change Everything

Even in the recent past, most information we received was at least hours old, and in many cases weeks old, unless we were watching it live on TV. The Internet, mobile devices, and social tech applications have changed this drastically. We now have citizen journalism, real-time news feeds, push delivery of chosen information–the game has changed. We talked in chapter 5 about building rivers of information; the rivers we are building today seem robust, but an even greater flood of real-time information is coming.

For that reason, information filtering will become critical as a companion to the real-time flow. Filtering will allow us to write rules that watch the information and yank out the really important things we need to know instantly–while further prioritizing the items we can wait until lunch to read versus those we should read before we go to bed. I will love this because I just like to seem smart to my friends. Others might love this because seconds count when learning information that could trigger actions–for example, when a possible star employee has left a competitor, or when a competitor has just stumbled in the market, opening up the door for you to grab market share.

7. Crowdsourcing Will Explode Across the World and Change Social Dynamics

There is a simple formula that makes this an easy prediction. We have millions of organizations that want to save money and get work done faster while developing higher-quality products. We have billions of people who would like to make more money. We have the Internet, cheap connection devices, and crowdsourcing sites that facilitate the work getting done. Add all this up, and you'll see that we're primed for an explosion in this new method of getting work done. We'll also see a rapid segmentation of the kinds of work that get sourced out to the Internet herd.

With crowdsourcing fully implemented and used across the globe, we will see huge shifts in where money flows. Anytime new money flows into an area, there are the corresponding social shifts. This has been evidenced by the changes going on in India because of the vast amount of outsourcing benefiting people there. Billions of dollars that used to pay people in the United States are now paying people in cities like Mumbai and New Delhi, and this fact is obvious when you see the growth of the middle and upper classes in those cities.

8. The Ability to Rate People Will Cause Havoc, Then Harmony

This prediction is also a simple extrapolation of current trends. We are already rating all kinds of professions and writing recommendations on career-oriented sites like LinkedIn. A couple of sites now in beta testing (e.g., Getunvarnished.com) are going to allow people to rate the individuals around them—just on what kind of people they are.

The creators of these tools are trying to be very careful to ensure that the commenters have credibility, and they are building scoring systems that make the system as fair as possible. Already journalists and bloggers are writing editorials about how terrible these sites are going to be—they will just become sites where people trash one another, and others will enjoy reading the negative instead of the positive.

OK, I get it—we tend to be attracted to the negative before the positive. I also get that people tend to write more negative reviews than positive reviews because anger is a stronger emotion than contentment. So yes, these rating sites will be a mess at first. But they will then sort themselves out and become useful—very useful.

The reality today is that we constantly meet new people in our personal and professional lives. We know very little about these people, yet we have to interact with them based on trust. We learn about them only as time goes on. This is a very inefficient system, and it's dangerous in some cases. Think about how the world will be different when you can just go online and see what other people have said about someone over the years. For this to be valuable, the comments through the years need to be honest and truthful from the writer's point of view; if a person being reviewed can game the system by having all their friends write glowing reports, the value of rating at all gets diluted. This clearly shows that we have to devise schemas so that ratings can be trusted. I could postulate forever about designing how this system will work, but for now, trust that it will be working soon.

9. Virtual Worlds Will Make a Comeback

I love the concept of the technology hype cycle, which shows the ups and downs of new technologies as they get overhyped, then get trashed, and then make a comeback as practical tools. Virtual worlds are a good example of a technology in the middle of this cycle. The early dynamics that made virtual worlds interesting have not changed: People like to interface with technology in real-world ways. We ingest information best immersively rather than from plain old text on paper (or screen). That is why people like charts and graphs better than text grids. People also like the concept of having an avatar that represents them visually.

We will first see the comeback at work, in virtual meeting rooms. Then we will see game worlds like *World of Warcraft* bleed over into commercial worlds, with stores increasingly selling products from within game worlds. E-commerce will figure out how to represent stores better in the virtual space, and without much fanfare, we will see the dominant interface on the Internet move away from 2-D pages and toward 3-D worlds. This *is* going to happen, my friends, so get your avatars built. (And please, quit trying to integrate animals into your themes—I'm tired of talking to squirrel girls and raccoon guys. Just stick to a human avatar that looks like you, without the wrinkles.)

10. Game Dynamics Will Move into the Real World

This one might make people who belong to the older generations a little queasy, but there is no reason to get freaked out about this trend. The science of digital gaming has been improving for a few decades now, and we are close to getting it down cold. The obvious evidence for this exists within the online gaming industry, which continues to explode—meaning billions of dollars in revenues for numerous organizations.

We have trained millions of young people in the concepts of game theory—whether they know it or not. We have taught them that there is a training-level sandbox where they can learn how to play the game in a safe environment. We have taught them that there are levels of achievement they can work through, and that each successive level will be so hard as to almost make them quit. Eventually, however, they will succeed and move on to the next level, giving them a feeling of pride. We have taught them the concept of heads-up displays that overlay real-time information about what they are looking at. We have taught them a reward system from which they can get new tools or money in exchange for small successes. The games they play allow them to assemble teams of strangers to go on a mission or quest with them. Their teammates create value based on their skills only; it does not matter what nationality, sex, or age group they belong to.

And the list goes on. If you are an astute observer of human beings, you can take this information about what people have learned inside gaming worlds and think about how it could apply to the business or education worlds. Think about how you could create a job-training path that mimics the ways games train people. Think about how you might change incentive programs to match the types of incentives used in games. What about imitating the game player's ability to form ad hoc teams to get projects done? There is a reason that online gaming is so successful—there is a methodology for grabbing someone's attention and keeping that person engaged, and it works. We should learn from that in the business world and use it to our advantage. Mark my words: This concept will not sound crazy to you in another few years.

* * *

I get excited whenever I write about the future of social technology, because I can see so clearly what my world will become, and it is a world that is more efficient, fun, and robust. Technology in general has had a powerful impact on the quality of our lives over the past twenty years, and that trend is not going to slow down. People always seem to think that we have arrived in the future with the tools we have today, that technology is as good as it's going to get. Thankfully, this is shortsighted.

A few final thoughts before you leave us . . .

If you have not yet visited the website (EnterpriseSocial-Technology.com), please take a few minutes and check out the Resources and The Crowdsourcing of EST pages. There are lots of tools and links to other pieces of content that extend the concepts discussed here.

I am very certain that social technologies will prove to be one of the technology innovations that has the largest impact on the human race. To put that comment in context, I predict social technologies will have far more impact than mainframes, PCs, word processing, e-commerce, e-mail, and many of the other basic technologies that have changed our lives thus far. I suspect we really have little understanding as to what the long-range impact of the social tech toolbox will be. Maybe the way to look at this is that Web 0.0 (the basic infrastructure of the Internet) and Web 1.0 (e-commerce) were just the build up to Web 2.0. The real difference being that Web 2.0 will touch everyone in the world both personally and professionally at some day in the future . . .

Now go forth and use the information in this book to move yourself and your organization forward. A tool left in the toolbox is worthless to everyone. Don't let social tech be something that you learn from your competitors!

The Crowdsourcing of This Book

 Let me identify myself: I am Corey Travis, the project manager for this book. This section is penned in my hand, so to speak.

Our goal as a team in writing this book was to create a thought-leading guide to social technology by actually using social technology—specifically, crowdsourcing.

We are aware that some authors have crowdsourced an element or two of their books, but to our knowledge we are the first to crowd-source a book project in its entirety. Working through this project, we found that crowdsourcing enabled us to create a book that was richer in content and insight than if it had been produced by a single author or an editor working with a group of preselected contributors. Not only that, but we were able to produce this book more quickly and more economically than if we had followed the standard publishing procedures. Our crowdsourcing experience with every phase of the publishing process proved to be a good example of how a company can successfully use enterprise social technology to redefine a process like book creation and marketing.

In brief, here's how our crowdsourced publishing process worked.

Scott originally came up with the idea of writing a book that would consolidate his views on how organizations could implement a holistic social tech strategy. With that thought in mind, he began toying with the idea of having the crowd help write the book, but not in the same way that other people have used the crowd. Instead of just announcing the subject and then having random people write on a wiki, he wanted to control the general message and coordinate the topics so that his ideas came through. He also wanted the crowd to provide interesting case studies—ones he was not familiar with—and to add their personal experiences and knowledge to his framework. With this in mind, we decided to figure out how to crowdsource every step of the publishing process, just to see how we could completely change the current model.

The decision to crowdsource the cover design was simple; it's a common practice that is done on many creative sites. Nothing hard about that.

For the content, we decided to heavily outline the chapters, then narrow the crowd by picking three potential writers for each chapter. We had them each write the full chapter and submit their version, and we then picked the best. We have no idea whether anyone has used this model before; we just believed it would help us create a stellar book, and we are really pleased with how it worked out.

The final decision was about how to crowdsource the publicity. This is the magic ingredient—we have not seen this done for a book before, but we believe we will get a great return on our investment. At first, we thought we would just offer bounties for getting us the traditional kinds of exposure—an interview with Oprah, David Letterman, or Jay Leno. We figured if we offered enough money, someone in the crowd would find a way to get the bounty. Then we rethought our approach, because we were pretty sure Oprah, David, and Jay have better things to do than have Scott on their shows to wax eloquent about social tech. That led us to the list of bounties we provide later in this section.

We also plan to see whether we can have the book converted into the various ebook formats through crowdsourcing. If you want to see how that went, you'll have to check out our website (Enterprise-SocialTechnology.com) and look for the Making of the Book tab on the main menu. We will continue to update this story with additional crowdsourcing results we get after the publishing date.

We are going to use traditional distribution methods and the traditional publishing model of selling the book through retail locations, because this system still has a lot of value and because many people still want a bound, paper book in their hands. Plus, for people who want a special message written inside, Scott figures it's hard to sign electronic copies.

We intend to create more books this way and have already thought of some topics that would best be written by the crowd, for the crowd. It is clear to us that there is a unique value proposition in having the crowd compete to write chapters and work from a coordinated outline to produce a book: The process is fast, it results in high-quality content, and it gives the book a unique texture.

Let's look more closely at how each stage worked.

Crowdsourcing the Cover

This part of the experience was by far our favorite. It was so exciting to walk into work every morning and view hundreds of cover submissions from designers who were spread across the world. It really was a great competition.

We started by choosing 99designs.com as our crowdsourcing partner. We did this because the company has a good reputation for employing designers who understand projects like book covers. We selected a bounty that we felt was a little higher than normal so that we would receive more attention. We then posted a brief with a description of what we were looking for. We gave details on what the cover must include and what elements we find aesthetically pleasing, and we also included some don'ts. We learned that a few designers don't read the instructions at all and that some don't take well to criticism, but I am still overwhelmed by the amount of great options we received.

If you were to have a book cover designed using traditional methods, you would pay something in the order of $5,000 and receive five to eight comps to choose from. Through crowdsourcing we spent $750 and received 330 comps. Imagine the possibilities of crowdsourcing other forms of creative designs when you are achieving metrics like that! And the pricing and large selection pool of comps weren't the only positives—the whole process only took two weeks.

The Winning Designer

When our two weeks were up, we narrowed our submissions to the top ten; presented them to our peers, colleges, publisher, and social networks; and asked for a vote. We assumed this would help us narrow it down to one, but it didn't; we had votes across the spectrum. At this point we had to step in and choose the cover we thought would be most pleasing from among the voters' three favorites. Two of the designs in the top three came from one submitter, Christopher Bridges, and he turned out to be our winning designer.

Christopher graduated from the University of Central Oklahoma in 2009 with a BFA in graphic design. In 2010, he received a local and district Gold ADDY Award for a book he wrote and illustrated, titled *Blip The Bot!* The same year, he also received an award of excellence from the university's College of Fine Arts and Design. While working as a designer for his current employer, Chris also freelance designs to supplement his income.

As a freelancer, Chris relies on crowdsourcing websites. Instead of using his time to find new clients and new projects, he goes straight to the projects and picks from a huge directory of work to find a job best suited to his skills. "I found out about this project from a friend who posted a link to it on their Facebook account," he explains. "It's strange to say, but practically all of my work comes from references through people who have seen my work online, or through friends hearing of projects and introducing them to me. It makes my job much easier when I can just concentrate on doing good work, as opposed to spending much of my time trying to find it."

Crowdsourcing the Content

It was difficult to pick a crowdsourcing site to assist us in getting the chapters written. The first site we tried out bombed; we received just one response.

Researching your crowdsourcing partner is very important. Be sure to pay attention to things like the amount of active projects available, the amount of writers and other creatives active on the site, and testimonials. The good thing about crowdsourcing is that if you are unhappy with the work you get, you can remove your project and get your bounty back. Make sure to pick a site that offers a satisfaction guarantee, and if you aren't having any luck, pull the project and start over with another site.

Fortunately, when we took a second shot and posted the project on crowdSPRING.com, Mike Samson, the site's cofounder, came to our rescue. He gave us some tips on how to manage the project and make it successful. We were able to gather a great list of diverse writers through this online marketplace for creative services, and we found working with crowdSPRING to be easy.

Mike is an entrepreneur in the true sense of the word. In his former life, he was an Emmy Award–nominated producer and production manager with more than twenty years of experience as a senior manager in the film and TV industries. He worked on dozens of feature film and television projects, including *Wall Street, Bull Durham,* Stephen King's *The Stand,* and *Men in Black II.* He says:

When we were approached by Corey Travis with Future Point of View to host the *Enterprise Social Technology* project, we jumped at the chance. We knew that our community of talented writers and designers (over 64,000 strong and growing fast) would want to be involved, contribute their ideas, and watch the process unfold.

As the aggregator for this book, Scott Klososky first provided an extremely detailed outline of all the content we wanted and provided in-depth instructions on how to write each chapter. Included in the instructions were samples and advice on the voice, tone, word count, expectations, and other details. This part of the project was serious work, and in many ways was the same process any author must go through.

It then took constant updating, feedback, and study of all the potential chapters we could have accepted in order to find the right versions for the book. In some ways, it would have been easier from an editorial standpoint if Scott had written the book from beginning to end. But relying on crowdsourcing delivered much richer content than any one author could have created on his or her own.

Let me share a little bit about what we went through in the first week after posting the project on crowdSPRING. The chapter requests were posted in the late afternoon, and we wanted to let it sit for a few days to see what happened. We had no idea that we would get the response we did. Within twenty-four hours we received 876 e-mails asking for permission to view the project. By the end of the project we had more than 1,040 applicants and fifty-eight entries. An *applicant* is a person who asks permission to view the project; they must sign a nondisclosure agreement before they are able to read detailed briefs of the project. This protects your work from being stolen. An *entry* is a submission for permission to work; in this case we asked for a three-hundred-to-five-hundred-word essay on why we should choose you for the project and which part of project you would like to work on. The entry is your formal application into the writing process. This may seem overwhelming, but keep in mind that there are tricks that make this process simpler. We chose applicants that we thought had the most potential based on the piece of sample writing they submitted. We looked for things like writing style, grammatical errors, interesting thoughts, background, and communication when choosing writers.

The editorial process for the book consisted of three parts. First, we set a deadline: one week before the final version of the book was due. We used this last week to give feedback to the writers and allow them enough time to make corrections and resubmit their chapters. A second round of edits came after we chose the final writers; with crowdsourcing you are always able to ask for revisions before you award the bounty, and we suggest that you take advantage of this time. Final edits were made by the aggregator and publisher.

The Writers

We ended up with eleven excellent writers who helped with various sections of the book, and who live all over the world. When reading through their backgrounds, you will see why it can be a benefit to have a book that has been partially written by the crowd! Let me share a little bit about them.

Adele Barlow

Adele cofounded yMedia, an Auckland-based initiative for nonprofit organizations. Winner of the 2008 "Judge's Choice" Computerworld Award for Excellence and a finalist in the Young ICT category, yMedia has worked with industry leaders such as Microsoft to help organizations with limited funding to build their

Web presence. Adele was the Australia/New Zealand project manager for internationally acclaimed digital media think tank X Media Lab and has also worked with Capability New Zealand, the New Zealand Computer Society, the New Zealand Centre for Social Innovation, and (in London) Pembridge Partners.

Lisa Neal-Shaw

Lisa is a freelance writer and a reference librarian at the Mark & Emily Turner Memorial Library in Presque Isle, Maine. In addition to writing through and about social technology, she serves as communications co-chair and secretary for the Maine Library Association. In the past she has worked in radio broadcasting, in editing, and with the Maine Department of Labor's Bureau of Employment Services. Lisa lives in northern Maine with her family, which includes numerous cats and a dog. Her website is lisamnshaw. gizapage.com.

Shashi Kadapa

Shashi holds a bachelor's degree in engineering and an MBA in marketing. He began his career working with Cummins India, Optics Balzers AG, Carborundum Universal, and other engineering companies in such diverse functional areas as production, design, operations, and marketing. He then worked with Patni Computer Systems, MicroWorld Technologies, Ectone, and other IT firms before becoming a full-time writer, freelance journalist, animator, and graphic designer. His portfolio includes marketing research papers, technology white papers, content for websites, and articles on processes, Flash animations, websites, and graphics.

Corwin Bermudez

Corwin Bermudez is a graphic artist, illustrator, designer, Web developer, author, painter, and creative writer from Londonderry, New Hampshire. He specializes in commercial and marketing graphics as well as Web design, illustration, digital rendering, and branding design. Although Corwin's specialties are art and design, he writes fiction and plays music as well.

Mike Wise

With more than twenty years in technology and sales in three different industries, Mike brings a broad spectrum of knowledge and experience to socially facilitated selling projects. He founded WebWisedom, an enterprise social technology, e-marketing, and e-business consultancy, in November 2009. Web-Wisedom helps sales and marketing organizations develop customized strategies to leverage social technologies within the unique environments of the organization and its markets.

Prior to founding WebWisedom, Mike led e-commerce sales efforts within the insurance industry for IdeaStar, primarily in the health and life vertical. Previously, Mike spent ten years with ADP in sales, sales training, and sales management in various locations across the United States.

Aubrey Sampson

Aubrey is a stay-at-home mom who regularly speaks at women's and youth ministry events. She has a bachelor's degree from Wheaton College in English literature and is currently working on her master's degree in spiritual formation and ministry at

Wheaton. She is also working on her first book, *Thoughts on Women's Identity and Belonging*. Aubrey lives in Illinois with her husband and two sons.

Grant Zellner

Grant is a freelance copywriter living in Oklahoma. He holds a bachelor's degree in business marketing and a master's degree in journalism, both from the University of Oklahoma. With more than five years' experience in marketing and advertising copywriting for businesses and nonprofit organizations of all sizes, he has worked on projects that include websites, magazine features and advertorials, sales letters, print and multimedia ads, and press releases.

Grant is the author of the copywriteZ blog, which discusses ideas in marketing, advertising, and business writing. Contact Grant via his website, copywriteZ.me.

Richard Stooker

Richard Stooker is an author, novelist, copywriter, infopreneur, and Internet marketer. He began selling information online back in 1996. He has a BS in accounting from Southern Illinois University (Edwardsville) and spent more than thirty years in a government cubicle, from which he thankfully escaped.

You can learn more about Richard by searching his name at Amazon.com or at the following places:

Facebook.com/richard.stooker
LinkedIn.com/in/richardstooker
RichardStooker.com

Christopher M. Locke

Born and raised in Boston, Christopher studied architecture in the mid-1980s and was first introduced to the power of the personal computer when he began using CAD (computer-aided design) drafting software. In 1995, he founded a Web design studio called Computer Graphics Unlimited. Over the past fifteen years, he has designed, developed, and consulted on more than three hundred fifty websites, from small mom-and-pop storefronts to multimillion-dollar websites. Currently he is a lead developer for MoreDirect in Boca Raton, Florida. Christopher spends his remaining time consulting on Web projects and helping clients develop e-commerce solutions, B2B apps, Facebook apps, and social tech and SEO strategies. Software development is his life's passion—second only to his three amazing children.

Grace Wall Conlon

Grace has been an independent contributing writer for newspapers and magazines for the past eighteen years and has broad experience in the corporate business world. Before launching her freelance career, Grace worked for twenty-six years with Lever Brothers Company, where she was responsible for developing computer-based strategic planning systems for Lever's consumer packaged goods division. After retiring from Lever Brothers in 1980, she consulted for twelve years, wrote for business periodicals, and was a columnist for *Advertising Age*. She has been a guest speaker at the Yale University School of Organization and Management, the University of Tulsa, New York University, and Polytechnic Institute of New York University.

Maximilian Suchy

Max is a freelance designer, writer, and creative consultant born and brought up in Europe and currently based in Florida. An avid technology fan and Internet user, he was attracted to working on this book because it is right up his alley. To check out some of Max's creative design work, please visit his online portfolio at www.maximilian.us.

* * *

As you look through these folks' bios, you might notice the wide range of backgrounds and areas of expertise. What you would not see is the dramatic differences they represent in ages and geography. We scaled the demographic continuum from the United States to India and from age twenty-seven to age eighty. One of the interesting aspects of crowdsourcing is that you really are dealing with only the talent on the other end of the line. We did not really know anything about these people until after we received their submissions. In some ways, this is the fairest way to contract for help, because there is no way to be biased against the providers.

If you are interested in seeing a couple of chapters that we did not select for the book but that were really good, go to Enterprise-SocialTechnology.com under the section "The Crowdsourcing of EST." These will give you a real sense of the quality of writing we were able to get in our crowdsourcing contest. You will also see why we say that it was really hard being unable to pick some of the writers who did excellent work, knowing they would get no benefit from us for all their positive effort.

Crowdsourcing Book Publicity

As mentioned previously, we are excited about the concept of rewarding members of the crowd for helping garner exposure for this book.

We thought long and hard about things people could help us do, things that would bring attention to the book in a positive way. We also tried to stay away from traditional publicity in most cases.

By the time you read this, we are hoping that some of the bounties will be taken. You may still have the opportunity to participate in our crowdsource publishing experiment, however, so check and see whether any of these bounties still available if you are interested.

For the latest information on bounties and a list of which ones have been won, go to EnterpriseSocialTechnology.com and click on "The Crowdsourcing of EST."

Get 250 people to wear social tech T-shirts and take a picture: $5,000.
Method for claiming it: Send us a high-resolution photo of the group.

Get Webster's to add *social technology* as a term: $5,000.
Method for claiming it: Press release by Webster's that makes the announcement.

Send link for the book's Amazon.com page to more than 2,000 of your social networking connections (first 100 people): $50
Method for claiming it: Show us a screen shot of your account and the connections, and a screenshot of what the delivered message looked like.

Get Michael Arrington (founder of TechCrunch) to read the book: $2,500 cash, or a $2,500 donation to charity of his choice.
Method for claiming it: Michael has to send an e-mail to scott@klososky.com, telling us that he read *Enterprise Social Technology* and what he thinks of the concepts it shares.

Get Robert Scoble (author of the Scobleizer blog) to read the book: $2,499 cash, or a $2,499 donation to charity of his choice (he gets $1 less so Michael Arrington is not mad at us).

Method for claiming it: Robert has to send us an e-mail to scott@klososky.com, telling us that he read *Enterprise Social Technology* and what he thinks of the concepts it shares.

Review a chapter of your choice on your blog (at least 200 words, and must have at least 1,000 subscribers): Five free books signed by the author.

Method for claiming it: Send us a screenshot of the blog and the number of subscribers you have.

For college professors—adopt the book as part of your curriculum: Twenty free copies (or $500).

Method for claiming it: Send us a copy of the syllabus for the course.

Publish an article in a major periodical (circulation of at least fifty thousand) about the making of the book (first ten people): $500.

Method for claiming it: Send us a copy of the printed article and the masthead of the publication the day it was published.

For organizations—purchase at least two hundred copies for employees and/or customers: $1,000 to the charity of your choice, and the purchased copies will be signed.

Method for claiming it: Provide a copy of the receipt, or contact us to provide the books.

Have the text translated into another language and published in another country: $2,500.
Method for claiming it: Send us written confirmation that it will be printed (from the publisher) and a copy in the language to which you have translated it.

Create a viral video about the book that gets at least ten thousand views (first person only): $1,000
Method for claiming it: Provide a screenshot of the video site with the number of views, so we can verify it.

Complete the twelve-step process described in this book at your organization, and send us a case study of the results (first five organizations): $500 to the charity of your choice.
Method for claiming it: Provide a written case study and allow us to interview the author.

If you have any ideas for nontraditional PR that are more interesting than ours, please let us know by e-mailing scott@klososky.com.

Overall, we had a great experience crowdsourcing this book. Defining this process proved to us that aggregating the thoughts, knowledge, and research of a group of people is a powerful way to produce content for cross-platform publication. We look forward to crowdsourcing many more books in the future.

ABOUT THE AGGREGATOR

Scott Klososky has founded numerous successful organizations, including two (Paragraph and Webcasts.com) that were sold for more than $200 million in aggregate. His unique insights into technology, business culture, and the future of business allows him to travel the globe as a speaker and consultant, advising senior executives in organizations ranging from Fortune 500 corporations to universities and nonprofits on topics such as IT strategy, social technologies, and leadership. He has previously worked with numerous companies—Cisco, Newell Rubbermaid, Lockheed Martin, Ebay, Volvo, The Hartford Financial Services Group, Great Clips, and Marriott, among others—as well as associations—the International Franchise Association, the Korean Ministry of Information, the Mortgage Bankers Association, the American Payroll Association, and the Association of Equipment Manufacturers.

Scott currently serves on the board of Alkami Technology, his latest technology start-up. Alkami is redefining online banking by creating a platform that allows banks and credit unions to deliver customized services to demographics like kids, senior citizens, and young married couples.

Scott is also the author of *The Velocity Manifesto: Harnessing Technology, Vision, and Culture to Future-Proof your Organization*, and he publishes a blog at www.technologystory.com. He can be found on Twitter at @sklososky.

30th May
5th July